International Mountain Rescue Handbook

FOURTH EDITION

Hamish MacInnes

FRANCES LINCOLN

Also by Hamish MacInnes
Scottish Climbs (2 Volumes)
Scottish Winter Climbs
Call-Out
High Drama
Look Behind the Ranges
West Highland Walks (4 Volumes)
Climb to the Lost World
Death Reel (fiction)
Beyond the Ranges
The Price of Adventure
Sweep Search
My Scotland
The Way Through the Glens
Land of Mountain and Mist
Mountain Disasters

Frances Lincoln Ltd
4 Torriano Mews
Torriano Avenue
London NW5 2RZ
www.franceslincoln.com

First published by Constable 1972 with revised editions 1984, 1998
Fourth edition published by Frances Lincoln 2005

ISBN 0 7112 2444 7

British Library Cataloguing in Publication data
A catalogue record for this book is available from the British Library

Printed and bound in Singapore

9 8 7 6 5 4 3 2 1

Contents

Disclaimer

Acknowledgements

The Author and Publisher accepts no responsibility for techniques, illustrations and descriptions contained in this book. By its very nature search and rescue poses risks to both rescuers and rescued far beyond those encountered in high risk sports and often there is a narrow safety margin in the evacuation of a casualty. The information contained in the International Mountain Rescue Handbook is designed only for the specific use of experienced rescuer/mountaineers, qualified to evaluate the suggested methods and techniques.

I am grateful to Blyth Wright, Glenmore Lodge, for bringing the chapter on "Snow Structure" up to date and to Professor Desmond Smith for casting a knowledgeable eye over the proofs. Also to Reg Phillips for clarifying the usage of S.I. Units and other mechanical observations and finally to mountaineers, artists and rescue team members all over the world, without whose help this book could never have been completed.

Preface to Second revised edition

Since the first edition of this book in 1972 there have been numerous changes in Search and Rescue worldwide. First there was the helicopter revolution, when the whole scenario of patient evacuation was speeded up dramatically. Following this came helicopter related rescue techniques and an increasing awareness of the rescuer's responsibility in technical application and competence. More recently patient care has taken prominence, or rather moved up to keep pace with the aspirations towards excellence.

Also the advent of off-shore related work with the oil industry and that of high rise building maintenance has evolved new techniques and equipment which has had spin-off for both mountaineering and technical cliff rescue. In the field of electronics the walkie-talkie and the mobile 'phone are the everyday tools of the rescuer and locating devices from avalanche bleepers to ground radar are used regularly.

The layman could be forgiven for thinking that in this electronic age a rescue could be enacted by activating a computer program and pressing the right buttons; far from it. As long as people fall in difficult places or get lost in large tracts of land they require the individual dedication of each rescue team member to find and retrieve the casualty. The helicopter, the rescue dog and the rest of the MR electronic armoury are but the tools of the rescuer. Inevitably, in the event of severe weather conditions much, if not all, the electronic and mechanical wizardry can become inoperative and the successful outcome of the operation reverts to the sweat and toil of the rescuer.

As I pointed out in previous editions of this book, the contents can only be a summary to the much wider subject of Search and Rescue.

There are many papers and books on individual aspects of SAR and there is a continuous exchange of ideas and techniques between teams and individual team members. This is the basis of development, how things are perfected and the way forward towards the common goal of evacuating the injured in the most expedient, safest and comfortable way.

It is not possible to embrace all the views and developments which have evolved over the years, but I have tried to steer an unbiased course through the labyrinth of ropes, knots, pulleys and clamps to give a good working basis for efficient rescue techniques.

This latest edition now makes much wider, if not quite exclusive use of the International System of Units of measurement, (S.I. Units), in recognition of the increasingly wide use now being made of the system, the desire for harmonisation of standards and statutory requirements of some countries. Having said this it is also recognised that many people of the rescue community have grown up and work perfectly safely with earlier systems of units and operate equipment still specified in familiar pounds, feet and so on. The transition to the sole use of S.I. Units will take some time yet to reach all rescue operations and techniques. Many guides exist already to the conversion from whatever system to

S.I. At the risk of going over old ground the basic rules for using the S.I. units are included again in this book. Within the chapter on Testing and Evaluation is a precise engineering statement for those concerned with design. For those whose practised language is to express rope loads in pounds, kilogrammes or such like units and to whom safe use of equipment, in accordance with its labelled loading limits, is the first concern, an appendix is also provided to serve as a 'Rescuer's Rough Guide to S.I. Units'.

A dog trained for mountain rescue work cannot operate to its full potential unless it is trained to negotiate dangerous terrain, often in darkness. Its human rescue counterpart is no different. To be an efficient member of a mountain rescue team, operating in difficult country, he or she should be a competent mountaineer. One has only to experience the trauma of being on a loose cliff face in the dark with rocks being dislodged from above by the incompetent to appreciate this basic requirement. The intricacies of specific mountain rescue techniques can quickly be grasped by the experienced mountaineer to whom rope management is second nature.

I should like to explain the reason for retaining in this book rescue systems which are largely out of date. This is mainly for historical reference. They illustrate how modern techniques have evolved and also, if the basic equipment is available to the do-it-yourself rescuer, such practices may be the only systems which can be deployed.

Lastly I would like to draw attention to the snowballing problem of rescue call-outs, not just in the mountains, but with all outdoor activities. It puts increasing pressure on rescue teams and makes considerable inroads into their free time and personal life, especially with volunteer groups. Employers of volunteers are also faced with this increase of call-out activity and the resultant disruption to productivity.

It is inevitable with the world-wide explosion in leisure activities that Search and Rescue will have to adapt to the proliferation in related accidents. Professional (i.e. paid, full time) rescue groups will, by necessity, evolve. This has already occurred in popular mountain areas but it doesn't diminish the importance of the volunteer rescuer's role in the most basic of human instincts, to help his or her fellow in distress.

Snow Structure

A snow crystal

Introduction

Mountains + Snow = avalanches. It is always worth re-stating this simple equation. It may, however, be worth re-phrasing it to say 'steep slopes + snow = avalanches', bearing in mind that avalanches may occur in certain circumstances in unusual places and at low altitudes. The worst avalanche accident ever to occur in the UK, it should be remembered, took place in 1836 in Lewes, in East Sussex, not a dozen miles from the English Channel.

Great strides have been made in the understanding of the avalanche phenomenon in the past ten to fifteen years. These have centred round the more widespread exchange of information and enlightened approach to co-operation between scientist and practitioner. The bringing to bear of computer science and technology upon the problem of avalanche forecasting has transformed this field from what was almost a black art, into a science which can no longer properly be described as inexact, unless one wishes similarly to describe meteorology, astrophysics and other disciplines. In fact, with some current computer-assisted forecasting systems, the potential exists for the avalanche forecast to be more accurate than the weather forecast upon which it depends.

Having said that, no system operated by human beings may achieve 100 per cent reliability. The sheer difficulty of gathering data in the hostile mountain environment is a serious limiting factor in the generation of accurate avalanche forecasts. Also, the input of the

Grain Shape Classification

Morphological Classification					**Process oriented Classification**		**Additional information on physical processes and strength**		
Basic Classification	*Symb*	*Sub class*	*Symb*	*Description of shape*	*Place of formation*	*Process oriented classification*	*Physical processes*	*Dependence on most important parameters*	*Common effect on strength*
Precipitation particles ✛	1				cloud				
	a	Columns ▱	cl	short prismatic crystal, solid or hollow			Growth at high supersaturation at -3 to -8˚C and below -22˚C		
	b	Needles ↔	nd	Needle-like approx cylindrical			Growth at high supersaturation at -3 to -5˚C		
	c	Plates ⬡	pl	Plate-like, mostly hexagonal			Growth at high supersaturation at -0 to -3˚C and -8 to -25˚C		
	d	Stellar dentrites ✳	sd	Six-fold star-like planar or spacial			Growth at high supersation at temperatures between -12 to -16˚C		
	e	Irregular crystals ⌒	ir	Clusters of very small crystals			Polycrystals growing at varying environmental conditions		
	f	Graupel ⨉	gp	Heavily rimed particles			Heavy riming of particles by accretion of supercooled water		
	g	Hail ▲	hl	Laminar internal structure, translucent or milky, glazed surface			Growth by accretion of supercooled water		
	h	Ice pellets △	ip	Transparent, mostly small spheroids			Frozen rain		
Decomposing & fragmented precipitation particles ╱	2								
	a	Partly decomposed precip. particles ╱	dc	Partly decomposed particles, characteristic shapes of precip. particles still recognisable	Recently deposited snow	Initial rounding and separation	Decrease of surface area to reduce surface free energy at low temperature gradients.	Speed of decomposition decreases with decreasing snow temperature and decreasing temperature gradient.	Strength decrease with time. The felt-like arrangement dendrites has a modest initial strength.
	b	Highly broken particles ╱	bk	Packed, shards or rounded fragments of precipitation particles	Saltation layer	Wind-broken particles. Initially fractured then rapid rounding due to small size	Fragmentation particles are closely packed by wind. Fragmentation followed by rounding and growth.	Fragmentation and packing increase with wind speed.	Quick sintering results in rapid strength increase.
Rounded Grains (monocrystals) ●	3				Dry snow				
	a	Small rounded particles ●	sr	Well-rounded. Particles of size < 0.5 mm often well bonded	Small equilibrium form	Decrease of specific surface area by slow decrease of number of grains and increase of mean grain diameter. Equilibrium form may be partly faceted at lower temperatures.	Growth rate increases with temperature and temperature gradient. Growth slower in higher density snow with smaller pores.	Strength increase with time, density and decreasing grain size.	
	b	Large round particles ●	lr	Well-rounded particles of size > 0.5 mm	Large equilibrium form	Grain-to-grain vapour diffusion due to low to medium temperature gradients. Mean excess vapour density remains below critical value for kinetic growth.	See above.	Strength increase with time, density and decreasing grain size.	
	c	Mixed Forms ◖	mx	Rounded particles with few facets which are developing	Transitional forms as temperature gradient increases	Growth regime changes if temperature gradient increases above critical value of about 10 C/m.	Grains are changing in response to an increasing temperature gradient.	Desintering could decrease strength.	

Morphological Classification					Process oriented Classification		Additional information on physical processes and strength		
Basic Classification	Symb	Sub class	Symb	Description of shape	Place of formation	Process oriented classification	Physical processes	Dependence on most important parameters	Common effect on strength
Faceted crystals $\square$	4				Dry snow				
	a	Solid faceted particles $\square$	fa	Solid, faceted crystals; usually hexagonal prisms		Solid, kinetic growth form	Strong grain-to-grain vapour diffusion driven by large temperature gradient. Excess vapour density above critical value for kinetic growth.	Growth rate increases with temperature, temperature gradient, and decreasing density. May not occur in high density snow because. of small pores	Strength decreases with increasing growth rate and grain size.
	b	Small faceted particles ◩	sf	Small, faceted crystals in surface layer; < 0.5 mm in size	near surface	Kinetic growth form at early stage of development.	May develop directly from 1 or 2a due to large near-surface temperature gradients.	Temperature gradient may periodically change sign but remains at a high absolute value.	Low strength snow.
	c	Mixed forms ⌂	mx	Faceted particles with recent rounding of facets		Transitional form as temperature gradient decreases	Faceted grains are rounding due to decrease in temperature gradient.		
Cup shaped and crystals; Depth Hoar ∧	5				Dry snow				
	a	Cup crystal ∧, ▲	cp	Cup-shaped, striated crystal; usually hollow		Hollow or partly solid cup-shaped kinetic growth crystals	Very fast growth at large temperature gradient.	Formation increases with increasing vapour flux.	Usually fragile but strength increases with density.
	b	Columns of depth hoar ∧	dh	Large, cup-shaped striated hollow crystals arranged in columns (< 10 mm)		Large cup-shaped kinetic growth forms arranged in columns	Intergranular arrangement in columns. Most of the lateral bonds between columns have disappeared during	The snow has almost completely recrystallized. High recrystallization rate for long period at low snow density and high external temperature gradient facilitates formation.	Very fragile snow.
	c	Columnar crystals ═	cl	Very large, columnar crystals with c-axis horizontal (10–20 mm)		Final growth stage of depth hoar at high temperature gradient in low density snow	Evolves from earlier stage described above. Some bonding occurs and new crystals are initiated.	Longer time required than any other snow crystal.	Some strength returns.
Wet grains ◯	6				Wet snow				
	a	Clustered rounded grains ⽊	cl	Clustered rounded crystals held by large ice-to-ice internal veins among three crystals or two-grain boundaries.		Grain clusters without melt-freeze cycles	Wet snow at low water content, pendular regime. Clusters form to minimize surface free energy.	Meltwater can drain. Too much water leads to slush. Freezing leads to melt-freeze particles.	Ice-to-ice bonds give strength.
	b	Rounded poly-crystals ♧	mf	Individual crystals are frozen into a solid polycrystalline grain. May be seen either wet or frozen.		Melt-freeze polycrystals	Wet snow at low water content. Melt-freeze cycles form polycrystals when water in veins freezes.	Particle size increases with number of melt-freeze cycles. Radiation penetration over time restores 6a. Excess water leads to 6c.	High strength in the frozen state. Lower strength in the wet state. Strength increases with number of melt-freeze cycles.
	c	Slush ◦◦◦	sl	Separate rounded crystals completely immersed in water		Poorly bonded, rounded single crystals	High liquid content. Equilibrium form of ice in water.	Water drainage blocked by impermeable layer or ground. High energy input to snow cover by solar radiation, high air temperature or water input.	Little strength due to decaying bonds.

Grain Shape Classification *continued*

					Process oriented Classification		Additional information on physical processes and strength		
Basic Classification	Symb	Sub class	Symb	Description of shape	Place of formation	Process oriented classification	Physical processes	Dependence on most important parameters	Common effect on strength
Feathery crystals $\vee$	7								
	a	Surface hoar crystals $\vee$	sh	Striated, usually feathery crystal; aligned; usually flat, sometimes needle-like	Cold snow surface	Kinetic growth form in air	Rapid kinetic growth of crystals at the snow surface by rapid transfer of water vapour toward the snow surface. Snow surface cooled below ambient air temperature by radiational cooling.	Increasing growth rate with increased cooling of the snow surface and increasing relative humidity of the air.	Fragile, extremely low shear strength. Strength may remain low for extended periods when buried in cold snow.
	b	Cavity hoar $\vee$	ch	Striated, planar or feathery crystals grown in cavities; random orientation	Cavities in snow; same form might grow in very low density snow with extreme T	Kinetic growth form in cavities	Plate or feathery crystals may grow in high temperature gradient fields in large voids in the snow. e.g. in the vicinity of tree trunks, buried bushes or below sun crusts.		
Ice masses ▬	8								
	a	Ice Layer	il	Horizontal ice layer	Buried layers in snow being melted and refrozen	Ice layer from refreezing of draining meltwater. Usually retains some degree of permeability.	Rain or melt water from the surface percolates into cold snow where it refreezes. Water may be preferentially held by fine-grained layer such as a buried wind crust.	Depends on timing of percolating water and cycles of melting and refreezing. More likely to occur if snow is highly stratified.	Ice layers are strong but strength decays once snow is completely wetted.
	b	Ice column	ic	Vertical ice body	Within layers	Icy column from refreezing of draining meltwater.	Water within flow fingers freezes due to heat conduction into surrounding snow at T<0°C.	Flow fingers more likely to occur if snow is highly stratified. Freezing greater if snow is very cold.	
	c	Basal Ice	bi	Basal ice layer	Base of snow cover	Ice forms from freezing of ponded meltwater.	Water ponds above substrate and freezes by heat conduction into cold substrate.	Formation enhanced if substrate is impermeable and very cold (e.g. permafrost).	Weak slush layer may form on top.
Surface deposits and crusts $\vee$	9								
	a	Rime $\vee$	rm	Soft rime: irregular deposit. Hard rime: small supercooled water droplets frozen in place	Surface	Surface rime	Accretion of small, supercooled droplets on to surface grains.	Increases with fog density and exposure to wind.	Thin breakable crust forms if process continues long enough.
	b	Rain crust	rm	Thin, transparent glaze or clear surface layer	Surface	Frozen rain water at snow surface	Results from freezing rain on snow. Forms a surface glaze.	Droplets have to be supercooled but coalesce before freezing.	Thin breakable crust.
	c	Sun crust, firnspiegel	sc	Thin, transparent glaze or surface film	Surface	Refrozen meltwater at snow surface	Refrozen surface layer partially melted by solar radiation. Short-wave absorption in the glaze is decreased. Cooling of the glaze by longwave radiation and evaporation. Greenhouse effect for the underlying snow. Water vapour condenses below the glaze. May develop into smooth, shiny layer of clear ice	Builds during clear weather (longwave cooling), air temperatures below freezing (not to be confused with meltfreeze crusts). Melting can occur below the crust in clean snow.	Thin, often breakable ice crust.

Grain Shape Classification *continued*

Morphological Classification				Process oriented Classification		Additional information on physical processes and strength		
Basic Classification	Symb	Sub class	Symb	Description of shape	Place of formation	Process oriented classification	Physical processes	Dependence on most important parameters	Common effect on strength
d	Wind crust ◖	wc	Small, broken or abraded, closely packed particles; well sintered	Surface	Wind crust	at surface. Fragmentation and packing of wind transported snow particles. High number of contact points and small size causes rapid strength increase through sintering.	Hardness of crust increases with wind speed, decreasing particle size and moderate temperature.	Hard, sometimes breakable crust.
e	Melt-freeze crust ◔	mfc	Crust of recognizable melt-freeze polycrystals	Near surface	Crust of melt-freeze particles	Refrozen layer (e.g. wind crust) which was wetted with water at least once.	Particle size and density increases with number of melt-freeze cycles.	Hardness increases with number of melt-freeze cycles.

Table 2, "Grain Shape Classification," from the preliminary draft of the new "International Classification for Seasonal Snow on the Ground," prepared by the Working Group on Snow Classification (see box on page 5), and issued by the International Commission on Snow and Ice of the International Association of Scientific Hydrology and the International Glaciological Society.

The preliminary draft of the new International Classification will appear in the next issue of *The Avalanche Review*. The final draft will be available by late winter by contacting either Sam Colbeck, CRREL, 72 Lyme Road, Hanover, NH 03755; or Dick Armstrong, CIRES, Campus Box 449, University of Colorado, Boulder, CO 80309.

experienced snow observer cannot, in the foreseeable future, be entirely replaced by the opinion of machines and computer programs, however advanced and sophisticated. Avalanche forecasters, themselves usually seasoned mountaineers or skiers, will therefore routinely seek feedback on snow conditions from MRT members, ski-patrollers, climbers and other members of the public who may have useful current information to offer.

Snow structure

In this chapter we examine the changes ('metamorphism') which take place in snow after it has settled on the ground. The layered snow cover produced by successive falls of snow is universally referred to by English-speaking snow and avalanche workers as the 'snowpack'. In trying to understand the processes which take place, it should be remembered that these are complex, particularly in climate regimes where temperature fluctuations are large or high wind speeds common. Thus, all other influences may be eclipsed by a sudden thaw, producing full-depth wet-snow avalanches. Alternatively, in a heavy snowfall event, accompanied by substantial wind transport, instability amongst the newly-formed surface layers may in itself be the dominant factor affecting avalanche hazard.

Snow crystals

Snow crystals form in the atmosphere. Although the basic habit of the crystal is hexagonal the detailed form is infinitely varied and is determined by the temperature and degree of vapour saturation at the time of formation. Much has been written about the process of crystallization, but from a practical point of view it is sufficient to know that the crystal form will have a profound effect on the subsequent changes which take place within the snow cover and on its propensity for avalanching. The behaviour of a layer of graupel, for example, in which the individual crystals lack any cohesion will be markedly different from a layer of stellar crystals whose delicate and complex structure is highly sensitive to change. Some of the main families of crystals are illustrated on pages 10 – 12.

For the grain shape classification, numbers *1–9* are used for the basic grain types, and letters *a, b, . . .* are used for the corresponding subclassifications. An alternate set of letters is given (e.g. *dh* or *mf*) for those who want symbols that suggest the corresponding English description. The two sets, however, are equivalent. If one has to deal with mixtures of grain types, proportions of the various types may be expressed as the number of tenths, e.g. *8F2aE0.5* and *2F1cE1.0*, where the first number is the fraction, *Fxx* indicates the shape and *Exx* indicates the size. The graphic symbols for the different types of a mixture can either be separated by commas or, if a metamorphic transition between the different types can be identified, arrows indicate the direction of transition.

Additional attributes can be used to refine the description of the grains. Examples of these attributes are grouped below and may be seen in Appendix E, which contains the photographs:

- General appearance: solid, hollow, broken, abraded, partly melted, rounded, angular;
- Grain surface: rounded facets, stepped or striated, rimed;
- Grain interconnections: bonded, unbonded, bond size, clustered, coordination number (number of bonds per grain), oriented texture, arranged in columns.

Grain size   **General symbol: *E***
The grain size of a more or less homogeneous mass of snow is the average size of its characteristic grains. If there is an obvious mixture of different grain types and sizes, the different classes may be characterised individually. The size of a grain or particle is its greatest extension measured in millimetres. Other definitions are possible depending on the application but have to be clearly stated. A simple method suitable for field measurements is to place a sample of the grains on a plate that has been ruled in millimetres. The average size is then estimated by comparing the size of the grains with the spacing of the lines on the plate. This estimate may differ from those obtained by sieving or stereology. Some users will need to specify the range or distribution of sizes.

The grain size of deposited snow is expressed in millimetres or alternatively by using the terms in Table 3. A grain size of 1 mm is classified as *E1.0*.

Table 3. Grain size.

Term	Size (mm)
Very fine	< 0.2
Fine	0.2–0.5
Medium	0.5–1.0
Coarse	1.0–2.0
Very Coarse	2.0–5.0
Extreme	> 5.0

Liquid water content   **General Symbol: *θ***
Measurements of liquid water content or wetness are expressed as a percentage by volume, which usually requires a separate measurement of density. Several methods are in use today for field measurements to determine liquid water content: hot (melting) and cold (freezing) calorimetry, dilution and dielectric measurements. A general classification of liquid water content is given in Table 4.

Liquid water is only mobile if the irreducible water content is exceeded. The irreducible water content is about 3 per cent by volume and depends significantly on snow texture, grain size and grain shape. This is the water that can be held by surface forces against the pull of gravity.

Impurities   **General symbol: *J***
This subsection has been included in the classification to cover those cases in which the kind and amount of an impurity have an influence on the physical characteristics of the snow. In these cases the kind of impurity should be fully described and its amount given as a percentage by weight. Common impurities are dust, sand, organic material and solubles. Very low amounts of impurities do not strongly influence the physical properties of snow but are of hydrological and environmental interest. These are normally given in parts per million by weight (e.g. acids). The graphic symbol for impurities is ▭▭

Table 4. Liquid water content.

Term	Remarks	Approximate Range of θ	Graphic Symbol
Dry	Usually T is below 0°C, but dry snow can occur at any temperature up to 0°C. Disaggregated snow grains have little tendency to adhere to each other when pressed together, as in making a snowball.	0%	
Moist	$T = 0$°C. The water is not visible even at 10 × magnification. When lightly crushed, the snow has a distinct tendency to stick together.	<3%	
Wet	$T = 0$°C. The water can be recognised at 10 × magnification by its meniscus between adjacent snow grains, but water cannot be pressed out by moderately squeezing the snow in the hands. (Pendular regime)	3–8%	
Very Wet	$T = 0$°C. The water can be pressed out by moderately squeezing the snow in the hands, but there is an appreciable amount of air confined within the pores. (Funicular regime)	8–15%	
Slush	$T = 0$°C. The snow is flooded with water and contains a relatively small amount of air	> 15%	

Table 5. Hardness of deposited snow.

Term	Swiss Rammsonde (N)	Order of magnitude strength (Pa)	Hand test	Symbol	Graphic symbol
Very low	0–20	$0–10^3$	fist	R1	
Low	20–150	$10^3–10^4$	4 fingers	R2	/
Medium	150–500	$10^4–10^5$	1 finger	R3	✕
High	500–1000	$10^5–10^6$	pencil	R4	//
Very High	>1000	$> 10^6$	knife blade	R5	※
Ice				R6	▬

Snow strength   General symbol: Σ

Snow strength depends on the stress state (compressive, tensile or shear), stress rate, strain and strain rate. In addition, strength depends on the sample volume because snow is imhomogeneous. To make measurements meaningful, all of these parameters must be considered. Moreover, strength types such as ductile, brittle fracture or maximum strength at low strain rates must be given.

Strain is dimensionless. The units are s^{-1} for strain rate, Pa for stress and Pa·s for stress rate.

Snow hardness   General symbol: R

Hardness measurements are subjective and produce an index value that depends on the instrument; therefore, the device has to be specified. A widely accepted instrument is the Swiss Rammsonde (cone tip angle: 60°; base diameter: 40 mm; weight: 10 N/m; ram weight: 10 N). Hardness is measured in newtons. It may be classified as shown in Table 5, which includes both the Rammsonde and the commonly used hand test. With the hand test, objects of different areas are gently pushed into the snow with a penetration force of about 50 N, which is easily executed with the hand.

Metamorphism

No sooner have they formed than snow crystals start to undergo certain changes. These may take place as the snowflake falls through the atmosphere, drastically altering the original shape, for instance by the addition of rime as the crystal falls through a moist layer, or they may take place as the snow accumulates on the ground. The nature and speed of these changes is determined by the prevailing temperature and pressure. In recent years, a new nomenclature has been adopted to describe the changes affecting snow crystals in the snowpack. The changes to crystals known in previous texts as 'destructive' or 'equi-temperature' metamorphism are now referred to as 'equilibrium forms'. The old 'constructive' or 'temperature gradient' metamorphism is now known as 'kinetic growth'.

Equilibrium forms – changes leading to stabilisation

In the normal course of events this leads to a simplification and rounding of crystal structure with the establishment of strong bonds between individual crystals and a shrinking of the whole snow layer. Equilibrium forms are thus created, a process known in common parlance as 'settling', and it is accelerated as the

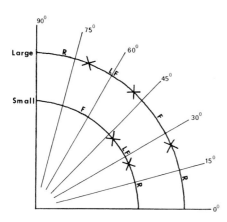

temperature approaches the freezing point. It is clearly a process which has a stabilising influence on the snow pack resulting ultimately in the formation of a single compact layer of homogeneous ice crystals known as spring snow or neve.

Kinetic growth – changes leading to instability

Under certain conditions, usually in cold regions or high altitudes where there is intense radiative heat loss from the snow surface, a strong temperature gradient exists between the relatively warm base layers in contact with the ground and the much colder surface layers exposed to the atmosphere. Under the influence of this gradient water vapour moves upwards, recrystallising at favourable localities within the snowpack.

The product of this process of vapour migration and recrystallisation is the formation of faceted (early stage), stepped or 'laddered' kinetic growth crystals, leading ultimately to the hexagonal, conical, hollow 'cup crystal'. Intermediate and later stage kinetic growth crystals are often referred to as 'sugar snow', while the term 'depth hoar' is still widely used to describe more or less any stage of development. A fairly wide latitude appears to exist in the use of these terms. The adoption of the International Commission on Snow and Ice's current terminology does not appear to be by any means universal, as the French, for instance, still refer routinely to 'metamorphose de gradient'.

It should be noted that buried surface hoar, in suitable conditions, has a development similar to that of true depth hoar. Furthermore, kinetic growth may occur and faceted crystals develop, much more quickly than generally appreciated.

Left: This illustration shows the frequency of both large and small avalanches in relation to slope angle. R = Rare; F = Frequent; LF = Less Frequent (K Spence)

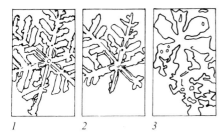

1   2   3

Equilibrium forms:
These illustrations below are of the same crystal maintained at a temperature of –9°C; separation time approx. three hours. The third illustration shows the same crystal after three days at –9°C

Precipitation particle sub-classes:
1 This shows the initial period of partial stability and at this stage the crystals are hooked together. This lasts only a short time – the period during a fall and shortly after (but not after the first sun or thaw)

2 This is a dangerous period of high instability which can vary from a few days to several weeks depending on temperature and conditions. The crystals are free to move as they have lost cohesion. This is the period for dry loose snow avalanches in alpine regions

3 Bonds are formed in the settled snow at their points of contact. This is the longest stage in the firnification process and eventually leads to firn snow (Eric Langmuir)

There is no need for a strong temperature gradient to exist throughout the whole depth of the snowpack.

Extreme gradients of 60–70°C/metre have been recorded on many occasions in Scotland, over sections of the snowpack depth. It appears that this is sufficient to produce faceting overnight, or certainly after a day or two. Layers of depth hoar are extremely fragile and may give rise to devastating avalanches when overloaded beyond their strength. Avalanches may also run on thin layers of kinetic growth crystals. In addition because they may form deep within the snowpack they can

Depth hoar crystal (Horska Sluzba)

only be detected by digging a snow pit to ground level or by computer simulation (see Crocus pp. 30 & 40).

Melt/freeze metamorphism – changes leading alternatively to stabilisation or to instability

In the spring the temperature of the whole snow cover may be just below freezing level. Because of radiation heat loss at night, the snow alternately freezes and thaws and this gives rise to the third process of change known as melt/freeze metamorphism. The effect of this is that the larger crystals grow at the expense of the smaller and that there is a very marked difference in the strength of the snow depending on whether it is in the melt or freeze phase of the cycle. The danger lies in the melt phase when water (rain or melt

SAIS — SURFACE PIT RECORD

DATE	20/12/93	TIME	10 10 Hrs	AREA	NORTHERN CAIRNGORMS	OBS	SB/TR	
LOCN	CISTE MHEARAD	GRID	011046	ALT	1100 m	ASPECT	15	DEKA°
						INCLIN	48	°

MET. INFORMATION

AIR TEMP	−5.3	WIND DIR	30 DEKA°	WIND SPEED	20 mph	CLOUD	O	%
PRECIP (SN/R)	NIL	DRIFT (Y/N)	TRACE	BEATTIE SCALE	2 5 3 / 1 2 2	IF CAT 3 +/-	Today	Tomorrow
					10 3 1 = 29		+	+

SNOWPACK INFORMATION

PEN FT	15 Cm	PEN SKI	10 Cm	PEN RAM	⟋ Cm	AVAL CODE	1

GRAIN TYPE: Basic Classification

1	+	Precipitation Particles
2	/	Decomposing and Fragmented Particles
3	●	Rounded Grains
4	□	Faceted Crystals
5	∧	Cup-shaped and Depth Hoar Crystals
6	O	Wet Grains
7	V	Feathery Crystals
8	▬	Ice Masses
9	∀	Surface Deposits and Crusts

Hardness
1. Fist
2. 4 Fingers /
3. 1 Finger X
4. Pencil //
5. Knife ✗
6. Ice ▬

Wetness
No Snowball — Drop III
Snowball I — Flooded IIII
Wet Glove II

Snow Temperature °C

Surface pit record showing a strong temperature gradient (maximum 25° C/metre) associated with faceting in the 80–90 cm layer. A gradient of about 10° C/metre is regarded as usually being sufficient to drive kinetic growth. The apparently positive snow temperature at the bottom of the pit is a result of a thermometer error.

Below: The effect of a vertical slope profile on the forces within the snow caused by creep. The tension and the compression are indicated by the spacing of the bars. CZ = Compression Zone; NZ = Neutral Zone; TZ = Tension Zone, where it is highly probable that an avalanche could start. The top line of arrows indicates creep and the lower line of arrows indicates glide. As mentioned in the text, it is possible for a full depth avalanche to slide on the ground, e.g. a grassy slope (K Spence)

Below: When the weight of a slab exerts a component of force parallel to the sliding surface greater than the shear strength of the bond the primary condition for the release of a slab avalanche is achieved. This condition can be reached by an increased snow load (a rise in stress) or by a decrease in strength caused by constructive metamorphism or crust disintegration. Stress can be calculated if the slab thickness, the slope angle, and the mean density of the slab are known: $T = Mg \sin \theta$
Where
  M = Mass of unit volume of snow
  g = Accel. of gravity
  T = Shear stress at bottom slab due to M
By the use of a shear frame, the strength of successive snow layers may be measured and the Stability Index may be calculated. (R Turner)

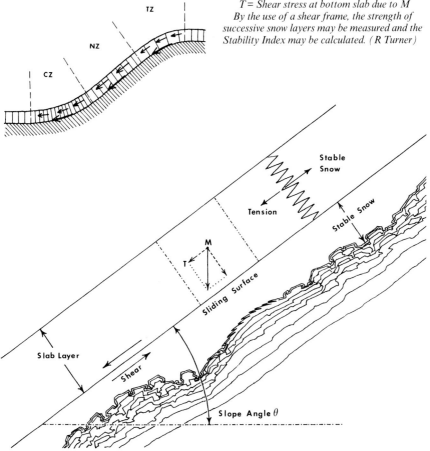

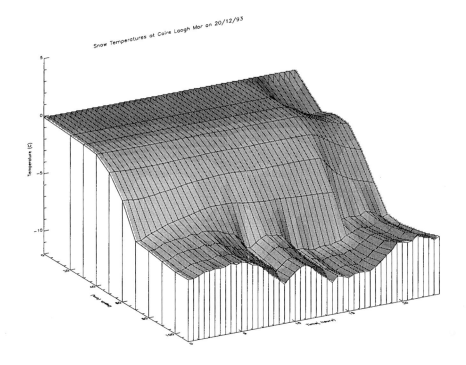

Snow Temperatures at Coire Laogh Mor on 20/12/93

24 hour Cairngorm graph: snow temperature against time and depth, Cairngorm 20–12–93.

water) percolates through the snow till it reaches the ground or an impermeable crust. Flowing at this level it may completely undermine the anchorage and provide an effective lubricant for any subsequent avalanche. However, when rain falls on the snowpack, as is common in maritime climates, avalanches may occur before free water is able to reach lower levels. The mechanism for this phenomenon remains to be fully understood but it is common following a fall of fresh snow.

These then are the three fundamental processes of metamorphism which determine the nature of the snowpack and which give rise to the infinite variations of its physical and mechanical properties.

Snowfall

What is it that causes snow to avalanche? First of all there has to be enough snow. The more there is and the faster it accumulates the more likely it is to avalanche and the larger that avalanche will be. Even 25 cm of snow can form an impressive slide.

Most avalanches occur during or immediately after a heavy fall of snow, so that this is a time to be particularly careful in the mountains. Evidence suggests that the rate of precipitation is as important as the total amount of snow which falls in a single storm. Precipitation intensities in excess of 2·5 cm/hr are usually regarded as hazardous. It will be appreciated that precipitation intensity is a measure of the rate at which a slope is loaded. In addition, new snow adds to the burden on the layers below and this can precipitate a

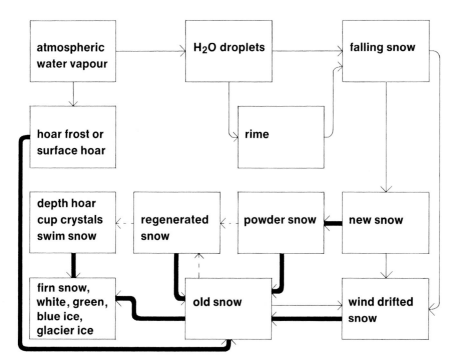

The hydrologic cycle *above*
Only in certain conducive climatic
conditions does falling snow reach the final
stage of glacier ice. This table shows the
phases of the hydrologic cycle and the ways
in which water vapour is deposited as a solid
on the surface of the ground. Due to sudden
thaw conditions the ice may revert to the
liquid phase by melting. Depth hoar is also
called 'Cup crystals' and 'Swim snow' in
certain areas. Dotted lines indicate kinetic
growth.

failure in them. Indeed, the most common
avalanche trigger is a fall of fresh snow.

Angle of slope

The slope must also be sufficiently steep to
allow the snow to slide. Generally
speaking, the steeper the slope, the more
likely it is to avalanche, but on very steep
slopes, say over 60 degrees, the snow rarely
gets a chance to accumulate, so large
avalanches on such slopes are infrequent.
The most dangerous slopes are therefore
those of intermediate angle, between
30–45 degrees. However, because
accumulations on lower-angles slopes may
be much greater, when in extreme
conditions they do produce avalanches,
they can be of exceptional magnitude.

Strength v stress

These two factors of weight of snow and
angle of slope are the main stress factors
tending to move the snow downhill. They
are resisted by the strength of the snow
which, in simple terms, can be regarded as
a function of the cohesion of the
individual crystals and the adhesion of the
various layers to each other and to the
surface of the ground below. Theoretically,
at least, when the stress factors exceed the
strength of the snow, failure will occur. In
practice affairs are a good deal more

European Avalanche Hazard Scale

	Degree of hazard	Snowpack stability	Avalanche probability
1	Low	The snowpack is generally well bonded and stable.	Triggering is generally possible only with high additional loads** and few very steep extreme slopes. Only a few small natural avalanches (sluffs) possible.
2	Moderate	The snowpack is moderately well bonded on some steep slopes*, otherwise generally well bonded.	Triggering possible with high additional loads**, particularly on the steep slopes indicated in the bulletin. Large natural avalanches not likely.
3	Considerable	The snowpack is moderately to weakly bonded on many steep slopes*.	Triggering possible, sometimes even with low additional loads**. The bulletin indicates many slopes which are particularly affected. In certain conditions, medium and occasionally large-sized natural avalanches may occur.
4	High	The snowpack is weakly bonded in most steep slopes*.	Triggering probable even with low additional loads** on many steep slopes. In some conditions, frequent medium or large-sized natural avalanches are likely.
5	Very high	The snowpack is generally weakly bonded and largely unstable.	Numerous large natural avalanches are likely, even in moderately steep terrain.

Explanations: * generally described in more detail in the avalanche bulletin (e.g. altitude, aspect, type of terrain etc.)
** additional load:– high: e.g. group of skiers, piste machine, avalanche blasting – low: e.g. skier, walker
– steep slopes: slopes with an incline of more than about 30°
– steep extreme slopes: particularly unfavourable in terms of the incline, terrain profile, proximity to ridge, smoothness of underlying ground surface
aspect: compass bearing directly down slope
natural: without human assistance

Davos, 5. Mai 1994

complex. Providing the overloading is not too sudden the snow may adjust by internal deformation (creep) or by the sliding of the whole snow layer along the ground (glide). These phenomena are well seen in the spring when the whole snow cover may become buckled and warped as a result of the plastic response of the snow to downslope pressure. It is the absence of such a response which allows the tension to build up to the point where slab fracture is the only way of restoring equilibrium to the system.

Slab avalanches

Slab avalanches constitute by far the greatest potential hazard in the mountains in winter and they are, more often than not, quite impossible to identify merely by a surface inspection. Unstable slabs can result from a variety of conditions, but it is in the attachment of the slab to the layer below that we must look for the underlying cause. In extreme cases there may be no attachment at all, the underlayers having contracted away leaving the slab completely unsupported over a considerable area. This situation makes it easier to understand the often hair-trigger sensitivity of slabs. More commonly, there will be some discontinuity between the slab and the layer below. This may take the form of a crust or an intervening layer of weak unconsolidated snow, or it may be that an earlier firm anchorage has been destroyed by the growth of a layer of depth hoar. In the spring the attachment of the whole snow cover to the ground becomes of increasing significance. Smooth surfaces such as rock slabs or long grass offer little support.

Probably the greatest single factor in promoting the development of slabs is the wind. Under its influence, snow is transported and packed into 'windslabs' which can vary in hardness from no more than firm powder (soft slab) to a consistency more akin to concrete (hard slab). The latter is associated with higher windspeeds greater than 30 mph/48 kph.

> *Recently formed slab is particularly unstable!!*

Avalanche prediction in Mountain Rescue

The difficulties involved in avalanche prediction have already been touched upon. It is clear that much can be inferred from the careful observation of recent and prevailing weather conditions and from a knowledge of local terrain and the location of avalanche paths. Nevertheless, it is only by a detailed examination of the whole snow cover from surface to ground that its various characteristics can be positively identified and an attempt made to estimate the likelihood of an avalanche. This will seldom be practical for mountain rescuers involved in the urgent necessities of search and rescue work.

Fortunately, in most Alpine and sub-Alpine countries, an avalanche forecasting network exists. Avalanche forecasters, as indicated earlier, will usually be experienced mountain people, who have had specialised training. They may have access to computer-assisted forecasting techniques and indeed, may themselves be mountain rescuers or former members of teams. It cannot be emphasised too strongly that close study of the current avalanche forecast and preferably, direct contact with the forecaster, should be the *first* resort of any MRT leader.

Having said this, areas still exist where no avalanche forecast network is in place. Also, in a prolonged rescue, weather conditions may develop in an unexpected way, invalidating the avalanche forecast. Therefore, it is necessary for mountain rescuers to be able to make their own judgements and to have a repertoire of techniques and tests which they can use to ensure their own safety.

Taking a snow profile in the Cairngorms, Scotland (E Langmuir)

Surface snow pits

It will generally not be possible, given the pressures of time in a mountain rescue, to perform the kind of detailed snowpit analysis carried out by avalanche forecasters. Indeed, there would be little point in doing this, as the interpretation of such data as temperature profile and hardness of layers (particularly the examination of a ram penetrometer profile) are a matter for the specialist. However, the snowpit may still be a useful tool, especially the quickly-executed 'hasty pit' or 'surface snow pit'. There, the implication is that the mountaineer is mainly interested in the snow layers which exist above the highest substantial layer of old neve or snow-ice.

A problem in any kind of snowpit examination or shear test is to ensure that the site being used is representative of the suspect slope. Thus the snowpit site should be of the same orientation and, as far as possible, altitude, as this. Digging a pit using shovel or ice-axe down to the first substantial neve layer, will then display any avalanche hazard which happens to be particularly obvious, such as air space between layers, unstable layers of graupel (hail) or windslab lying on icy crusts.

It should be possible to identify individual layers, find out whether any are particularly soft or whether there are any radical differences in hardness between adjacent layers. Wetness of layers may be tested by taking a handful of snow from each layer and trying to make a snowball. With very dry snow, no snowball will form. However, as a rule of thumb, if it is possible to squeeze water drops from a snowball formed from any layer, then serious instability is likely to exist at that level.

Particular caution should be observed when there are accumulations of fresh windslab. As already stated, this is particularly unstable and significant shear planes may exist in soft surface layers where it is not possible to identify any change in hardness or crystal type between layers. It should be seriously questioned whether it is reasonable to proceed on to steep slopes in these circumstances.

Shovel test

Despite the name, a shovel is not necessary. Your ice axe and gloved hands will suffice. To perform the test, isolate a wedge shaped block, cutting down to the top of the next identified layer. If the top layer slides spontaneously, a very poor bond exists between the layers. If it does, then try to rate the ease with which you can pull the snow block off by inserting your shovel/ice axe/hands behind the block and pulling. Do this for each suspect layer in your pit. In marginal conditions, several shovel tests may be

necessary before an opinion can be formed.

Performing this test many times will help you to build up a 'feeling' for the stability of the layers. As you climb, digging stances, cutting steps or placing deadman, all give you an opportunity to make a quick check on surface layers.

These techniques should enable you to make an educated risk assessment. Remember that your observations will hold good only for slopes of similar orientation to your test site.

You will need to extrapolate for situations higher up, for instance below cornices where surface windslab layers may be much thicker. An attempt should be made to rate the slope Safe, Marginal or Unsafe. Even if a slope is Marginal or Unsafe, it may be possible to choose a safe route by careful selection.

A different form of shovel test is current in North America, where the loaded column test is also used (Tremper, Schaerer et al).

Ski Rutschblock test

The Rutschblock test, originating from Norway and Switzerland, has gained a certain vogue partly because a system now exists for quantifying the results. It is said that it provides a better index of the propensity of a slope to avalanche, because it necessarily takes into account the loading effect of all the snow layers, while the shovel test progressively removes these. In practice, researchers report a good correlation between shovel and Rutschblock test results.

As with the shovel test, the use of the Rutschblock must be hedged around with caveats. Does the site selected represent the avalanche situation which actually threatens? In other words, the stability of the main slope may be acceptable, but the weakest point may be higher up, where deeper deposits of fresh slab may lie below a ridge crest which must be approached. Again, the possibility of a spontaneous

Avalanche
Classification System
(G Hunter)

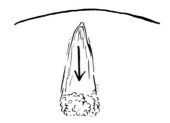 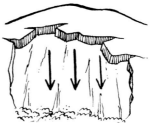

Criterion

1 Type of breakaway   Loose snow avalanche   *Slab avalanche*

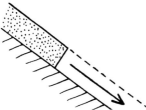 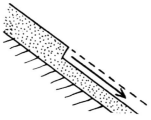

2 Position of
*   sliding surface   Full depth avalanche*   *Surface avalance*

3 Humidity of
*   the snow   Dry snow avalanche*   *Wet snow avalanche*

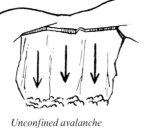 

4 Form of the
*   track in*
crosssection
*   Unconfined avalanche*   *Channelled avalanche*

5 Form of
*   movement   Airborne powder avalanche*   *Flowing avalanche*

Right: A powder snow avalanche at Alta, Utah, USA

Below right: This church, outside Davos, Switzerland, is built in a regular avalanche path. Note the massive splitting wedge at right hand end (E Langmuir)

Left: The 'Shovel' test. This test can be done with an ice axe, or even with your hands to test the stability of the snow, see text. (P Moores)
Inset showing close-up of snow block. (P Moores)

avalanche coming from above must always be considered, even if shear tests indicate that the slope examined is safe.

Tests show that a single Rutschblock may give only about a 65 per cent probability of establishing the slope median value. However, two such tests, performed at least 10 m apart, will give a 90 per cent chance of establishing this. This practice is therefore *recommended*.

A further difficulty with the Rutschblock test is that, traditionally, it is said that it must be performed on a slope of 30 degrees or more, in order that the propensity of layers actually to slide could be observed. However, recent tests in Canada have established that an extrapolation may be made from a site of less than 30 degrees angle if one step on the Rutschblock scale is subtracted for each increase in angle of 10 degrees. Thus, a value of 4 gained at a site of 25 degree angle low down on a slope, could be extrapolated as giving a value of 2 on a 45 degree slope higher up. This, of course, makes the large assumption that snowpack factors are similar at the two sites. Finally, it should be noted that Rutschblock tests may give little information on soft surface layers. In this case, the shovel test may give useful indications.

Because the column isolated in this test is larger than that used in the shovel test, it may be assumed that it gives a better

average for the condition of layers on a given slope. Having isolated the block by the use of a shovel, ski or snow saw, an attempt is then made to dislodge it. The ease with which it fails is judged according to the following scale:

1. Fails when isolating the column.
2. Fails when approaching the column.
3. Fails when standing on the column.
4. Fails with soft jump.
5. Fails with one hard jump.
6. Fails with several hard jumps or taking off skis and jumping.
7. Does not fail.

Modified or walking Rutschblock

Given that in some countries, such as Scotland, rescuers are seldom on skis, a modification of the ski Rutschblock may be found useful. This was first described by Tremper, who used a block of 3 to 4 feet square. SAIS Observers on Cairngorm use a 1 metre-square block, tapering to 80 cm at the upslope side. A similar scale is used to quantify the slope stability, but in the absence of skis, the observer kneels on the block, in order to circumvent the problem of excessive foot penetration.

This test is found to correlate well with ski Rutschblock tests. In the same way as with the skis tests, two tests more than 10 metres apart should give a 90 per cent chance of finding the slope median. This is therefore the *method of choice* when conditions are suitable.

Route choice

Experienced rescuers and other mountaineers can undoubtedly operate and survive in areas of high avalanche hazard. This ability is due partly to developed understanding of snow conditions, but also very largely to a capability in choosing safe routes. Thus, in conditions when avalanches are likely, steep open slopes and gullies are to be avoided. Routes which follow ridges and buttresses will invariably be safer, particularly as they in addition give the possibility of belaying on rock rather than snow. On mountain ridges, the windward side may be preferred to the leeward, even if a cornice is not present, as it may be scoured free of new snow. Convex slopes are notoriously more prone to avalanche than concave ones. In particularly unstable conditions, or when exceptional snow accumulations are present, then the possibility of greatly extended avalanche run-outs should be borne in mind.

Computer forecasting

In recent years, much effort has been devoted to devising computer-assisted avalanche forecasting systems. This work has taken place mainly in France and Switzerland, although McLung in Canada and others in Norway and elsewhere have also been active.

As computer models ideally require data from representative fixed sites, such systems are often used in conjunction with automatic weather stations, along with

Damage to ski tow and parked car near Davos, Switzerland (E Langmuir)

snow depth and temperature monitoring equipment.

Perhaps the most impressive system is the French SAFRAN/CROCUS/MEPRA complex, in which SAFRAN is the data gathering element, CROCUS models the snowpack evolution and MEPRA is an expert system which basically uses shear calculations to establish snowpack stability. The accuracy with which CROCUS simulates the evolution of the snowpack using only meteorological data, is a source of amazement for most beholders.

For their centrally-produced forecasts, the Swiss use two models (MODULL and DAVOS), of which MODULL, a neural network system, is perhaps the most intriguing. However, the overall accuracy of neural networks is limited to about 80 per cent (in itself a very good average), by the problem of over-training on a given data set.

There is now great interest in local forecasting systems at the level of an individual ski area, using models which will run on a PC. Of these, the Swiss NXD Nearest Neighbours is probably the most widely used. It is a statistical model, which compares a range of meteorological and snowpack variables forecasted for a given day, with similar data for all available days in the past. A 'distance' between the forecast day and those past days is then computed and the ten days in the past 'nearest' to the forecast day are displayed, along with information as to avalanche activity. If more than 30 per cent of the past days are avalanche days, the forecast day should also be an avalanche day. Information as to altitude and slope aspect of past avalanches is also available.

The French ASTRAL model is very similar in conception, but appears at the moment to be less widely used.

AVALOG is an 'expert', or rule-based machine-intelligence system, used mainly in France. It produces an index of avalanche probability for individual slide-paths controlled by explosives.

Currently under development in Switzerland, but being tested also in France, Italy and Scotland, is the NX. LOG system, which is a combination of expert and statistical approaches and which will ultimately evolve as a 'computer learning' system, creating its own corrections to the rules in its database.

Good results with computer-assisted forecasting systems depend on accurate data. Results up to 90 per cent overall accuracy with close to 100 per cent on avalanche days, have occasionally been achieved over a season's operation. As yet, however, nó system has been devised which can exclude the final judgement of the human observer.

Other computer assistance exists in the field of data recording, management and transmission. The most comprehensive system is probably the French ADIPRA program, some versions of which incorporate the PRELA analogous days forecasting system. The AVALINK/ WINPIT system used in Scotland, linked to the NXD forecasting model, is similar to this, as is the proprietary ADICLHIMA system, used in some French ski resorts. The SNOWLINK program from Utah is essentially a data management tool.

Current research includes the use of GIS (Geographical Information Systems) for calculating avalanche release time and run-out, as well as modelling and quantifying wind transport of snow. Three dimensional modelling has also been linked to NXD output to display avalanche hazard in graphical form. This method of displaying the avalanche forecast, perhaps with hands-on 'fly-through' capability at key user points, should be available to the public in the near future.

Rescuers probing debris of a large wet snow avalanche, Ben Nevis, Scotland, for buried climbers. It is possible that this avalanche was triggered by a helicopter passing on another rescue operation (H MacInnes)

Below: Slab release occurs when stresses at top, sides and bottom of the slab exceed the strength properties of the snow. This is the secondary condition for slab release (R Turner)

Bottom: Avalanche search: Showing the probable burial areas of an avalanche victim. A indicates the point when avalanched. B the point when last seen. P and P indicate possible places of burial, usually in a continuation of a line drawn between A and B (G Hunter)

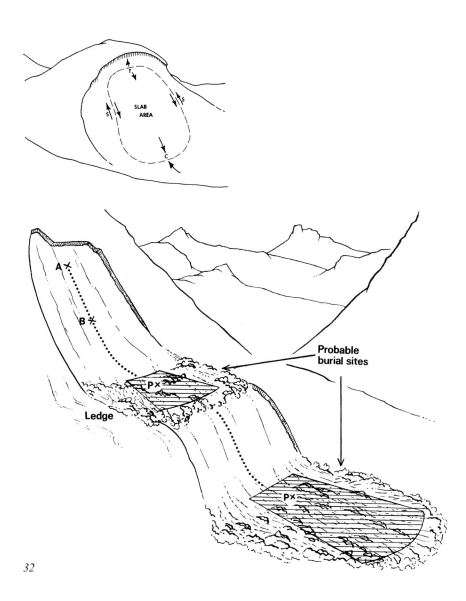

Avalanche hazard scale

As well as co-operation in the creation and testing of computer forecasting systems, the western European avalanche agencies are involved in other joint projects. One of these was the formulation and adoption of the common Avalanche Hazard Scale.

This now avoids the difficulties which arose for ski-tourers in particular, who might be crossing national boundaries into countries where different scales were in use.

Types of avalanche

An avalanche is a complex dynamic phenomenon which is not easily pigeon-holed into one category or another. Many of the larger ones defy classification, comprising, as they do, a series of consecutive events each one triggered by its predecessor and involving one layer after another until the whole snow cover is on the move. Nevertheless, it is possible to

Below: Hard slab avalanche, Lochnagar, Cairngorm, Scotland (Laraig Club)

describe most avalanches by reference to a set of five criteria. This simple system, recognised internationally, is illustrated on page 25.

Within this system it is possible to identify a number of recurring types which merit some further consideration.

I. Dry powder or airborne-powder (aerosol) avalanches

This type of avalanche prevails in cold, dry conditions. At such times slopes, especially north-facing ones, may be hazardous for weeks until the snow has settled. Windward slopes may settle after a few days of good weather, although it must be remembered that wind-transported snow may form slabs elsewhere. The higher the altitude the greater and more prolonged the hazard.

Features: Most so-called 'powder' avalanches in fact start off as soft slabs. Gathering momentum and material on the way, they produce a fast-moving mass of powder snow. If a powder avalanche attains a velocity of around 65 kph, it may become airborne or partly airborne (mixed motion). Such avalanches have been recorded as achieving velocities of between 300 and 400 kph. The mechanism for this probably involves the creation of a suspension of air and snow dust at the snow surface, enabling the avalanche to gain in mass from the snow over which it is travelling. 'Ground-cushion effect' has also been propounded as a mechanism for at least some of these avalanches.

It appears more or less impossible to predict when an airborne, as opposed to a flowing powder avalanche will occur. However, experience in Scotland, where airborne avalanches are relatively rare, indicates that on many occasions when such avalanches have been observed, a high percentage of graupel (hail) has been present in the snowpack. It may be that this provides a very mobile layer, which may allow the avalanche to accelerate quickly enough, even on the relatively short slopes available in Scotland, to achieve the threshold velocity.

Indications: As little as 20 cm of snow in the starting zone can pose a threat, though, as mentioned previously, the precipitation intensity is also of critical importance. As a rough guide, an accumulation rate in excess of 2·5 cm per hour is a dangerously high value. Typical circumstances include: new snow falling on a surface crust or on a layer of surface hoar; new cold snow falling after a period of cold weather.

II. Soft slab avalanches

These are the most common of winter avalanches and are associated with the rapid accumulation of fresh snow on lee slopes under the influence of winds of 16–48 kph. After heavy falls the danger may not be confined to lee slopes and all slopes should be treated with suspicion till the snow settles. This may occur in a matter of hours or it may take several days if conditions remain cold. Extensive sloughing is a sure sign that settlement is taking place.

Features: Although it may be released as a unit, the soft slab, by definition, pulverises in motion and if it is large enough may develop into a powder avalanche – see above. Initially, it involves only the surface layer of snow, although its release may trigger off other weaknesses within the snow cover. It is as well to remember the dictum that most soft slab avalanches are released by their victims.

Indications: Soft slabs are most easily recognised by reference to the weather conditions which favour their formation. Since they are surface phenomena it is usually possible in the field to dig through the surface layer and examine the attachment to the underlayer. In a suitable test location the slab will often respond to a kick with a boot or ski by breaking away

A hard slab fracture wall with curtains of blown snow. Lochnagar, Scotland (Laraig Club)

in straight-edged pieces. The same kind of practical test on a larger scale involves 'test skiing' in safe locations which nevertheless have a similar exposure to the avalanche-prone slopes. It is important to remember that in the absence of fresh snow, drifting alone can build up soft slabs on lee slopes.

III. Hard slab avalanches

The hard slab presents one of the greatest hazards in the mountains, not because of its frequency, but because its deceptively solid surface gives a false sense of security to those passing over it. The combination of high winds (>48 kph) and high humidity favours the formation of hard slabs on lee slopes. If it remains cold the danger can persist for some time and may be obscured by subsequent snow falls.

Features: Release is much the same as for soft slabs and may be accompanied by a sharp cracking noise. In this case, however, the slab breaks up into a jigsaw of angular blocks, many of which remain intact on

Right: The tail end of an ice avalanche, Caucasus, Russia (P Nunn)

Below: This photograph illustrates the angular blocks of a large slab avalanche in Czechoslovakia (Horska Sluzba)

the journey down the slope. It need hardly be said that a large hard slab avalanche possesses enormous destructive power.

Indications: Hard slab has a dull, chalky appearance and occasionally emits a booming noise when walked upon. A lack of adhesion to the underlayer is characteristic of all hard slabs and indeed in some cases the slabs are not attached at all over considerable areas. Such circumstances give rise to sudden local subsidence which can be most alarming even on the flat. Hard slabs are frequently associated with strong temperature gradients and a consequent build-up of depth hoar. A dangerous slab exhibits an almost hair-trigger sensitivity and may be released by the passage of a skier or mountaineer or spontaneously, by a sudden rise in temperature.

IV. Climax avalanche

So called because it is the result of changing characteristics deep within the snow cover over a prolonged period of time. It could be described as a 'delayed action' avalanche caused by the failure of some weak layer overloaded beyond its strength. The overloading is almost invariably caused by a fall of new snow and more often than not the weakness is a layer of depth hoar. It will be clear that such avalanches usually involve the entire snow cover and for this reason can reach devastating proportions.

Indications: Surface indications are useless. The only sure way of recognising the danger of a climax avalanche is to dig a snow pit to ground level or by computer simulation.

V. Wet avalanches

Common in spring and following thaw conditions at any time during the winter, wet avalanches result from thaw or rainfall

Inset: An avalanche off the northern slopes of Huascarán Norte which fell between the Llanganuco Lakes, on 31st May 1970. Fourteen members of a Czech expedition are buried under the debris (H Clark, American Alpine Club Journal)

The enormous avalanche which fell off Huascarán Norte 31st May 1970. The main branch on the right destroyed Renrahirca. The minor branch on the left wiped out Yungay. About 17 million cubic metres of ice and rock fell a vertical height of 13,000 ft/3,965 m. Due to the high pressures generated much of the ice turned to water. It reached a speed of almost 200 mph/320 kph. A portion of the avalanche which swept uphill some 650 ft/198 m, spilled over a hill into Yungay. Although this was a mere trickle compared to the main avalanche which destroyed Renrahirca, it killed some 3,700 people and entombed them in 40 ft/12 m of debris. Ten years later the town of Yungay was virtually flattened with the loss of 18,000 lives in an earthquake (Dr Walter Welsch, American Alpine Club Journal)

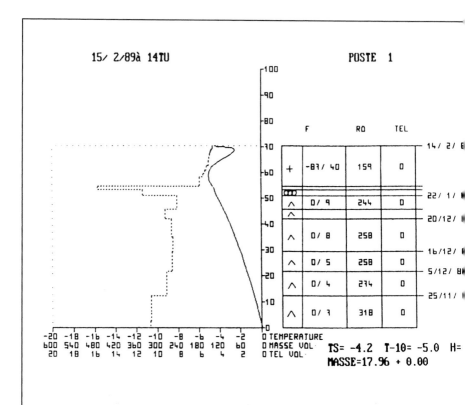

15/ 2/89à 14TU   POSTE 1

		F	RO	TEL
+	-83/ 40	159	0
⟅⟆			
∧	0/ 9	244	0
∧			
∧	0/ 8	258	0
∧	0/ 5	258	0
∧	0/ 4	234	0
∧	0/ 3	318	0

14/ 2/ 8
22/ 1/ 8
20/12/ 8
16/12/ 8
5/12/ 88
25/11/ 8

0 TEMPERATURE
0 MASSE VOL
0 TEL VOL

TS= -4.2   T-10= -5.0   H=
MASSE=17.96 + 0.00

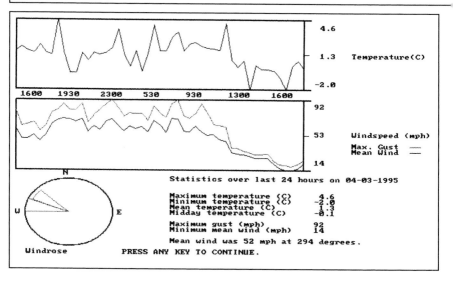

4.6

1.3   Temperature(C)

-2.0

1600 1930 2300 530 930 1300 1600

92

53   Windspeed (mph)

Max. Gust ——
Mean Wind ——

14

Statistics over last 24 hours on 04-03-1995

Maximum temperature (C)   4.6
Minimum temperature (C)   -2.0
Mean temperature (C)   1.3
Midday temperature (C)   -0.1

Maximum gust (mph)   92
Minimum mean wind (mph)   14

Mean wind was 52 mph at 294 degrees.

Windrose   PRESS ANY KEY TO CONTINUE.

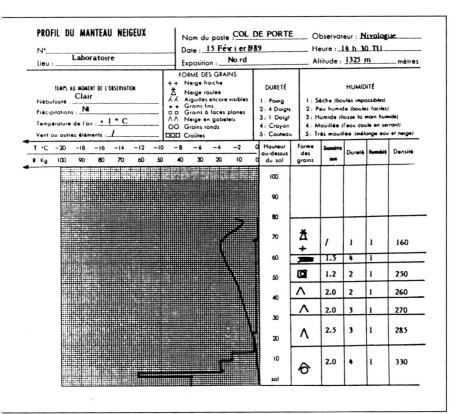

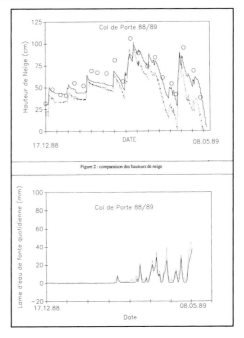

Comparison of CROCUS simulation of the snowpack (left) and manually observed snow profile (right). The similarities between the temperature profile, layering and densities are particularly striking.

affecting the snowpack. Obviously, they can only occur when the snow temperature is close to freezing point. Depending on the degree of saturation they can start on shallow angled slopes (20 degrees and occasionally less than that). The danger is especially great after a heavy snowstorm which starts cold and finishes warm.

Features: Wet avalanches may be loose or slab in form. They travel at relatively low speeds and can sometimes be outrun by a competent skier or occasionally by making a fast exit on foot out of the avalanche path. Great turbulence is set up as the avalanche flows down the slope, producing snow boulders which gouge long grooves in the bed surface. A big wet slide acts like a giant bulldozer picking up a mass of debris on the way: trees, shrubs, rocks etc., all of which add to the very considerable destructive force. In a channelled avalanche the debris sets like concrete immediately on stopping and this greatly reduces the chances of survival of anyone caught in it, as well as impeding the rescue effort. These avalanches can be very big with debris accumulating up to 100 ft/30 m deep.

Indications: This is possibly the easiest hazard to anticipate because of the conditions which initiate a wet avalanche cycle; a rapid temperature rise after snowfall, usually late in the winter and often in damp, overcast weather. Rain, wet snowfalls, warm winds and melting are all contributory factors. A snowpit may reveal layers of wet snow on top of crust, or a layer of depth hoar which may be dangerously weakened by percolating water. There is likely to be little, if any, temperature gradient between the bottom and top of the snow cover. Local small scale avalanching, cracks in the snow, excessive sunballing activity are some of the visible warning signs.

VI. Cornice collapses

Cornice collapse is a specialised form of avalanche. In addition many avalanches are cornice triggered and in general, climbing below cornices should be avoided:

During snowstorms or heavy drifting. Immediately (24–48 hours) after these. During heavy thaw or sudden temperature rise.

When walking above cornices, take care to give them a wide berth.

VII. Ice avalanches

Ice or glacier avalanches are the direct result of glacier movement. In the present state of knowledge they are quite unpredictable and can occur at any hour of day or night. They vary from the fall of an individual serac to the collapse of a whole mountain-side. Pages 38–39 show one such occurrence in the Peruvian Andes which resulted in the deaths of 3,700 people.

Features: Large blocks of ice and often masses of earth and rock. Additional debris may be brought down by avalanches triggered off by the first one. They may be accompanied initially by a cloud of pulverised ice but in later stages become a flowing river of mud, rock and ice.

Indications: Overhanging ice, seracs etc., are obvious danger spots as are large sections of ice above cliff tops or ridges. Heavy rain entering crevasses and lubricating the undersurface of the ice may accelerate ice movement and therefore increase the danger.

Spring avalanche, Coire an Lochain, Cairngorm, Scotland (E Langmuir)

Avalanches, avalanche search

Avalanches: the survivors

A rapid search of the avalanche tip and any accumulation of avalanche debris should be done as quickly as possible. The survivors should split up into groups for this, if there are enough in the surviving party. Studying the illustrations in this book will help to acquire a knowledge of the most likely places to search. A projection past the point where the victim was last seen, from the point at which he was avalanched, often gives an indication of the probable burial place. Trees, boulders or tracks across the hillside under the snow cover can often arrest the fall of a body. Ski sticks, used in reverse, or those with detachable baskets, can be used as probes.

If the avalanche victims cannot readily be located, the survivors must make the decision: either to continue searching for the buried persons, or to go for help.

Should there be several survivors, one or two can go for assistance as soon as the initial search has been completed, leaving the others to continue the search. It is essential to keep as quiet as possible, giving perhaps an occasional shout in a likely burial area and then listening, for anyone buried in an avalanche and conscious can hear people on the surface some distance away, and he in turn may give a call for help. This, however, is often very faint. A constant look-out must be

---

IF YOU SEE A BURIAL

1. Check for further danger
2. Mark entry and last seen position of victim/s
3. Start *immediate* search
4. Look for signs of victim/s, quickly covering all of debris
5. Start transceiver search

If no transceivers worn:

6. Start probe, using all personnel, most likely sites first
7. Make systematic coarse probe
8. Send for help
9. Continue searching until rescue team arrives
10. *Don't give up!*

ACTION IF CAUGHT

In most avalanches defensive action is very difficult. Movement relative to the debris is often impossible. However, some of the following may be useful:

1. Try to delay departure by plunging ice axe into the undersurface. This may help to keep you near the top of the slide
2. Shout; others may see you
3. Try to run to the side, or jump up slope above the fracture
4. If hard slab try to remain on top of a block
5. Get rid of gear, rucksacks, skis, etc
6. Try to roll like a log out of the debris
7. Swimming motions sometimes help, sometimes not
8. As the avalanche slows down you may be able to get some purchase on the debris. Make a desperate effort to get to the surface, or at least get a hand through

A large slab avalanche in Czechoslovakia. Note the rescuers digging trenches in the avalanche tip (Horska Sluzba)

An avalanche victim rescued after a twenty-two hour burial in the Cairngorm, Scotland. (Daily Express)

If caught in an avalanche, swimming motions give a certain amount of help, especially if you can face upwards and do a back stroke. It has been found that the limp body of an unconscious victim is usually buried to a greater depth. One would expect the human body, which is denser than the flowing snow, would sink deeper and deeper into the avalanche. Many complex factors, however, are involved, such as the type of terrain over which the avalanche flows, turbulence, and the victim's own efforts, such as swimming, which can increase the buried person's lateral motion and make his final location more difficult to find. The moving avalanche in many ways resembles a fluid.

Items of equipment attached to the body, e.g. skis, rucksack (even climbing rope it it is attached to someone else who is also buried), can make self-extraction from the avalanche more difficult. If there

kept for items of clothing etc. which may be among the avalanche debris, and the locations of these items noted and marked. The point from which the victim was avalanched should also be clearly marked, as well as the point where he was last seen. These are all important guides for the rescue team. The search should be continued until the arrival of the rescue team.

Access to avalanche site

The rescue team going to the scene of the avalanche should always choose a safe route. However, this is sometimes not possible, as certain access slopes may also be in a dangerous condition. Have avalanche tranceivers switched on. Avoid bunching together, as there is less chance of all the party being buried if the rescue team is in single file and a reasonable distance apart, at least 45 m approx.

The edge of a channel gouged by a large avalanche in the Tatra (Miroslav Hladik)

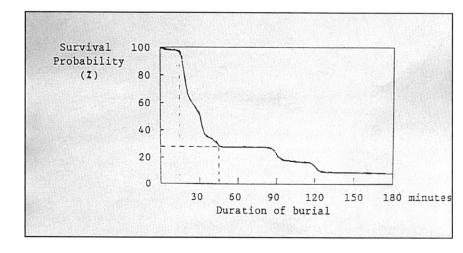

Survival Probability (%) vs Duration of burial (minutes)

Using a magnetometer to detect burial avalanche victims. Virtually all avalanche victims have some metallic objects on their persons. However it was found that there were too many false 'finds' of minerals and other metallic objects to justify its continued use.

is any avalanche risk such items should be ready for quick release in case of emergency; wrist loops of ski sticks should not be worn and rucksack straps can be slackened off for quick jettisoning if need be. A study of the illustrations and text in the Snow Structure section will give indications of potentially dangerous slopes.

Though swimming is probably the best method of keeping nearer to the surface of the avalanche, it is very important, that a hand is held over the nose and mouth to allow a breathing space and to avoid swallowing further snow. In the case of a dry snow avalanche, it may be necessary to do this in preference to swimming as the danger of breathing in quantities of powder is very great.

As the avalanche tip and debris of a wet snow avalanche freezes almost instantly on stopping, the breathing space round the mouth and nose is most important. The avalanche tip consists largely of snow boulders and there is sometimes enough air trapped between the snow boulders, or still filtering through between them, for the victim to survive.

Avalanche search, teams

When the rescue team arrives at the scene of an avalanche, the most likely places should be searched first, i.e. the areas with accumulated avalanche debris. If the missing party has transceivers a search using these should be implemented immediately. If there are survivors, they may be able to give indications regarding the place where the buried victim was last seen and the point where he was struck by the avalanche. Should an avalanche dog be available, it should be employed as soon as possible on an initial rapid search of the likely areas. A trained dog can do this much faster than a rescue team without transceivers. If the initial search is to no avail, a more thorough search must be conducted.

Should information be available regarding the victim's position at the time of avalanche release, and the point where he was last seen, the debris in the area of the trajectory of these points – especially areas with deposits of avalanche debris – should have first priority.

A rapid systematic search of the avalanche debris surface should be made for further clues, e.g. items of clothing, gloves, helmet, hat etc. Such things tend to be pulled off in an avalanche.

The rescue organiser should decide which area to search first. This can usually be established upon inspection of the avalanche, together with the evaluation of information from the survivors, etc. An avalanche dog, when available, should be employed in the most likely area for a more thorough search, as soon as the rapid initial search has been completed. If there is no trained avalanche dog, an initial coarse probe must be made of the high priority areas. This will have to be followed with further probes in other likely areas of possible burial, should the person not be located.

The coarse probe should be repeated as long as a live rescue remains possible. The areas probed should be marked clearly and, if the same area has to be covered several times, the starting line should be varied, by commencing just a short way behind the initial starting point (or finishing point, if the debris is level) and slightly to one side, so that the pattern of probing on successive runs is staggered.

A fine probe should only be resorted to when the probability of locating someone alive is slight.

A further aid for rockfall/landslide/earthquake rubble search is the 'Life Detector'. The equipment is marketed by Wandel & Goltermann Ltd and the instrument can detect small vibrations (ground waves) or calls for help (sound waves) from buried people. It works on a seismic principle and can have up to six sensors. Extraneous sounds can be filtered and differentiated from the distress calls/vibrations such as knocking. Sensors are also able to absorb infrasound from 1Hz upwards. The absorbed vibrations are electronically amplified and made audible to the human ear. Signals are received through headphones/loudspeaker or from an optical display. Extra sensors are available and a directional microphone as well as an alternating two-way intercom.

The TPL 310/B is a similar unit made in Tel Aviv by Elpam Electronics Ltd and claims are made for its use in avalanche search as well as rubble/landslides etc. though the author has not had the opportunity to test it for avalanches.

Several of the above steps can be conducted simultaneously, and in the case of a large avalanche both avalanche dogs and probing teams can work, once the dog and handler have conducted the initial rapid search. The dog handler should advise on this, for he is an expert on the use of his dog. The parties must work some distance apart, of course, and in positions such that their scent won't interfere with the work of the dog. Time is the all-important factor in avalanche rescues. The chance of survival diminishes to about 25 per cent an hour after burial. Priority for taking a trained dog and

Right: Avalanche victims, Japan. Note bodies still frozen. The simple lightweight Japanese snow shoes can be seen on the rescuers' rucksacks (E Haneda, Japanese Alpine Club)

Below right and opposite page: Wet snow avalanche tip, Japan. Digging for victims presumed dead (E Haneda, Japanese Alpine Club)

Below: Wet snow avalanche, Japan. Conditions are very similar to other areas in the world which are influenced by warmer ocean winds (E Haneda, Japanese Alpine Club)

handler to the avalanche burial site in the first available helicopter is a vital requirement in the overall rescue plan.

An avalanche rescue party should always carry a climbing rope with them, as the traversing of dangerous slopes can be safeguarded by using belays. Often avalanches, which can occur in deep powder conditions, can lay bare large expanses of hard snow or ice and crampons may be necessary to negotiate such slopes.

Skis can often provide a fast means of approaching an avalanche accident and these, for rescue team members, should be equipped with skins. Snow shoes also offer a fast means of traversing deep snow, and the large Yukon-type plastic models are excellent for this purpose.

Mention is made elsewhere of the use of oversnow vehicles, and the use of helicopters in such emergencies cannot be overstressed. However, as with normal mountain rescue, too much reliance should not be placed on such mechanical

Mt. Tamgawa, north of Tokyo where over 600 fatalities have occurred. In such areas park and civil authorities are sometimes justified in imposing more rigorous controls (E Haneda, Japanese Alpine Club)

Inset: The memorial plaque at Mt. Tamgawa with more than 600 names on it. It is doubtful if such a sombre reminder of the danger of the hills has much effect on careless walkers and climbers (E Haneda, Japanese Alpine Club)

aids in view of possible mechanical faults and restrictions imposed by weather and terrain.

The call-out arrangements for avalanche rescue can be similar to those of the average rescue evacuation. Priority should be given to trained avalanche dogs and handlers. Time is a most important factor in avalanche burials. Fumes from the helicopter can affect scent. The rescue controller should attempt to reach the scene of the avalanche as quickly as possible, as the search must be fast, systematic and thorough. At base, the full machinery of a rescue emergency must be put into operation regarding extra assistance when required, first-aid tents in the event of a major avalanche involving a number of people, etc.

The majority of buried avalanche victims are carried to the area of maximum deposition, which is usually the tip of the avalanche. As mentioned, boulders, trees, paths (if it is a ground avalanche) and other terrain features which can catch the snow can also catch the victim.

In the case of a channelled avalanche, the bends in the gully which show deposition should be searched. The likelihood of a person being buried at a given bend is proportional to the quantity of avalanche debris deposited there. Victims can sometimes be buried directly behind natural obstacles, as such objects could have delayed the victim's motion.

Friction reduces the flow velocity of an avalanche at the sides, and the maximum speed of flow occurs in the avalanche centre. If the victim's trajectory is near the centre of the flow he may be buried deeply.

A person who is carried away close to the fracture line of an avalanche will usually be buried closer to the surface than someone who has been engulfed in an avalanche near the bottom of the slope.

In the case of an airborne powder avalanche there is a possibility that victims may be hurled into the air, and there have

been cases where they have been found in the branches of trees.

If there is a possible danger from further avalanches, a lookout should be posted at a suitable point. Transceivers should be set to 'Transmit'.

Probing

Probing for an avalanche victim requires the minimum of equipment which is easily transported and light. In areas of relatively small avalanches a probe of 3 m approx. will often suffice. In areas where larger avalanches are more common, the probe length should be at least 3–4 m long and up to 9 mm in diameter. Longer probes should be sectional, unless they are cached, at a rescue post, in a known danger area, where they will not have to be transported far in the event of an avalanche accident. The probe should be made from steel: the only successful aluminium alloy probes are those made from thick-walled aluminium alloy tubing which has been fully heat treated.

Most current designs of collapsible probes have a thin steel wire running through the centre of tube, which is tensioned, when the sections are joined at their ferrules, by means of a wing nut at the top end. Probes are available made from carbon fibre. Military tank aerials can sometimes be used as probes, but they are not so robust as the specially designed probes. Probes have been made with small barbs at the end to pick up fragments of clothing, and others are of a slightly larger diameter so that oxygen can be passed down through the probe for deeply buried victims, where some time could be spent in digging them out.

On any given probe line, the probes should be of equal length, as this enables the rescue controller to calculate the cubic area probed, for it is possible, should the victim not be found (in the case of a very deep avalanche), that a deeper probe may have to be conducted at a later date.

A victim is located under the snow

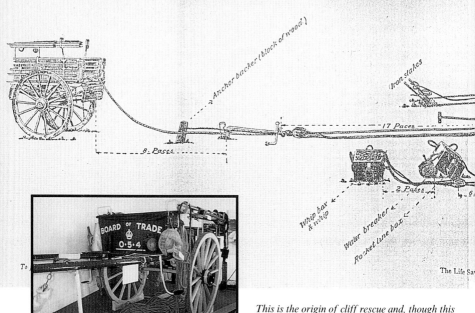

This is the origin of cliff rescue and, though this Costguard rescue layout dates from the mid-19th century, it has striking similarities to modern-day cliff evacuation techniques. The equipment was primarily used for shipwrecks but, as many of these took place on rugged rocky coastlines, often a cliff top was used as a 'belay' station and the survivors hauled up. The breeches buoy technique was a forerunner of the modern MR cableway, and the tripod a common tool of the Coastguard unit.

Inset: The horse-drawn two-wheel rescue cart was used in preference to the four-wheel models for ease of access in certain areas. This rescue cart was based in Greencastle, Co. Donegal, Ireland from 1878–1955, where it can still be viewed. A tractor superseded the horse in 1955, when, in an emergency, it took half-an-hour to catch the horse! Note the rocket launcher, for firing a lifeline, above the wheel and also the wicker safety helmet. In days when there were no two-way radios the rescuer, with the aid of a bo'sun's whistle stored in the mesh of the wicker helmet, relayed signals to the belay party on the cliff top. (B. McDermott)

Above: The German Bergwacht rescue vehicle c.1935. It was in this Mercedes Kompressorwagon that they drove through the night from Munich to Grindelwald for an Eiger North Wall rescue.(E. Gramminger)

Right: On the 1936 Eigerwand rescue attempt the German Bergwacht had a special plane at their disposal.(E. Gramminger)

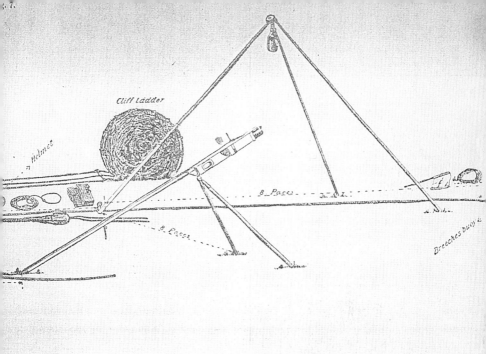

Cliff ladder

Helmet

8 Paces

Breeches buoy

8 Paces

...atus correctly placed for action,

cover when using probes because his body resistance differs from that of the avalanche debris. It is sometimes difficult, however, to differentiate between a body and, say, a rucksack or grass under the snow cover. Bodies have in fact been pierced by probe poles on actual rescues.

In theory the prober requires no previous training, but because of the difficulty in the 'feel' of various objects whilst probing, it is advantageous for each rescue team member to have training in this work. It is essential that the rescue organiser/team leader is experienced in the various methods and where and when to use them.

If an object is encountered, the probing line should not be interrupted, and two assistants following behind, with shovels, should investigate these 'finds' independently.

Though one has more sensitive 'feel' using bare hands on the probe, if it is cold,

Use of artillery for triggering avalanches

Below: A 75 mm pack Howitzer which was used at Alta, Utah for slopes which cannot be reached by fixed mount recoilless rifle, now obsolete (G F Horton, US Forest Service)

Bottom: Ready to fire. An observer with binoculars observes the effect of the mortar bomb, now obsolete (Hanstruol)

the numbness caused by the cold can have a detrimental effect on the sensitivity of the hands of the prober.

Probes should not be left inserted in the snow for any length of time, as they can sometimes freeze in, and be difficult to extract. Anti-freeze mixture, silicon, wax, etc., on the probes will prevent them from sticking, for a short time at least.

Marker cords should be used for keeping the probing party in line. Once the line becomes ragged, the probing will not be so concise and even. The rescue controller, or the person in charge of the probing line, must exercise strict discipline. A loud hailer can be useful for avalanche

Sighting a mortar which was previously used for avalanche control, Davos, Switzerland, now obsolete (Parsenn-Rettungsdienst, Davos, Switzerland)

Above: A climbing conditions board which was used in Glencoe, Scotland. Though the information in this case is hypothetical, such serious conditions do arise from time to time. Sonic boom should be taken into account in regions of possible avalanche (H MacInnes)

Right: using a 75 mm recoilless rifle for avalanche control in Utah, USA (G F Horton, US Forest Service)

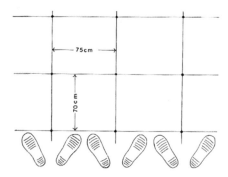

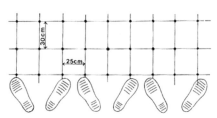

Above left: The coarse probe. The dots indicate the insertion points for the probe. The figures are in centimetres (R Turner)

Above right: The fine probe. The black dots indicate the points of insertion for the probes. The figures are in centimetres (R Turner)

Above: It is possible for a probe to be deflected by a buried object such as a lump of ice or a rock (K Spence)

rescue operations.

Approximately 20 probers per line is usually enough to control at any one point. If more help is available, with probes, a further probing line can be started.

If there is a shortage of manpower, the marker cord should be omitted, but the area probed must be marked clearly.

Under the control of the rescue controller, or whoever is in charge of the probe, the probing party should move uphill, as it is much easier probing in a steady advance uphill than downhill.

The rescue controller will advise the depth to which the probe should be made. If the avalanche is shallow, there is no point in trying to insert the probe the full distance into, perhaps, an underlayer of snow which has not moved.

Coarse or fine probing?

A coarse probe should be used during the initial stages of an avalanche search, when live recovery is anticipated. As the name implies, it is a form of wider spacing of probe insertions with the emphasis on speed. With a fine probe, which takes about four times longer than a coarse probe, one is almost certain to find the victim. In deep avalanches it is possible, when the probe is deeply inserted in the debris, that deflection may occur, caused usually by the probe striking the side of a snow boulder or rock etc.

Below: Showing the possible position of a buried climber wearing an avalanche cord. Probably the best type of avalanche cord is made from polypropylene. It should be marked every 2 m with an arrow indicating the distance and direction of the buried man. Avalanche cords are seldom used now and their reliability is doubtful (G Hunter)

Bottom: Avalanche rescue exercise in Switzerland. Note the flag markers which are used to indicate the area covered (E Wengé, Institut für Schnee-und Lawinforschung Weissfluhjoch, Davos, Switzerland)

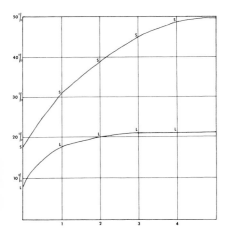

Number of probe runs

This graph shows the relative chances of finding a buried avalanche victim alive using coarse probing. The top line S indicates a small avalanche and the line L indicates a large avalanche. The bottom line shows the number of passes with the probes, L taking one hour and S taking 15 minutes. Always use the coarse probing technique if there is hope of finding the victim alive (A Fyffe)

Left: The possible search procedure at a large avalanche. At the top right of the drawing a slab fracture line can be seen. Further down the path of the avalanche, a dog and handler are shown conducting a rapid, initial search of likely burial places (these are marked P). This is done before the dog and handler conduct a fine search of the avalanche tip. Meantime, the main search party could start probing (A). The area which has been probed should be marked. The two figures at each side of the probing party are using a line to mark the point at which to probe; this enables a more accurate series of insertions by the probes.
F = a first-aid tent, situated on a safe site. W = wind direction, for reference for dog search and for location of helicopter smoke canister, situated at 'S'. The helicopter landing zone should be marked (if on snow, this should be stamped down). R = extra search personnel. T = the line of a summer track across hillside, which could also be a possible point where a body could be deposited. L = a lookout, in case of further avalanche danger

Coarse probe

The coarse probe is conducted as follows: probers are spaced in like, elbow to elbow, in hand on mid-thigh position. A single insertion is made. Usually one signal is sufficient by the rescue controller for the insertion of probe, the extraction and the step forward. Probers should, however, await the command to insert so that the line can be kept in order. As mentioned elsewhere, the probers should keep silent and there should be strict discipline.

The coarse probe gives approximately a 76 per cent chance of finding a victim.

Fine probe

The probers take up the same arrangement of line-up as for the coarse probe. Each rescuer probes in front of his left foot, in the centre between his feet, and then in front of his right foot. On command the line advances 30 cm and repeats the three insertions. It is usually

Bottom: Probing a large avalanche requires a great number of people. Whenever possible a trained avalanche dog should be used initially, or use tranceivers, Switzerland (M Schild)

Opposite page: Trenching a large avalanche in Czechoslovakia. Rescue team members are seen digging trenches whilst probing is carried out (Horska Sluzba)

Drawing: When an avalanche is too deep to be searched properly with probes, the avalanche should be trenched through the deep sections, working uphill. The trenches should be 1–2 m wide. The trenches can be up to 6–7 m apart. The probing is carried out both vertically and obliquely (K Spence)

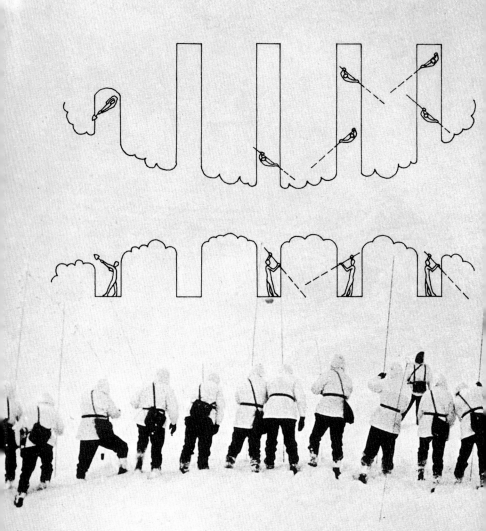

Right: An exercise in probing. Note the sectional construction of the probe and at the top there is a handle to facilitate pushing it into the snow (Horska Sluzba)

Far right: A member of an Icelandic mountain rescue team locating a buried body by dowsing. In several parts of the world this method is deployed in avalanche search (B Wright)

Below: A ski pole probe, a useful item for the ski-tourer (Blyth Wright)

Below: The 'snow tred'. This type of snow shoe is good for traversing deep powder snow. The toe of the boot passes through the wide webbing loop, which has cord lacing, and a heel band is also provided. A further necessary modification is a cord over the arch of the boot to prevent the heel loop working loose. The snow tred is made from light and rigid plastic. There are many types of snow shoes and indeed skis used in mountain rescue work and rescue team members will know the most suitable soft snow aids for their particular area.

Opposite page left: Victim of a wet snow avalanche. Note the small snow boulders of the avalanche tip. Scotland (H MacInnes)

Opposite page right: Digging out avalanche victims, Scotland. Wet snow avalanche (H MacInnes)

Opposite page below: An avalanche victim being given oxygen and cardiac massage. Wet snow avalanche, Scotland (H MacInnes)

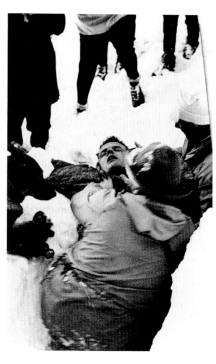

Above: Digging out a volunteer for a dog training avalanche search exercise, Switzerland (H MacInnes)

Right: Removing the victim of a slab avalanche, Scottish Highlands (H MacInnes)

better to have separate commands for each insertion and each move forward. A marker cord should be used for a fine probe; it can be attached to an ice axe or ski-pole at either side of the probers and is moved forward by two other rescuers. This will ensure an accurate line of insertions. All insertions by the probes must be done behind the line or cord, which will be accurately moved by the two assistants.

Discipline must be even more rigid during a fine probe.

The fine probe has a theoretical 100 per cent chance of finding a buried victim.

When the speed of a coarse probe is weighed against its loss of thoroughness, calculations show that the chance of finding a victim alive is greatly increased if the avalanche search is started with the coarse probe (see illustration).

The coarse probe should be repeated over and over again until the victim is found. If the repetition of the coarse probe is to no avail after a time interval which leaves the victim only a very slight chance of survival, the position changes (see table of survival in avalanches).

When the position is reached where the chances are that the victim is in fact dead, the fine probe should be resorted to. It should be borne in mind that there have been some cases of people surviving very long burials and hope should not be given up prematurely.

The chances of locating a victim by repeated passes using the coarse probe technique are significant in small avalanches. The results are not so good, however, for large avalanches.

In the case of larger avalanches the probing depth should not be reduced to under 3 m approx. except in the case of obvious evidence which indicates a shallower burial depth.

Searcher starts here

First contact: Stop, rotate bleeper for aerial alignment

Probable direction (increase in signal strength)

Victim

Reduce volume

Direction 100% clear

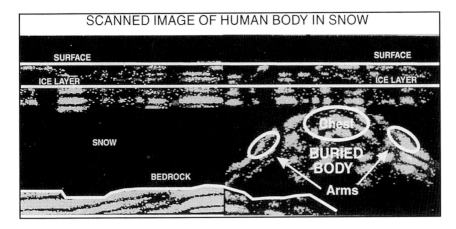

SCANNED IMAGE OF HUMAN BODY IN SNOW

SURFACE — SURFACE — ICE LAYER — ICE LAYER — SNOW — BEDROCK — Chest — BURIED BODY — Arms

Above: A copy of a scan using ground probing radar where the body of a climber was located after many months' burial. During periods of the early search for the missing man, the snow at the point of burial was approx. 20m deep. The body was recovered in August, after a 2 hour, 20 min search of a snow-filled corrie (Peter Suskins, Oceanfix International Ltd)

Left: Oceanfix ground penetrating radar being used to locate a dead climber, initially buried to a depth of 20 m for eight months (H MacInnes)

Only 19 per cent of all persons completely buried in an avalanche survive, irrespective of the means of rescue.

Many ideas have been put forward for the location of the buried victim in an avalanche, from reflected sound, reflected electromagnetic radiation, dielectric effect, magnetic detectors, radioactive tracers, high frequency radio emission and many others, but the avalanche dog and the simple probe remain both the cheapest and the most effective methods of avalanche search. Transceiver equipment, which uses audio frequency induction field, shows considerable promise, but the buried person must have a transceiver himself, switched to transmit. The use of transceivers is now much more widespread and they are essential items of equipment for the rescue team.

Ground Radar

This form of Radar (GPR) was developed for detecting buried plastic mines in the Falklands. An impulse radar system is a wide-band video-pulse radar which transmits energy over a frequency band in contrast to pulse radars operating at one frequency which is turned on and off. The difference between the two is that ground radar operates over a much shorter distance and can penetrate the ground to depths of 30 metres. GPR has been used successfully to locate buried bodies in snow and the equipment is available in certain countries, though often deployed in a system not portable enough for SAR work. Emrad Ltd, an English firm have however, managed to develop a unit which can be carried as a backpack. This technology as well as being used for pipe and archaeological location has been successfully used for finding mass murder victims and buried valuables.

The principal application of GPR at the present time is to locate buried victims (avalanche etc.) when all other means have failed but it is just a matter of time before miniaturisation and the reduction of costs make it a common tool for SAR teams.

The most commonly used avalanche transceivers in use today are the Skadi (American), the Autophon (Swiss) and the Pieps (Austrian). Teams should be familiar with the use of transceivers and they should be taken by team members as routine during winter rescue operations. It is estimated that one rescuer using a bleeper will search an area as fast as 490 people using avalanche probes

The illustrations show a Pieps transceiver in its carrying case (right) and the Autophon and Skadi (below). These are dual frequency transceivers operating on both 2·275 and 457 kHz.

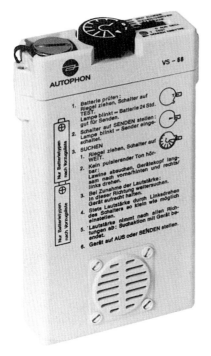

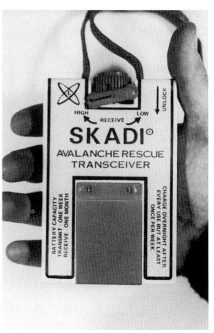

RECCO

This system is in use in several European ski resorts. It is a radar, which relies on the buried victim wearing one or more special reflectors. It is effective, but can be affected by shielding, depending on how the victim is lying in the snow. Thus, more than one reflector, for instance in a jacket as well as a boot, may be helpful. The scanner is best employed from a helicopter, but may also be used on foot. Reflectors are relatively cheap and the main restriction on the wider use of Recco appears to be the reluctance of the public, or clothing manufacturers, to employ reflectors more widely.

Avalanche air-bags (balloons)

This equipment is mainly applicable to the off-piste ski-ing situation. The principle is that the skier wears a rucksack containing the deflated air-bag and a compressed gas cylinder. Pulling a rip-cord in the event of an avalanche incident inflates the air-bag, which reduces the relative mass of the skier and makes him/her more liable to remain on the surface. Tests have been conducted with the equipment at the Swiss Federal Avalanche Institute at Davos. These tests revealed a number of problems, but did indicate that, if the avalanche victim retained the presence of mind actually to pull the rip-cord in the absence of malfunction, then there was indeed an enhanced chance of the victim staying on the surface. However, air-bags are unlikely to recommend themselves to ski tourers, already burdened with much equipment, or to winter climbers. For the off-piste skier, they may present an added safety aid, but the cost, at present about four times that of a transceiver, may also be a deterrent.

Avalanche transceivers

These devices are essentially small radios transmitting a signal or bleep, which in the event of a burial, can also be switched quickly to receive or search mode. They give considerable added security and are the technology currently recommended by most avalanche safety agencies. However, there are a number of points to bear in mind. The transceiver is of no use unless switched on to transmit. Therefore, it must be switched on before leaving base in the morning. This may seem excessively cautious, but many avalanche accidents occur when their victims least expect it and this is the only real way to cater for this problem. Secondly, it must be securely attached to the body using the harness provided. Cases have occurred when jackets or rucksacks containing transceivers have been successfully rescued, but because these have been torn off in the avalanche, their owners have not been located in time to save them.

Finally, the wearing of avalanche bleepers can lead to a dangerous feeling of invulnerability. The majority of buried victims still die, so avoidance of accident is still the only policy.

It is essential to carry the transceiver using the harness supplied by the manufacturer. It is useless to have the transceiver in your rucksack, as this can be lost in an avalanche. Also, ensure that you switch it to *transmit* before leaving base, or at the start of the operation. It goes without saying that the batteries should be in good condition and the units working properly (tested before starting out).

Provided the victim is wearing an avalanche transceiver in good working order and switched to *transmit*, he has a better chance of being located quickly than by any other method. For example, in an area 100 m square, when buried 3 m or less, he has a 98 per cent chance of being found within ten minutes.

Searching with avalanche transceivers

The rescue bleeper or beacon is not a directional finder, though you will obtain a more powerful signal when the two antennae are parallel. When a signal is first picked up you can orientate your bleeper until the signal is loudest.

Before starting a search, everyone should have his or her set at full volume. If there is possible danger from further avalanches, a lookout should be posted to advise searchers of impending danger. In the event of a further avalanche, the searchers should quickly switch their bleepers to transmit and beat a hasty retreat.

A search is conducted by those with bleepers spread out at intervals of not more than 30 m. The search can be conducted in any direction, as long as it is done in straight parallel lines. If the avalanche is large and there are only a few instruments a zig-zag pattern should be adopted.

It is important that every fifteen paces or so the whole party should stop on command from the avalanche search-controller, so that the searchers can listen carefully and not be distracted by boots moving on the debris and other noises. As with other methods of avalanche search, silence is important. As soon as a signal is picked up two further rescue-team members should track it down with their bleepers while the main search party continues in the established search pattern. If only one person is missing, two searchers should be used to track him down finally, whilst the rest organise for digging him out.

Pinpointing the burial position

Meantime, the two searchers assigned to finally locating the victim should keep going in the same straight line with their transceivers orientated for maximum signal strength. The sequence is as per the diagram, and teams should practise the technique at least once per season. One transceiver, or several, can be buried or hidden in grass, etc., to simulate actual burials, and it will be found that team members can soon reach a high standard of efficiency. For example, three searchers

should be able to pinpoint a transmitting bleeper in a search area 100 × 200 m in less than six minutes. Avoid having metal objects close to the transceiver. The Skadi has also been deployed to locate cavers underground by using other Skadis on the surface.

Avalanche dogs, rescue dogs

WOLVES is a system incorporating microwave link technology with a police/security/rescue dog, developed by The Link Detector Company. It can be used for locating missing persons in darkness and in confined/dangerous places. Though designed primarily for police work it has an application, when fitted to a small trained dog, for searching rockfalls/earthquake rubble etc.

The unit comprises of a body and head harness; head and chest mounted cameras, microwave transmitter, infra red lamp, integrated receiver-video recorder, helical antenna, rechargeable batteries and charger. The dog body harness weighs 3 kg fully equipped and the unit has an operating range of 75 m inside buildings etc and 1 km in open areas (Cumbria Constabulary)

A SAR dog being fitted with a GPS to monitor its search pattern. (Trimble Navigation Ltd., California)

By employing rescue dogs a rescue organiser can reduce the number of human searchers required on a given operation, as a fully trained dog is capable of doing the work of 20 men, sometimes even more.

A search may take place over a vast snow-covered mountainside where the victim can be quickly covered by drifting snow, or hidden from view in a boulder-field. The rescue dog is trained to find humans on their air-borne scent by means of its highly developed olfactory tract. The human body emits odour which, depending on wind and weather conditions, can be carried up to 300 m on air currents.

Although dogs can be trained to discriminate between countless humans if given an article bearing a particular human scent, rescue dogs are not normally trained by this method, except for special teams using bloodhounds which have proved highly successful for tracking in California and other areas. The rescue dog is trained to find any human being in a given area, working across or into the wind. If rescue dogs were trained to discriminate between various human scents, in certain situations, where a party had gone missing, a rescue dog might ignore the scent of one or more of the victims if it did not correspond with the scent it was seeking. In rescue work anyone within the search area must be checked out by the dog, whether victim or not. In some instances persons unconnected with the search, but found in the area, have provided vital information.

A dog being tested for the A grade in Norway after a bivouac in the mountains. The dog is judged by a panel of three instructors (Norwegian Red Cross)

Dog selection

There are many types of dogs, intelligent, stupid, good and bad. Certain breeds are more adaptable to rescue work than others. The sex of the animal matters little, as both males and bitches work equally well. However, a bitch will not be fit for work twice a year for at least two weeks. Handlers of male dogs are not overjoyed with a bitch 'in season' working alongside their dogs.

Internationally the German Shepherd is the most popular rescue dog. The St Bernard, though traditionally associated with mountain rescue from the seventeenth century, has gone out of favour owing mainly to its size and unsuitability to steep terrain. Scottish Border Collies have been used with considerable success. The Border Collie has no equal for ranging over rough terrain at a great distance from its handler.

Among the prerequisites for the ideal rescue dog are:
(i)   Good temperament
(ii) Exceptional scenting ability
(iii) Intelligence and strength
(iv) Compact build and thick coat
The animal must be taken regularly on to the hills from an early age, in all weather conditions. The SAR dog is a member of the handler's family.

Training

Trained dogs are used extensively in Europe for avalanche searches, and they can work many times faster than a human search party using probing rods. There are over 500 trained avalanche dogs in Europe. Switzerland operates a highly organised rescue-dog system, in conjunction with the Swiss Air Rescue Guard, whereby anyone may dial '11' and the nearest avalanche dog will be flown to the scene of the incident immediately. At Davos the Parsenndienst Ski Patrol maintains kennels of avalanche dogs in close proximity to ski areas. Countries

These four photographs illustrate the second stage of avalanche dog training, where the dog's handler is covered by a small amount of snow (H MacInnes)

The shallow 'grave' which has been dug is used again for burying the dog's handler

A small amount of snow is used to cover the dog's handler. Note the aluminium alloy shovels

where there is not such a high incidence of avalanches, but many searches, also deploy their trained avalanche dogs for open summer search work. They can also be used for earthquake/landslide/water and wilderness search.

This ensures that the dogs have a wider work-range than if they were used solely for avalanches. The United Kingdom has five separate Search and Rescue Dog Associations, operating 70 trained dogs. In the USA various state Rescue Dog Associations, including those of Washington, New York, New Jersey, New Mexico, Texas and Virginia, have banded together to form the American Rescue Dog Association. Another effective dog unit is called WOOF or Wilderness Finders Incorporated of California. These units are on call 24 hours a day and their dogs, all German Shepherds, have received multi-purpose training.

The system of grading dogs varies throughout the world. In the Alps dogs are rated Class A, B and C and a dog will be about three to four years old before achieving Class C. A similar A, B and C system is used in Scandinavia and most other countries.

The United Kingdom dogs are graded 'Novice Dog' and 'Rescue Dog'. Stringent tests ensure that only the best dogs are chosen. In Scotland, for example, only 50 per cent of entrants get through the preliminary course. There only the best are accepted for operational work and are classed 'Novice Dogs'. After 12 months they are given more advanced training tests to attain the 'Rescue Dog' grade. Any dog failing this test is automatically rejected for rescue work. Successful dogs are re-tested every three years.

Puppy training

Ensure first of all that the dog is not affected by hip displasia, a deformity of the hip joint. It is difficult to detect in

The dog must be brought to a high pitch of excitement both by the dog's master, calling it as he goes towards the 'grave', and by the assistant holding the dog. He must tell it to 'seek' its master

The dog is released by the assistant to find its handler. Note that here the dog is tracking, but this does not matter at this early stage. For further sequences see text

young dogs and it is therefore advisable to obtain the pup from an accredited breeder (in the UK, one holding a BVA/KC Certificate). Alternatively, have it X-rayed, when a year old, by a veterinary surgeon. If it is affected in the slightest by this disease the condition will only be further aggravated by working in mountains and there is little point in persevering with training.

The young dog must not be asked to attempt serious search training until at least a year old. However, there is no reason why it should not be trained in simple obedience exercises before commencing search training. It should be taught to 'dig' on command by burying tit-bits in snow and then commanding it to dig for them. If possible, it should 'speak' on command before attending the first training course. This will help with the 'indication' when it finds a victim in subsequent training. Every time a dog does any exercise well, it should be praised immediately so that it becomes aware of the things that please its handler. It cannot be stressed too strongly that the dog must be happy throughout these games or exercises. It shouldn't become bored or frustrated and every game should end on a successful note for the dog. There is no need for harshness in training a young dog.

Novice training

Throughout the training the dog and handler are assessed as a team. The acceptance or rejection of a dog team is the responsibility of a panel of assessors: their decision is final.

The dog must enjoy the training and respond to it quickly. To help achieve this the handler should have a genuine liking and respect for the dog and do everything to help him. It is a two-way process and while the handler is teaching the dog he is also learning much from it. He must learn

Below: A dog can search an avalanche area 100 m square in 25 minutes. A team of 20 men coarse probing takes four hours. A fine search using a dog would take two hours compared with 20 hours taken by a probing party doing a fine probe. During a two-hour fine search with an avalanche dog, it would have to be rested at intervals due to the high concentration of the fine search (H MacInnes)

Above: The avalanche dog must be encouraged to dig and it is advantageous to have the dog trained to do this before it attends the basic course (H MacInnes)

to 'read' the dog, recognising signs when the dog makes a find, and adapt his search strategy to suit his dog. Regrettably, many a good dog has been turned down because of a bad handler.

Basic training

The object of this training is to stimulate the dog into, (a) seeking the source of a human scent, (b) working out search patterns and (c) giving a positive indication once it has located a victim. In addition, the dog is tested on its reliability with livestock and in basic obedience exercises, which are essential to the trained search dog. Due to their MR role, in the United Kingdom, dog teams must be competent on mountains, especially in snow conditions. In Scotland, for example, it is stipulated that the dog/handler team must be capable of negotiating difficult terrain in both winter and summer. A similar degree of competence from the handler is also required in other countries. It is not expected that the dog team will search severe climbs but it does ensure that when negotiating rough mountain terrain both dog and handler can cope competently.

It is difficult to lay down a rigid programme for training without regard for the character and ability of individual dogs. A training manual only provides the basics: everything hinges on the handler's getting the best out of his/her dog. Most dog trainers will disagree with some training methods: they know what will work for them. When they have problems with a dog they don't run to a book but try variations and study the dog in the hope of finding a means of getting it to work.

Open-country search work

This is, briefly, the training to be followed when starting a dog searching for a victim who may be lying hidden by brush or boulders. The trainer should have two or three assistants to help him.

Phase One: The dog is held by the assistant while the handler moves away, exciting the dog as he does so by calling his name and clapping his hands, etc. When about 9–18 m away, the handler lies down out of sight of the dog, which is given the command 'Seek' by the assistant as it is released to find the handler. The dog will immediately dash to where the handler has disappeared from view. When it finds the handler, the dog should be praised.

A circular wide-mesh harness net for lifting rescue dogs by helicopter winch. The animal's legs go through the mesh and the rope loop is taken up round the body to be secured with karabiners. The suspension points should be above the dog's centre of gravity. Two mesh sizes are necessary to cover various dog dimensions

Phase Two: The handler now holds the dog and the assistant walks away, at the same time attracting the dog's attention. The assistant then drops out of the dog's view at the same spot where the handler had hidden, and on releasing the dog the handler gives the command 'Seek'. If the dog appears hesitant or unsure of what to do the assistant should whistle or call. On reaching the assistant the dog should be praised by its handler, who has followed closely behind.

Phase Three: The distance from the starting point to where the assistant hides is now increased to about 45 m. The dog is allowed to see where the assistant goes out of view and when released by the handler is encouraged to 'Seek' him. As soon as it reaches the assistant the dog receives praise from the handler.

Phase Four: This time the dog is taken aside

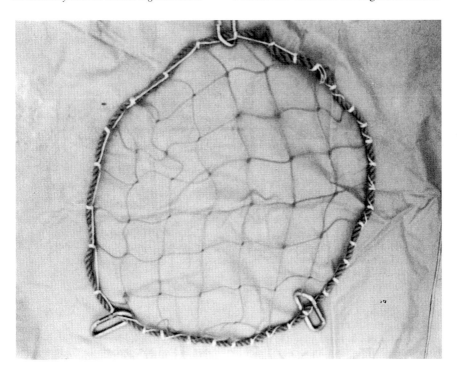

and not allowed to observe the assistant going into hiding. When released by the handler the dog will be encouraged to 'Seek' and will be allowed to work the problem out for itself. On finding the assistant it should be praised by the handler.

Phase Five: The help of a second assistant is required for this stage. Both assistants go into hiding on opposite flanks – about 45 m from the starting point. The dog is not allowed to see them hide and the handler releases the dog with the command 'Seek' as before. When it finds the first assistant the dog should be praised and then set to find the second one. (The first assistant should take the opportunity whilst the dog is being praised to slip out of the search area, otherwise the dog will be totally confused by his presence.) As soon as it finds the second assistant the dog should receive further praise. This phase helps the dog to learn to quarter an area when searching.

Search and Rescue dogs often have an identification 'waistcoat' as well as a harness when working. These dogs and handlers are part of the Russian SRDR rescue dog service (Slava Usov)

Phase Six: Several additional assistants can now be introduced to the training, hidden on both flanks at varying intervals. As the handler moves forward the dog is encouraged to quarter the ground ahead. After each successful find the dog is praised and urged to continue with the search until the last assistant is located. The handler must keep close behind the dog to correct, reassure and praise it as required.

A natural progression of this training is to increase the distance between the 'hides' and the time interval before setting the dog off to start the search. The assistants cease attracting the dog by calling or whistling. The handler now walks in a straight line down the centre of the search area, keeping well behind the dog, thereby allowing it to quarter to either side. In all training the handler keeps the dog's interest alive by ensuring that each search is successful and giving the maximum praise after each find. Most important is that allowance must be made for wind direction so that the dog is always working across or into the wind.

Avalanche search work

One of the main problems in winter is to locate missing persons quickly before death sets in, particularly those buried under snow. The Austrian avalanche dog training method is described.

Prior to attending a training course prospective handlers should not attempt to carry out snow burials for avalanche work. Such burials must be properly supervised during the training course, otherwise the 'victim' could be endangered as well as the dog ruined for further avalanche training.

In training, assistants are buried in snow-holes or 'graves' to represent avalanche victims, and the greatest care must be exercised to ensure that they are not asphyxiated. The hazards of a badly constructed snow-hole cannot be too strongly emphasised; even one that has been too well hidden can be a death-trap if it is not found in time. A soldier in the Austrian Tyrol died after acting as 'victim' in an avalanche exercise. He was buried under 60 cm of snow for only 20 minutes and was unconscious when uncovered. On training courses in the United Kingdom 'victims' are never buried more than two feet deep (people suffering from bronchial complaints should not be buried). In the initial stages of training the snow-hole must be large enough for two people, with a short tunnel or overhang at one end to enable the 'victim' to keep his head clear of snow when the 'grave' is filled in by the assistants, as well as to provide extra air-space. All potential handlers are thoroughly instructed in their

construction at the start of the course in view of the potential danger.

Once the dog has mastered the open-country search techniques it will have learned much that is required for avalanche work.

Sequence of training

The trainer is helped by two assistants as the dog and handler are taken through the various phases of avalanche training:

Phase One: The dog, the first assistant and the handler start at a point some 30 m from the previously prepared snow-hole. The handler leaves the dog held by the assistant while he walks away in the direction of the snow-hole, calling the dog in an urgent tone and bringing it to a high state of excitement. The assistant also encourages the dog to find his handler, using the command 'seek'. When the handler lies down in the hole out of sight of the dog, the assistant releases him, saying 'seek, seek'. The dog rushes to the 'grave', where it will be praised by the handler. It is then returned to the assistant.

Phase Two: The handler goes back into the 'grave', calling the dog as before. On this occasion a second assistant shovels loose snow over him, burying him under a few inches as quickly as possible. After completing the burial the second assistant returns to the starting point, passing close to the dog so that it can identify his scent. The dog realises that this is a stranger and that his handler is still lost.

The dog is released by the first assistant. It rushes to the snow-hole to find that instead of the handler there is only snow. Either it immediately puts its nose to work and begins to push the snow aside, or it stands perplexed. In the latter case the first assistant must give immediate help, pointing to the 'grave', telling the dog to 'dig', and digs himself with his hands. The dog will soon realise what is required of

A large-scale sweep search using search and rescue dogs in the Cairngorms, Scotland. Winds of 150 mph/240 kph are recorded in this region (H MacInnes)

him and also start to dig. It should be encouraged by both assistant and handler, the handler calling its name from beneath the snow. When the handler is uncovered, he must praise the dog enthusiastically. Once more the handler returns the dog to the first assistant at the starting point.

Phase Three: The second assistant accompanies the handler to the 'grave' this time, while the dog is left with the first assistant at the starting point. The handler will call and whistle to the dog as both he and the second assistant get into the 'grave'. The trainer will then bury both under loose snow in such a way that the second assistant is nearest the opening and will be found first by the dog. The best way to do this is for the second assistant to lie on top of the handler. The trainer returns to the starting point, ensuring the dog gets his scent as he

passes. Again the dog is released with the command 'seek'. It will rush to the 'grave' and dig out the second assistant, who will praise it and then get out of the 'grave'. The dog will be worried about its handler and should be encouraged to dig further until the handler is also uncovered.

Phase Four: After praising the dog the handler should, without any delay, take it back to the starting point. As he does so the second assistant is buried in the 'grave' by the first assistant, who then returns to the starting point. The dog is now under the command of its handler, who tells it to 'seek'. The dog should be encouraged to again rush to the 'grave' and 'dig'. Once it indicates that the assistant is beneath the snow it should be praised and urged to dig further until the assistant has been uncovered.

Left: A mountaineer buried in drifted snow, Scottish Highlands (H MacInnes)

Below: Some SAR dogs can locate corpses after prolonged burial, even in hard packed snow. This find on Ben Nevis was after a period of several months and the corpse was at a depth of 4 m. (B McDermott)

Right: Winching rescue dog and handler into an RAF Wessex helicopter prior to a search operation (R Smith)

Below: Search and rescue dogs en route to an avalanche search after being off-loaded from a Wessex helicopter, Ben Nevis, Scotland (H MacInnes)

Avalanche dog training in Norway. Here a dog is being tested during a training course. In Norway 'victims' are buried to a depth of 3 m for advanced training. They keep in touch with the instructors by walkie-talkie (Norwegian Red Cross)

N.B. All four phases should be done as quickly as possible to enable the dog to connect each phase with the previous one. When Phase Four is completed the dog should be rested for two to three hours before going on to Phase Five. This stage should only be attempted once the dog has fully mastered the earlier ones.

Phase Five: (a) Burying an assistant in the same hole – out of sight of the dog.
(b) Burying out of sight of the dog in a fresh 'grave' about 13 m from the old one.
(c) Burying out of sight of the dog in various places to right and left of the original 'grave'.
(d) Burying out of sight of both dog and handler.
(e) Deeper burials – but never deeper than 60 cm.
(f) Gradually increasing the size of the search area.

Many trainers advocate tit-bits or rewards when the dog finds a victim, and this is commendable in the early stages of the training. In the United States many units employ the 'tug of war' inducement, using a favourite plaything belonging to the dog.

Indication

Each handler should know when his dog has found a victim by certain signs in the dog's bodily attitude: ears erect and well forward, the tail held high, excitement as it 'homes in' on a scent source. On reaching the buried victim the dog should give a further indication by digging where the person is buried. In the case of a victim lying in the open the dog should return to its handler, who should with experience learn to 'read' his dog and be alert to when the dog has located the victim. Sometimes the handler fails to do this. When the dog is searching out of sight over a ridge, in

A search and rescue dog at work in the Scottish Highlands. The dog, a Border Collie, is seen above and slightly right of handler (H MacInnes)

mist or in darkness more positive indication of a 'find' is required. The dog should be trained to 'speak' by barking loudly once it has located the victim. Some dogs have difficulty in learning to speak on finding a victim. It is an aspect of training requiring patience, but is of vital importance.

Search and rescue operations

There should be no delay in summoning trained dogs to assist on a search, and it should not be left until the initial search has failed. The trained dog is the finest of search instruments. Also, in an avalanche search, the dog is the most successful method which does not depend on the victim carrying a locating bleeper. The majority of skiers, climbers, etc., do not carry such devices.

The dog is not infallible. Like its human counterparts, it has limitations; though when a mistake has been made by a dog team, it is usually on the part of the handler. Their efficiency can be influenced by wind conditions, i.e. when the wind is turbulent in a corrie or basin, or even when there is none. They can also fail to find corpses in wet snow avalanches as well as frozen bodies. However, even in the worst conditions the dog offers the best chance of locating the live victim. Over half of avalanche victims in Switzerland are located by dogs.

To be effective the dog should work at a distance from other search parties – any extraneous scents, such as searchers urinating on avalanche debris, can confuse even the best dog. The dog should be used in high priority search areas.

The handler must be properly briefed by the rescue organiser with all relevant information and be clear as to his search area. He must quickly ascertain his search

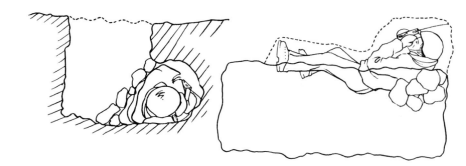

Above: This shows an end elevation of the 'grave' for the handler and the assistant, as used for avalanche dog training. Note that the grave is undercut on one side to enable the buried person to have the protection of the 'cave' thus formed. Loose snow blocks are then placed round the head end to allow him sufficient air. The loose blocks should preferably extend up to the snow surface level. The dotted wavy line indicates the level of the filled-in grave (G Hunter)

Above right: This is a plan view of the grave for rescue dog training. The 'victim' is actually under an overhang of snow, which has been dug out of one wall of the grave. Loose blocks should be built round the head up to the snow surface level and the victim can also have a walkie-talkie for keeping in touch with the training instructor. A hand should be kept over the mouth and nose to prevent loose snow restricting breathing (G Hunter)

Right: Avalanche dog training course, Switzerland (H MacInnes)

area once on the ground: check boundaries, memorise features and hazards. In view of the essentially lone role of the dog team the handler should be equipped with a walkie-talkie. It is vital that he is in contact with rescue control and advised of developments. He will also be able to notify control should his dog make a 'find'.

The most important factor is wind direction. When working the dog the handler must take advantage of wind, as the dog ranges in a zig-zag quartering pattern. Obviously, it is advantageous to work either across or into the wind, as either method allows the dog to detect scent – depending on the strength of the wind – whilst the victim is still some distance away. If working upwind the dog may be more reluctant to home in on a scent, as this will take it in the opposite way to the search direction. Not all dogs behave in this fashion but it does happen with less experienced animals.

Night operations

The victim's scent is more easily detectable in the cool of night than during the heat of day. The rescue dog should be an immediate choice at night, as it can carry on working when other search agencies find it unjustifiable or impractical.

Some handlers fit small lights to the dog harness to monitor its movements in darkness. Coolites can also be taped to the dog's harness. The tube contains two chemicals which when mixed emit a fluorescent glow, visible for a considerable distance and lasting approximately 12 hours. The tube gives off no heat. Coolites have other rescue applications, such as marking danger areas, paths, etc. during night work.

In Russia SAR dogs have been operating many years and have been involved in major disasters from earthquakes to avalanches. For searching in hard neve conditions rescue dogs have 'dog gloves' to protect their pads. These are of an elasticised nylon with small holes to allow their claws to protrude, like fingerless mitts. Another interesting aspect of their dog handling is that the dogs nostrils are cleaned if they have snow or dirt in them. This is done with, water, a rag or a fine small brush.

Dogs and Helicopters

The SAR organiser should arrange for the dog teams to be conveyed by the fastest means possible. When helicopters are available they should be used to transport the dog team/s. Dog/s and handler/s can be landed/winched down to the search area fresh to commence work.

Winching dogs and handlers together presents no real problems. The 'grabbit' or gated winch hook is clipped into the dog's harness, then the handler clips on. (See Helicopter sections.) When being winched into the helicopter the handler should arrive at the cabin entry facing outwards, holding the dog across his chest. The crewman guides them on to the door sill where the handler can swivel in whichever direction his dog is facing and push it into the aircraft. Care should be taken to avoid trapping the dog's paws between handler and sill. The handler should then immediately clip the dog's harness to the inside of the aircraft.

When being winched out of the aircraft the procedure is reversed, the handler being seated on the sill with the dog across his lap. The crewman winches in, suspending them below the winch before lowering.

When alighting from the machine the handler should allow the dog a few minutes before working. After it has been travelling in cramped, noisy conditions, with fumes, it needs time to adjust. Fumes can seriously affect the dog's olfactory system for up to an hour afterwards. (This also applies to dogs travelling in other vehicles.) Because of this, the dog should be kept clear of areas where the helicopter has landed, as fumes linger. Down-draught, especially from large helicopters, can disperse scent and thereby it may be undetectable until the concentration builds up again.

Pyrotechnics

Avoid firing signal rockets/pyrotechnics near rescue dogs. Some dogs are nervous of such sudden noises.

The Wandel & Goltermann 'Life Detector' can be used in earthquake/landslide situations, detecting minute vibrations or calls for help working on seismic principles.

There can be up to six sensors. Sensors are also able to absorb infrasound from 1Hz upwards. The vibrations are amplified and made audible to the human ear. The The TPL 310/B is a similar unit made in Tel Aviv by Elpam Electronics and claims are also made for avalanche search.

Belays, pitons, etc.

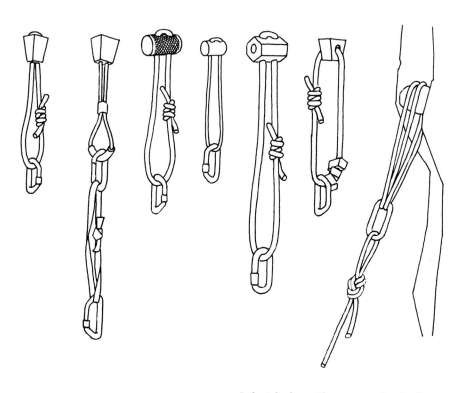

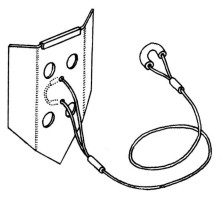

Left: A deadman. The swages on the wire sling are shown and those behind the deadman give the correct angle of pull when the deadman is located in the snow. The alloy plate of the deadman is shaped so that any accidental pull from the side will allow it to re-align. See further illustrations for placing a deadman (R Turner)

Above right: A selection of 'friends' for belaying in cracks. The approx. breaking load of a Friend is in the region of 10 kN.

Above: A selection of alloy artificial chockstones, with a natural chockstone belay on the right. For rescue work, wire chocks should be used where possible. For tapered vertical cracks, chock belays are superior to pitons (R Turner)

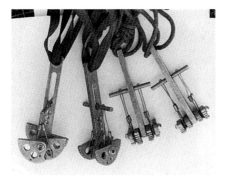

Below: Using a horizontal metal-shafted ice axe belay for snow lowering work. The rope can be attached to the shaft using a clove hitch, slightly nearer to the head end. The axe should be pushed down firmly into the trench and can be packed in with snow. The groove for the anchor rope 'A' should be kept as low as possible and on easy angled slopes the axe should be about 7 m approx. from the belayer. In softer snow an indirect belay should always be used for stretcher work using this method, but in hard snow, it is a very secure belay. Axes of 70 cm approx. and upwards can be used for this technique (R Turner)

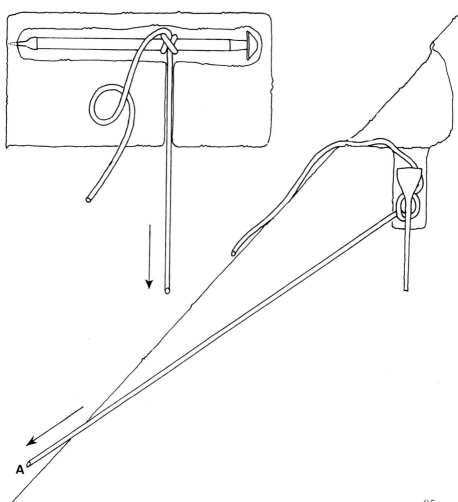

A

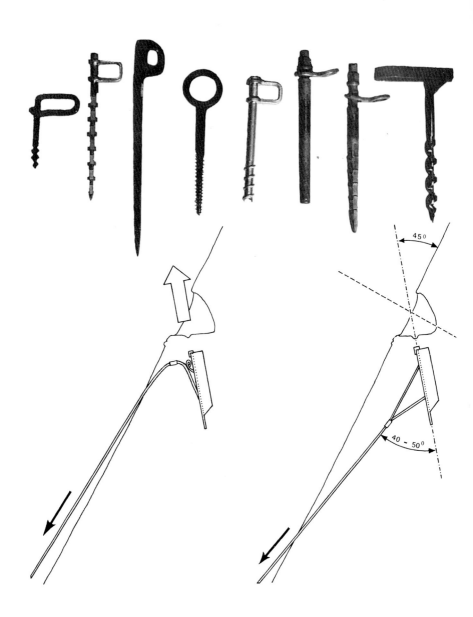

Above: The deadman belay. The illustration on the left shows the deadman incorrectly inserted. The illustration on the right shows the correct angles. The deadman should be at least 30 cm below the snow surface and the belay rope should be as long as possible (extended beyond the length of the wire). Ensure that the slot for the wire is deep enough to allow a straight belay length. Always test the deadman after insertion to ensure that it 'bites' correctly (R Turner)

Opposite page, top: A selection of ice pitons and screws in use in various countries today. The peg on the right has a swinging belay arm to facilitate insertion and extraction

Below: A selection of modern pitons used in rescue work (R Turner)

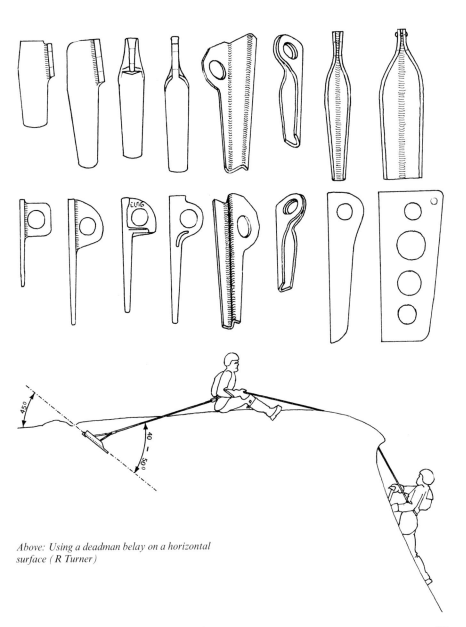

Above: Using a deadman belay on a horizontal surface (R Turner)

A Bosche battery operated hammer drill with a Red Head expansion bolt and hanger. At least two batteries are required if several bolts have to be placed (H MacInnes)

The sequence of placing an expansion bolt using a low voltage battery drill. Note drill with depth gauge and a sling should be fitted to handle for attachment to one's harness. Drill hole at right angles to rock and blow out dust from hole before entering bolt. Ensure that you use the specified drill size for the bolt and that the hole is the right depth. When using Red Head type bolts, the nut and hanger should be fitted to the bolt before driving in. Do not over tighten. Practise the technique before you do it for real.
(E Donaldson)

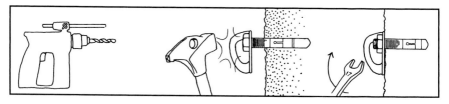

Expansion bolts

Though inserting expansion bolts causes damage to the rock, it is sometimes necessary to use them, or to have fixed bolts at rescue 'black spots'. There are several efficient rock drills available today, Bosche and Hilti are but two.

Types of bolts:

Hammer-In 1. Compression, split shank, either Screw Top or Buttonhead.
2. Wedge, Externally Threaded (stud). Internally Threaded (self drive).
Torque-In 1. Pull-Type; RAWL or Metolius
2. Push-Type

There are also 'Chemical Bolts' set in with epoxy resin. The Rawl is the only 'bomb-proof' bolt available, though it does require a large hole for its shank size. In Europe the drive-in Red Heads are the most popular, but one must be experienced at placing all expansion bolts and also to ensure that the correct drill size is used and that the drill depth gauge is used. Don't rely on guess work, lives may be at stake. When placing the bolt make sure that it will be loaded correctly when deployed.

Hangers can be made, or purchased, to suit requirements, use titanium or stainless steel (also bolts) if used in the long term and on sea cliffs. Ensure that hangers exert the minimum leverage on the bolt shank. Practise bolting on rock which will not cause controversy and test the inserts using a Tirfor, or suitable winch in conjunction with the cableway load meter.

> **Warning:** It has been found that there can be corrosion problems with fixed expansion bolt anchors, even with stainless steel bolts, and great care must be exercised. Fixed anchors must be checked and replaced periodically.

Bivouacs

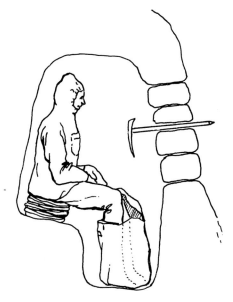

The making of snow-holes and igloos can be quite involved and as they are seldom used in connection with rescues they have not been dealt with here. For the manufacture of snow caves etc. a snow saw can be of great assistance. If the entrance to a snow-hole is blocked for warmth, it is essential to leave a ventilation hole, or an ice axe, which, when rotated from time to time, will allow enough air in as the shaft is oval. By sitting on a rope with feet in rucksack etc., a reasonably comfortable night can be had should a bivouac sack not be available. If a cap is kept across one's face, with the anorak hood drawn tight, the exhaled warm air will be kept within the anorak or cagoule. When possible excavate the snow-hole in a steep bank free from avalanche danger
(R Turner)

Below: A snow cave. The ice axe through the door of snow blocks ensures ventilation when it is rotated periodically. The roof of the cave should slope towards the entrance to allow drips to descend to the entrance. Two channels can be made down each side of the sleeping ledge to carry condensation from the walls and a further small channel along the rear of the hole or cave to connect these. A deeper trench at the door allows a sitting position for cooking etc.
(R Turner)

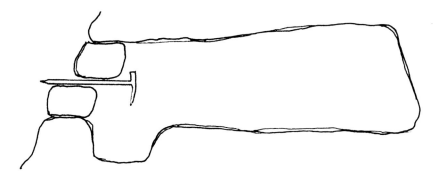

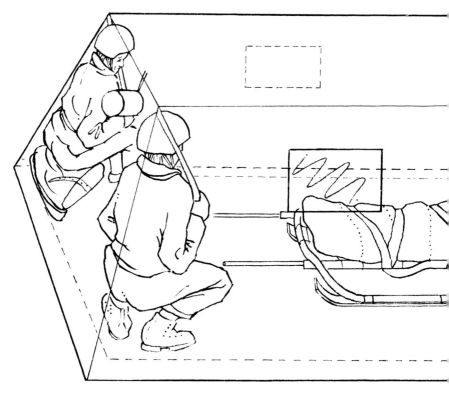

A large bri-nylon rescue team bivouac tent. These can be made with plastic windows and should be made from fluorescent material when possible. Such a tent is excellent for sheltering a critically injured person in severe weather conditions. The tent is held down by rescuers sitting on an internal ground flap and holding onto corner tapes. Two ventilators are necessary (G Hunter)

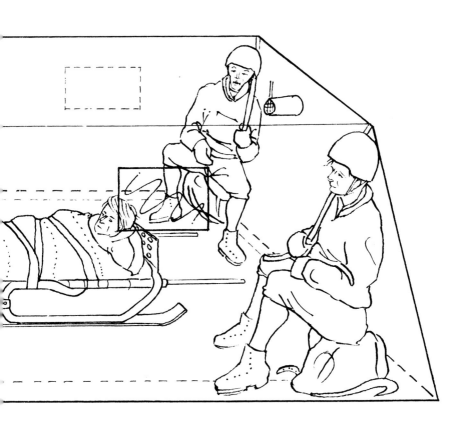

Call-out procedure

Reserves

Ambulance

Doctor

Helicopter

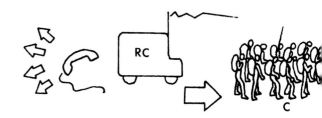

The call-out

As mentioned elsewhere in the text, the precise details of an accident obtained from a survivor, though often in a state of shock, are of the utmost importance. He must be questioned calmly and carefully and if possible given a hot sweet drink and first aid if required.

The following details should be obtained from him whenever possible:

a) The exact location of the accident, map reference if possible, and in the case of a climbing accident the part of the climb where the accident occurred.
b) Time of accident.
c) Number of people involved.
d) Injuries sustained.
e) Any other useful information, e.g. colour of clothing, weather, snow conditions.

These questions should be asked by someone with an expert knowledge of the area or the particular climb.

Once this information has been given it must be acted upon speedily. The normal call-out procedure must start.

If it is possible to get an advance party out right away so much the better. All team members should have their personal equipment at home with them and in most areas there is no reason why an advance party cannot be ready to start off within fifteen minutes of getting the call.

If at all possible the survivor should be asked to accompany the rescue team when there is doubt as to the exact location of the accident.

An advance party

When the location of an accident is known, the advance party is an important vanguard to the rescue team. Not only can it save life by rapid medical attention at the scene of the accident, but accurate details of the accident can be relayed by RT to the following main party or to base (which will have been established meantime and will have made known its requirements for equipment etc. to evacuate the injured). Obviously if the difficulties and the scale of the operation are great, there will be no advantage in an advance party which, in fact, could perhaps endanger following groups with rockfall etc.

However, on most mountain accidents on smaller mountains the advance party is

A straightforward rescue operation. A = Advance party with first aid, casualty bag, RT, etc., approaching the victim V. B = the main stretcher party, fully equipped with stretcher, further first aid, RT, etc. C = a further support party of late arrivals to help on the last stages of evacuation thereby relieving the main group. Both the main party and the return journey support party should go up as organised groups under a group leader who has a note of their names, etc. Rescue control, when possible, should be close to a telephone, or be in touch with someone with a walkie-talkie standing by a telephone for further assistance when required. A mobile/satellite phone is also an essential item of equipment and a fax machine is desirable. (K Spence)

a very great asset. A party of four is usually adequate for this task, but each must be highly competent, capable of overcoming any technical difficulty of access, being able to judge the requirements of the main rescue team and able to administer immediate first aid to the injured.

The equipment they take with them will be related to the available details of the accident. In the case of a rock climbing accident, with the injured still in a difficult situation, pitons, slings, rope clamps, karabiners etc., will have to be available in greater quantity than on, say, an easy evacuation from a snow couloir. A casualty bag should always be taken by the advance party, for even if the patient may think he can walk down with assistance, often he eventually needs to be carried. First aid and a walkie-talkie must be included in the advance party kit.

Not only is it necessary that all rescue team members are well versed in first aid, but the advance party must be highly competent as they often have to deal with situations which could be difficult for a doctor.

Probably the greatest hazard facing the advance party, and to a lesser degree the rescue team, is avalanche rescue. Time is an all-important factor in avalanche search and the advance party, even when using bleepers, can be in imminent danger from subsequent avalanches. The advance party on an avalanche accident should, whenever possible, include a trained dog and handler as well as first aid, oxygen equipment, probes, shovels, etc., in addition to personal equipment.

System of call-out

The call-out of team members should be given careful study. Not only can time and lives be saved by an efficient system, but it will ensure that the maximum number of personnel get called out at a given time.

Various systems of call-out are used, from walkie-talkies, air raid sirens to a series of maroon rockets and even church bells. Individual telephone emergency lines can be installed by certain telephone companies, but the usual call-out medium is the telephone or pagers/mobile 'phones.

It will be found that there are accident 'black spots' and that calls for help will often come from particular areas. The team leader or an experienced team member should question the survivor as fully as possible over the telephone (if it is not possible to do this in person immediately). As soon as the facts are ascertained he should contact one of several rescue call-out personnel (several must be deployed in case of absence, telephone faults etc.), or an efficient switchboard; or police, military etc., who have been previously thoroughly briefed on calling out the team. This will enable individual team members to arrive at a pre-arranged rendezvous with the necessary equipment in the shortest possible time, without having to bother calling out a fellow team member.

Mobile base

The possession of a base vehicle which contains all team equipment, can be invaluable. It should be available at the base of operations in the shortest possible time with all necessary equipment ready for use.

Large detailed photographs of the possible search/rescue areas should be kept in the mobile base for pinpointing location and for helping a survivor to retrace his movements to obtain the precise location of an accident.

With the exception of personal team equipment and individual RT sets etc., all communal equipment can be stowed in this truck, which can also be fitted out for providing meals and be an operations centre on a large-scale rescue. Often certain items of equipment are called for by the rescue party or advance party, which may otherwise entail a journey of some distance to collect them and this would waste valuable time.

It is important that directions to Team members in respect to a call-out are concise and accurate. If the operation (as in the case of missing persons) continues to another day/s, it is of prime importance to give all rescuers and the authorities, precise written details of the factors concerning the incident as listed at the start of this section. These details and the schedule for the next day's search should be entered, preferably in a computer and copies issued to all personnel/aircrew taking part in the operation. Photocopies of a map of ground searched and indicating new areas to search are necessities and will provide a permanent record of the call-out for statistical purposes. The 'call-sheet' should be updated each day and the new instructions issued. A fax machine (satellite facsimile machines are available) mobile 'phone, laptop computer/printer, etc. as mentioned above are all useful tools. The Operational Base should have a power source, low voltage off a vehicle, mains/generator or solar chargers for remote regions. These are especially good for radio equipment.

The Rescue Controller has one of the most demanding tasks on a large scale call-out. He has to anticipate the sometimes specialised equipment which may be required, from a chain saw for cutting through an avalanche tip of solid ice to the possible acquisition of recent satellite photographs to study a wilderness search area.

Another strange request which comes up from time to time is a lubricant, such as washing up liquid, to free a climber's knee or ankle from a crack. A pack of butter was used for this on one occasion! Even explosives for neutralising hazardous avalanche slopes have been deployed.

Homicide

It is possible during the career of a mountain rescuer that he or she will be faced with a suspicious death, though most rescue teams now have a member of the police or law enforcement agency in their ranks as a working team member. On fatalities the police usually require photographs of the deceased, and of the locus, as well as statements. Many regions follow up a fatality, and sometimes an

accident, with a Court of Inquiry. Certain countries, too, deploy a panel of experts to determine if there was negligence on the part of the group leader or the rescued party, and may impose fines related to the overall cost of the operation. The police may also use their facilities to determine if there was any motive for a fatality or accident, eg. insurance or inheritance. Gravity is a formidable accomplice!

A Forensic Specialist investigates the remains of two bodies found in the Grand Canyon. Soil samples containing maggot larvae, where the bodies had decomposed were taken. The larvae samples were studied to determine the date and time of death (K Phillips)

Stretchers,
casualty evacuation,
stretcher lowers,
cableways,
snow lowers, etc.

For the latest developments in
stretcher design see pages 348–9

As with other items of rescue equipment,
certain stretchers are more suited for
specific areas than others. It is only with
trial and error that a rescue team will
establish the optimum model for their
specific needs.

Stretcher design

For general mountain rescue evacuations
which involve carrying over rough terrain,
runners are required on the stretcher.
These should be broad enough to allow
easy movement in powder snow/sand and
be approx. ¾ the length of the stretcher. A
transport wheel is useful for long
evacuations and even on steep terrain can
be used to advantage. Various types of
wheels have been used, some with built-in
engines, double and treble wheels in
planetary formation. The two most
popular are the specially strengthened
70 cm 'mountain bike' type wheel with
puncture proof inner tube, or the wider
section all-terrain type. Both work well,
the cycle-type wheel offering lower rolling
resistance and the wider, better
performance over bogs, soft snow and
deep sand.
   The stretcher which is used for general
mountain rescue evacuation should have
carrying handles, preferably extending to
70 cm beyond the ends of the stretcher.
These can be either telescopic, folding or

An early MacInnes folding stretcher. This stretcher is made from Hiduminium tubing and weighs 14.5 kg. The stretcher uses a pre-stretched terylene patient bed which reduces wind resistance when carrying. It is fitted with a head and a back protector and hinges in the centre for ease of carrying. Stirrups, chest harness and very long wrap-around patient strap are standard equipment. The shafts are telescopic and are supplied with four shoulder harnesses. The wheel unit is fitted with a hub brake (H MacInnes)

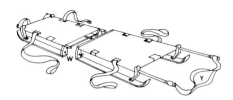

Split Thomas stretcher. This stretcher splits in two sections for easy carrying. The carrying straps serve as a rucksack-type straps. The stretcher bed is made from either plastic coated wire mesh or canvas. The shafts are telescopic and the complete stretcher weighs over 18 kg. The two parts of the stretcher are locked together with a bolt at W, as marked on the drawing. A mesh head guard is also available for this model. Y = carrying yoke. A Thomas splint can be attached to the bottom cross member (K Spence)

retractable transverse shafts. Some lock in positions most convenient for carrying. Weight and portability are important characteristics and some form of headguard which can quickly be hinged back or folded is vital for protection. The stretcher bed should be set below the outer frame member to help retain patient/corpse on the stretcher bed. Though this makes it more difficult to install the patient on the stretcher, a light-weight inner stretcher, spinal splint or vac-bag can be deployed (see illustrations) for immobilising casualties with suspected spinal/neck injuries. The use of an inner stretcher fitted with helicopter lifting harness obviates the main stretcher being taken to hospital by the helicopter/ ambulance. The main stretcher can therefore be retained in the area where it may shortly be required.

It is also desirable to have some form of shoulder carrying yoke or harness for clipping onto the shafts for strenuous evacuations. Some stretchers have packframes for transporting the stretcher sections to the scene of an accident. These can double as stretcher carrying yokes when the bottom loops of the shoulder straps are clipped to the stretcher shafts.

The bed of the stretcher should be of a composite material or plastic coated aluminium/titanium. This enables the base of the bed to act as a toboggan in deep powder snow and prevents snagging in bush or jungle terrain. It also acts as a rigid splint and affords protection to the casualty when sledging the stretcher.

Patient straps should provide adequate security for retaining the patient, even if accidentally inverted, or if the stretcher is suspended from one end as in the case of a vertical lower. The straps should preferably be capable of adjustment to avoid injured parts of the casualty's body. A cheststrap can be used when no adverse strain will impair the patient's breathing or aggravate an injury.

In the case of a split stretcher, or one which dismantles for carrying to the scene of the accident, it is very important to ensure that the sections are entrusted to fit, efficient team members, as there have been instances of one half of the stretcher not reaching, or arriving late at the locus.

There are many stretchers available today and for cliff/face evacuation a lightweight, rigid compact stretcher or inner stretcher may be more suited. If the injuries are not severe a heavy duty casualty bag can be utilised as a stretcher. For raising or lowering in the absence of spinal injuries/fractures the heavy duty casualty bag must have suitable suspension slings to maintain horizontal trim.

Helicopter lift cables/strops

Stainless steel cable with copper swaged end loops should be used, or custom made nylon strops available from rescue gear manufacturers. Either four or six slings should connect the stretcher to the

(Text continued on page 132)

Top: A single track powered 'wheelbarrow' used for patient evacuation. This machine runs on a single wide track and is steered and controlled by handlebars at the rear (H MacInnes)

Bottom: A badly injured climber being evacuated using a transport wheel on a Mariner stretcher. Note the two rear holding ropes, one either side of the rear stretcher bearer (A Contamine)

Below: Fitting the transport wheel to a Mariner. Note the leg traction frame on the stretcher. Weight of the stretcher (including the leg splint) 25 kg. Wheel and stays 5 kg (A Contamine)

Above: Using the Perche Barnarde stretcher on easier ground. The front stretcher bearer can be seen using the handlebar-type carrying handles across his shoulders (A Contamine)

Right: The Stokes Litter stretcher as used in the USA. Its weight is 22 kg though an all alloy model is now available. The model illustrated is fitted with a wheel (J Duff)

Opposite page top: The Perche Barnarde stretcher. The square sections of the main tube are held together by the pins marked '2'. The patient is suspended in the canvas bed marked '1'. Though many difficult evacuations have been done using this stretcher, for the severely injured patient with, say, a spinal injury, evacuation would be most uncomfortable (H MacInnes)

Opposite page, bottom: Doing a horizontal lower using a Perche Barnarde stretcher. The weight of the casualty is taken on a square section pole via a suspended canvas bag and handlebar-type handles can be clipped onto either end of the pole for two-man transport on easier ground (A Contamine)

Right and opposite page, top: A method of tying the stretcher lowering rope to one corner of the stretcher. A clove hitch is used on the runner upright and on one of the cross members and the end taken forward and further secured with a bowline (R Turner)

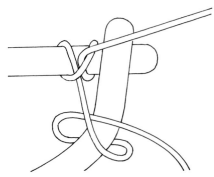

Above: A temporary rescue station as used in Norway. Note the helper sledges, which can be used by a dog team when necessary, or which can be quickly made up from the injured person's skis with a simple, lightweight kit (Norwegian Red Cross)

Right: Ullswater Fellbounder MK5: This machine was used for patient evacuation using a compact power unit (Sqn Ldr L Davies)

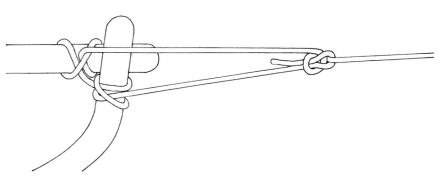

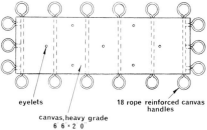

eyelets

canvas, heavy grade
6 6 × 2 0

18 rope reinforced canvas handles

Above: Traversing glaciers can present many problems. Often very rough sections in icefalls must be negotiated (A Contamine)

Left: The Tararua stretcher is made from stout canvas (2 m × 0.6 m approx.). Long poles such as lancewood or straight branches can be threaded through the side loops and the carrying poles are kept apart by two smaller branches lashed at right angles to the main carrying poles. This is used in the New Zealand bush for rescue work (D Craig)

113

Neil Robertson stretcher

Below left: A modified Neil Robertson stretcher with two tubular steel runners attached down the rear of the stretcher. H = a haulage point for lowers etc. S = a helmet mounted on an adjusting frame, which telescopes into the runner tubes. C = carrying handles. F = adjustable foot rest. The standard Neil Robertson stretcher is made from wood laths and canvas. Five tie-round patient straps are attached to the stretcher (K Spence)

Right: A Neil Robertson stretcher being used to lower a casualty down an ice face on La Perouse, New Zealand (M Bowie, Chief Guide, Mount Cook)

Below right: The Neil Robertson stretcher. This stretcher is popular for use with helicopters as it is very compact. The lowering slings and ring are seen at the head end (D Craig)

Rescue capsule

Opposite page: A glass fibre rescue capsule designed by the author. The patient is enclosed in the shell of the stretcher which has a small window at the head end. The stretcher splits into four sections for ease of transport to the scene of the accident. The suspension rig for stretchers using cableways is shown in inset photo, which also relates to the capsule photograph. 1 = quick link connecting stretcher suspension to belay rope. 2 = wide pulley, the cheeks of which pivot on the pulley spindle independently for quick use. Two holes are made at the cheek ends for two

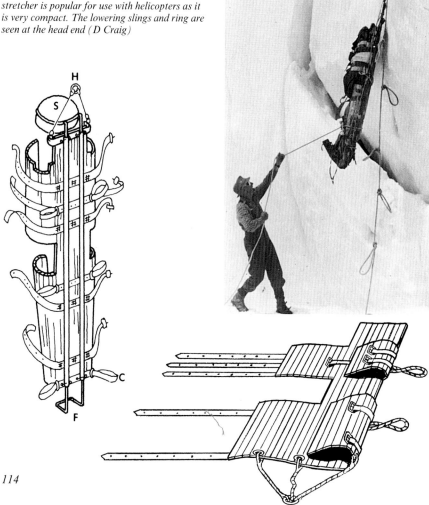

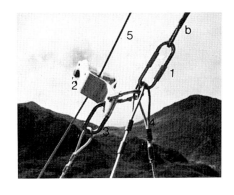

karabiners/quick links, for hanging stretcher and
for connecting front and rear pulleys.
3 = connecting karabiners and sling between
pulleys. 4 = wire suspension slings for stretcher,
rear slings being slightly longer. 5 = suspension
wire, which can be extended by coupling a further
cable. Even with quick links used as connectors
these will run through wide pulleys, with a central
locating groove such as shown – (2).
b = lowering rope (H MacInnes)

Right and below: The Branchard Piguillem stretcher which folds and can be carried by one person (weight 14 kg). The stretcher is fitted with helicopter lift wires and it has a 'built-in' casualty bag (Glenmore Lodge)

Opposite page, top: The MacInnes Superlite stretcher showing it with the 'All Terrain' wheel. The stretcher fitted with the two ball wheels can be taken over boulderfields and very rough ground. The balls are at low pressure and punctures can be repaired using a hot soldering iron, piton etc. The stretcher is in three hinged sections and can be folded for transport. Weight 11 kg. The fluorescent stretcher bed has a built-in casualty bag i.e. outer windproof/waterproof cover. The stretcher is fitted with helicopter lift wires (H MacInnes)

Opposite page, bottom: A motor vehicle ATV wheel utilised as a single stretcher transport wheel. Pressure is under 14 kPa (2 psi), which allows it to mush over rocks. Ribs prevent side-slip on slopes (Riverside MR, California)

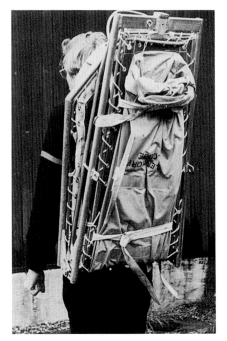

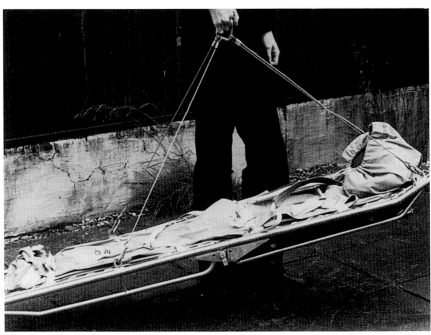

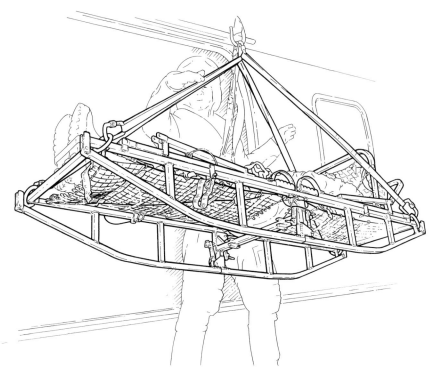

The stainless steel Bell Mountain Rescue
Stretcher has hinged handles and splits in two.
Two pack frames are used for transporting the
stretcher to the accident scene. These can be
assembled to make a small stretcher for
emergencies. The complete stretcher weighs 20.42
kg. Three sizes are manufactured.
(Peter Bell)

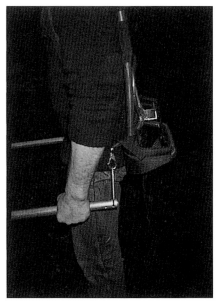

Above: The MacInnes split stretcher Mk6. This unit has a six-point detachable stainless steel suspension system with flip-back s/s head protector to which patient monitoring equipment can be attached. Length 218cm, weight 24kg. Two special packframes are used for carrying the stretcher halves, which double as carrying yokes when clipped to the telescopic shafts. A custom-built puncture-proof wheel unit is supplied. The Mk6 has an optional Inner Stretcher (right), again with six-point winching attachment. It is of heat-treated alloy tubing and carbon fibre; weight 7kg and fits into the Mk6. It is highly portable and can be winched or lowered horizontally independently of the parent stretcher. The advantages are the ease with which a patient with spinal injuries can be slid on to it, and that only the inner stretcher need be taken to hospital, leaving the Mk6 in the rescue region

Left: The packframe/shaft attachment for the MacInnes Mk6 stetcher.

119

The Ferno Split Basket stretcher being used on a horizontal lower (Ferno)

Inset: The stretcher, Model 71, weighs 13 kg, is 213 cm long and has a polythene shell with an alloy frame. A harness set and four-point lifting bridle are available.

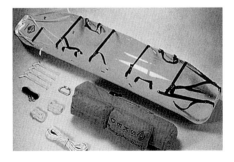

The Sked, a compact lightweight stretcher (Skedco Inc)

Right: A Stokes style aluminium stretcher made by DHS of Sydney which is used in Australia (Stuart McLeod)

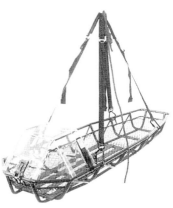

Above: The Heli-Lift stretcher. Closed cell foam material; length 210 cm. Like the Cocoon and similar models, this is a lightweight model which can be used as an 'inner' for the main MR stretcher (Isola)

Left: A CMC Vertical Evac adjustable stretcher harness. Note the head protector fitted to the Stokes litter. This stretcher also comes in a split version. Weight 14.52 kg (CMC)

The stretcher well clear of the ground and obstacles on the suspension cable (A Contamine)

A horizontal lower using a Troll stretcher, Veedawoo National Park, Wyoming (Dave Allport)

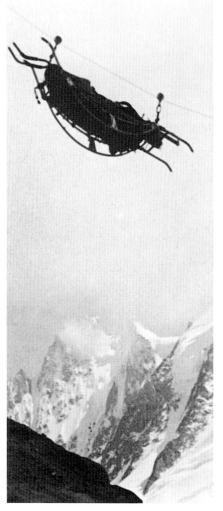

Sledging a stretcher down scree using short anchor ropes to the rescuers behind stretcher. Such treatment is rough for the patient and can only be used when he has minor injuries. Note how the anchor ropes are 'V'd'out for greater control (L Gramminger)

Left: A tragsitz can be used for transporting a casualty on easier ground as well. Extra security can be given to the bearer by having one or two back ropes (A Contamine)

A horizontal lower using an Akja stretcher suspended from four slings. It is important to have the suspension points on the slings adjusted so that the stretcher remains on a horizontal plane when it is pulled out from the face by the two 'barrow boys' and that all the slings are taut. A separate belay rope is being used for the barrow boys. This technique is much more difficult to use than the cableway system described elsewhere in the text. This practice lower was done in British Columbia, Canada (D Cuthbert, Vancouver)

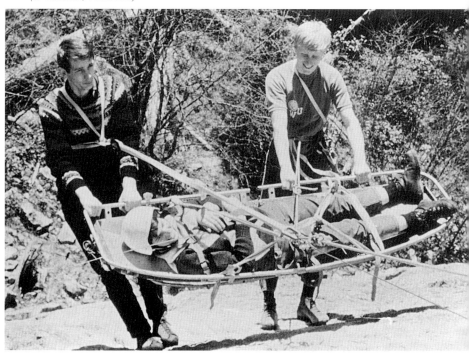

Right: Rescuer and casualty being lowered, using tragsitz, off the Grepon, French Alps. Rescuer is seen using a further guide rope for the descent, to which he can hold when necessary (A Contamine)

124

Patient and rescuer being lowered down an arete (tragsitz being used). Care must be exercised when doing such a lower as it is possible for the lowered party to pendulum either side of the arete or buttress (L Gramminger)

Left top: A rescuer being lowered with tragsitz. Note the walkie-talkie aerial and the swivel on the wire rope (L Gramminger)

Left middle: A cableway being used to evacuate a patient down a snow slope, where otherwise there would be serious delays due to the nature of the terrain. Cableway belays however must be from solid rock due to the high loads involved (Austrian Alpine Club)

Left bottom: Banff National Park. A rescuer being transported across a canyon by means of the standard rescue cableway. It is often advantageous, after the casualty has been lowered, for members of the rescue team to descend using the same cableway, leaving only two climber rescuers to return by another route after they have lowered the cableway rope (B Engler)

Below and opposite page: Launching the stretcher on a cableway in the French Alps (A Contamine)

A cliff lower using a single cable from a brake block. For a lower such as this, at least two turns round the block are necessary.
1 denotes a separate sling to the harness of the 'barrow boy', Banff National Park, Canada (B Engler)

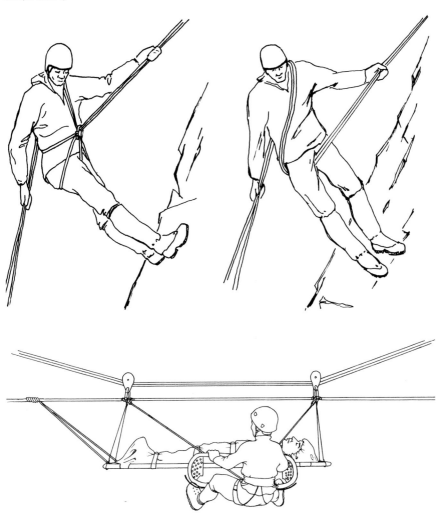

Abseiling, using the sit sling technique. A screw-gate karabiner should always be use for this (E Grieve)

Double roping without a sling. Gloves should always be worn when double roping (E Grieve)

A double rope traversing/cableway stretcher rig. This system can also be used for traversing cliff faces. Note from the haulage rope attachment that direction of travel is from right to left. The

'barrow boy' is attached to the pulleys by adjustable slings and the pulley karabiners are connected by the haulage/tail rope. These should be independently belayed. (E. Donaldson)

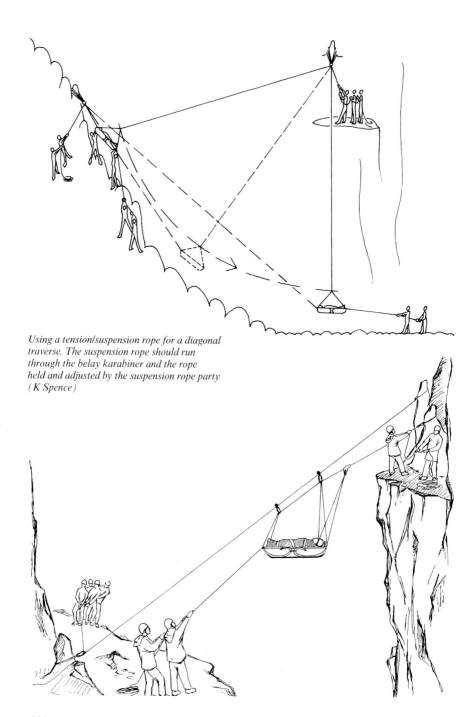

*Using a tension/suspension rope for a diagonal
traverse. The suspension rope should run
through the belay karabiner and the rope
held and adjusted by the suspension rope party
(K Spence)*

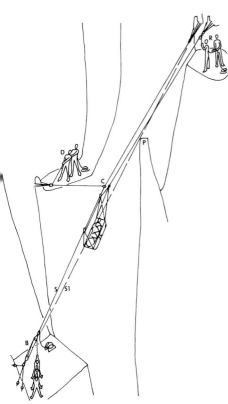

Left: This illustration shows a cableway with a 'change of direction' rope being used. This change of direction rope is operated by party D. This technique enables the stretcher to be cleared of obstacles in the path of the lower, and it can even be used for changing direction round a buttress. The obstacle shown here is a pinnacle, 'P'.

The change of direction rope used by party D has a karabiner or pulley on the end, which runs free behind the suspended stretcher, by gravity, or is attached to the stretcher if it is long enough to go to bottom party.

The bottom party can alter the tension on the suspension rope as required if a block and tackle is used. S1 indicates the suspension wire in a straight line from belay to belay and S shows the altered suspension cable or rope held out by the change of direction rope. Many variations of this technique can be used. Care should be taken that the suspension rope is not over-tensioned and the block and tackle should not be tied off. Before tension is put on the suspension rope by party D, the tension on the suspension rope should be eased. Consult the table re tension on suspension ropes before using this technique and other techniques illustrated. It is safer to use a further safety rope from the lower end of the stretcher to the bottom belay and to have this taken in on a lowering device. Great care must by used with this technique as the rope operated by party D can greatly overstress the suspension rope unless it is released by party B. Radio (R) communication is essential for this technique (K Spence)

Left: These cableway/lowering techniques, including the helicopter winch extension systems were evolved by the author and have been practiced since the 1960s. Evacuating a patient by cableway, tensioned by rescuers through a pulley or karabiner. The rescuer at the top, on the ledge, lowers the stretcher using a lowering device. His helper feeds the rope to him to avoid snagging. The stretcher is suspended from two pulleys, using slings, which allow the stretcher to descend on a horizontal plane. The lowering rope also connects the two pulleys to avoid jerky descent and at the top end a jumar-type clamp or Prusik knot is used on another sling, which is attached to the two rear corners of the stretcher. The stretcher is helped down by the two bottom men, who guide it to the required position. Having only four men holding the suspension rope in this way ensures that it won't be overstrained. Do not overstress suspension rope. In practice there would be considerable sag in the suspension rope
(E Grieve)

helicopter winch swivel/suspension rope/s. Ensure that the stretcher trim is correct with a patient aboard; the head end being slightly higher than the feet end. Try this out in training to make sure that various weights of patients suspend correctly.

Lowering/hoisting in safety

With the plethora of modern equipment one could be forgiven in thinking that a cliff lower or a winching operation would be child's play these days. This is not the case; it is fraught with hazards. Not only are there restrictions on what equipment can be taken to an often difficult or dangerous location, but often mountain accidents occur in bad weather, where even reaching the location can be a major expedition.

There are problems and limitations with all rescue rigging systems in current use. Some of the older rope clamps can damage or even sever the master rope under severe loading. The alternative in the rescue armoury, the Prusik knot, can sometimes inexplicably slip. It may be that the knot has worked loose and is not as snug on the master rope as it should be, or perhaps inadvertently has been used in conjunction with a coated lowering rope. In many parts of the world cliff rescue is often done in severe winter conditions. At all times, should there be heavy atmospheric icing, or ropes running (or cutting through) snow edges, there is a danger of a clamping device or Prusik creeping or slipping. Fortunately where this is a frequent occurrence rescue teams are capable of dealing with it.

Always try to take extra rope to further safeguard the stretcher and the rescuers who accompany it.

There is still a great deal of research to be done on rescue equipment. Many modern climbing aids were designed for mountaineering and not for the exacting task of rescue operations. Fortunately the experienced rescuer takes this into account.

As mentioned above and throughout the text, rope clamps have been used for technical rescue work for many years. But, many rope clamps were not designed for the heavy punishment found in a rescue rig, but within certain parameters they can provide a rapid means of expediting a rescue operation where climatic conditions may present a serious risk to the rescue operation.

Cardinal rules: When using Prusik's, use a low-stretch 8 mm kernmantle cord on 11mm kernmantle rope.

Use either polyester or nylon Prusik's on polyester rope and nylon Prusik's on nylon rope.

When used in tandem, the knots should have a spacing of at least 10 cm on the master rope.

Use a load releasing hitch in the circuit, between the tandem Prusik's and their anchor. The LRH acts as a shock absorber and can extend by 250 per cent under load and allows the tandem Prusik's to obtain a better grip on the master rope.

Always use flexible cord for the Prusik's and there should be a dedicated Prusik Knot Minder, who ensures that at all times, the knots are snug and not deformed.

When rope clamps are used by experienced rescuers they can as mentioned above, facilitate a rescue, but slack must be eliminated at all times on active ropes to avoid shock loading. Experienced mountaineers who jumar in icy conditions or muddy environments, such as climbs in jungle regions and when there is excessive sand, often carry a small, fine wire brush to clean the cams of their ascenders. This is worth bearing in mind for rescue work too.

(Text continued on page 158)

Using direct manpower to raise a crag-bound climber or casualty. A jumar-type clamp is used to secure rope and control of lift is directed by a rescuer at edge. The hauling party can be in various positions depending on the terrain. Inset shows an Edge Roller (G Hunter)

The two illustrations on this page show the method of evacuating a casualty from a cliff face where there are no belays directly above or below. Two rescuers climb up, or descend, to the casualty. They take with them the end of the suspension wire/synthetic fibre rope. This can also be done by clipping a karabiner and rope to the suspension rope, which has already been established, and they can pull this across to the casualty when they reach him. The rescue/first-aid party should take enough rope with them to the casualty to reach the bottom end of the cableway.

When the casualty is secured to the stretcher/casualty bag, which can be pulled up or lowered down the cableway, he is suspended using the sling attachment shown elsewhere in the text, and a further rope from the top belay party is attached to the stretcher for lowering. By using radio communication the bottom end of the suspension rope can be tensioned and the top lowering rope paid out together with the rescue first-aid party rope. Some form of lowering device must be used by the two lowering parties. Care should be exercised that the suspension rope is not over-tensioned and if a Simpul Sport winch is used a Russian clamp or a brake block must be used for safety behind this, preferably on a separate belay. If sufficient rope is available, a further bottom safety rope can be used on the stretcher and belayed as the stretcher descends (E Grieve)

Opposite page, top: Using two columns of rescuers to drag an injured climber over snow. The stretcher is the snow toboggan type (E Hameda, Japanese Alpine Club)

Opposite page, below left: Lifting a casualty out of a gully or ravine. An intermediate pulley P is used on the end of a further rope which runs through two runners and is held by a rescuer. The haulage rope is secured by a jumar-type clamp J. A further rescuer R controls the evacuation (E Grieve)

Opposite page, below right: Evacuating a casualty from a gully or ravine using the mechanical advantage gained by using pulleys. P = pulleys, J = a jumar-type rope clamp for securing haulage rope, K = a separate rope for keeping haulage rope clear of cliff edge (E Grieve)

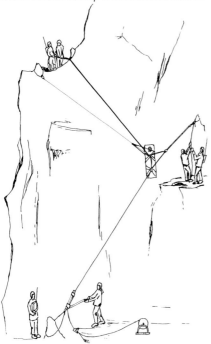
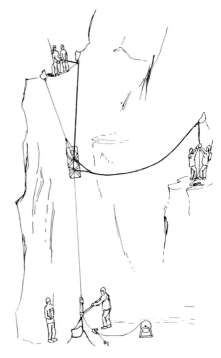

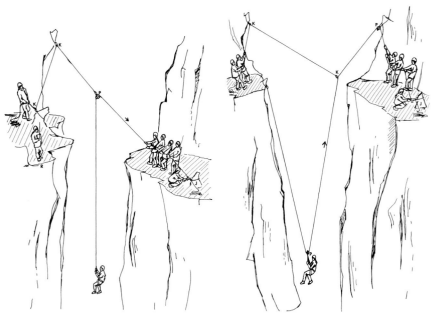

135

1. *This sequence shows a technique for raising a casualty out of a gully or couloir. If the rescue party can gain access to each side it should be possible for two rescuers to abseil down into the bed of the gully on doubled ropes. One of the rescuers takes with him the end of a long rescue rope (wire or synthetic fibre). This is marked R in the diagrams. The abseil ropes are A1–A4. Rope B safeguards (if need be) the rescuer, who places the sling for the pulley on the end of rope 5. He returns to the main ledge M taking with him the pulley which is attached to the end of rope 5, and threaded through the karabiner, which is attached to the bollard (or piton). On the ledge L one rescuer allows the rope R to run off drum. A further rescuer prepares a belay K for the end of the rescue rope R.*

The abseiling rescuers take with them a walkie-talkie and first aid (E Grieve)

2. *The rescuers who have abseiled down have administered first aid and the end of abseil rope A4 has been attached to the end of rescue rope R and hauled up to ledge M. The end of the rescue rope has been taken through pulley P and rope 5 has been tensioned and pulley P pulled out into the required position. The other end of rescue rope R has been attached to the belay on ledge L. The stretcher is being prepared with suspension slings and pulleys, ready to be lowered to the party with casualty . On ledge M a rope clamp has been attached to a belay. This clamp is better locked both front and rear ends as illustrated elsewhere in the book. Radio contact is maintained throughout the operation (E Grieve)3. Abseil ropes A2 and A3 have been tied together, pulled up and attached to the ends of the stretcher and this is pulled out to the centre of the gully and lowered. Other necessary equipment can be lowered to the casualty party at this stage, e.g. casualty bags, splints etc. (E Grieve)*

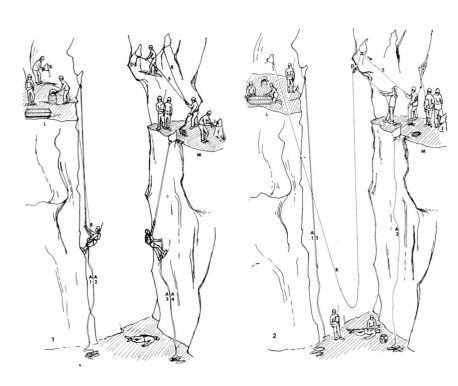

3. *Abseil ropes A2 and A3 have been tied together, pulled up and attached to the ends of the stretcher and this is pulled out to the centre of the gully and lowered. Other necessary equipment can be lowered to the casualty party at this stage, e.g. casualty bags, splints etc. (E Grieve)*

4. *The lifting operation. Rescue rope R is taken through the stretcher suspension pulleys when the casualty has been secured on stretcher. Ropes A2 and A3 are left on. (It is better to have a 'V' attachment onto the stretcher corners for these ropes by utilising two slings, each end of equal length, and having the ropes A2 and A3 attached to the ends of the slings. This will enable the stretcher to be kept on an even keel when*

assistance is given in the raising operation by means of these two ropes.) This illustration shows the stretcher in two positions, the lower one is where the L ledge party would be assisting by pulling on rope A2 and on ledge M one man is shown assisting with rope A3. The others haul on R. When the stretcher is hauled up to a point level with or above the ledges, A2 and A3 can be with plastic pulley in place of a standard karabiner, makes this task easier (G Hunter)

Warning: *care should be exercised to avoid overloading suspension ropes. If possible use a double rope cableway. It is also advantageous to have the anchors above the belayers. If in doubt use a load meter on suspension ropes. (E. Grieve)*

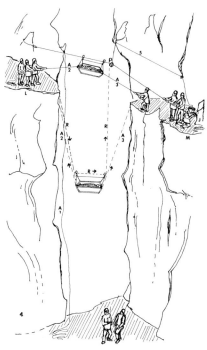

Below: An easy evacuation using a long rescue rope with a change of direction pulley being used (R). L = the rope drum and frame.

B1 = belay 1, with a lowering device or karabiner brake (brake drum, if wire rope is being used).

B2 = belay 2. The rescuer is ready to attach the rescue rope onto the lowering device, which is already attached to the belay. J = a jumar-type clamp (or Russian clamp for wire rope) which has a sling attached to the belay. The clamp will hold the stretcher securely until the rope is attached to the lowering device. In this way almost continuous movement can be maintained by the stretcher party, for as the top belayers run out of rope, the bottom rescuer/belayers are ready to take over. The rescue rope should be allowed to run down the hillside and should not be coiled up by the top belay party, who have just completed their lower. Instead, they should hurry down past the stretcher to take up a new belay position within the span of the rescue rope. S = a rescuer with a searchlight who illuminates the terrain for the stretcher party as well as lighting the way ahead (E Grieve)

Opposite page: The advance party ascending fixed rope using jumar-type clamps. The first two climbers fix the long rescue rope at various points for the remainder of the party. Usually, the person carrying the stretcher needs a separate safety rope on very steep rock and ice. The last man on the advance party going to casualty unties the belays en route *so that the rope can be used for lowering if required (G Hunter)*

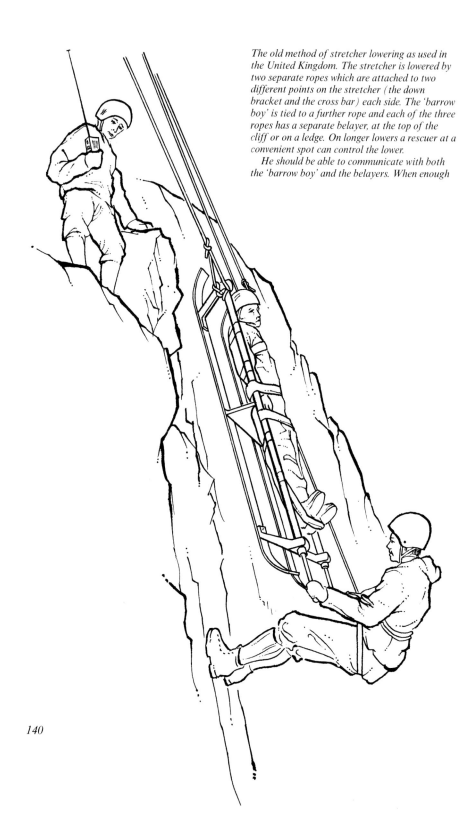

The old method of stretcher lowering as used in the United Kingdom. The stretcher is lowered by two separate ropes which are attached to two different points on the stretcher (the down bracket and the cross bar) each side. The 'barrow boy' is tied to a further rope and each of the three ropes has a separate belayer, at the top of the cliff or on a ledge. On longer lowers a rescuer at a convenient spot can control the lower.

He should be able to communicate with both the 'barrow boy' and the belayers. When enough people are available, it is advantageous to have a further party at base of cliff to receive stretcher and to continue with evacuation whilst the top belayers drop the ropes (unless one is needed for abseiling) and join the bottom party by a route which will not endanger those below with falling stones.

On longer lowers, the 'barrow boy' will find it more convenient to have a length of sling, or the end of his safety rope, taken from his waist, twice round the bottom cross bar of the stretcher then back to his hand which is holding a stretcher handle. This allows him to be attached to the stretcher, but at any time, by letting the rope end in his hand go, he can be free (G Hunter)

Using a climbing rope for a carrying seat. The patient can be further secured by a sling round both the casualty and the rescuer at chest height. The rescuer can be belayed down a slope with two rear ropes 'V'd' out and secured by the remainder of the party (G Hunter)

Rescuer and patient being lowered (or raised) using a tragsitz. Note the swivel on the rope above attachment point (G Hunter)

A simple ski stretcher using two or three anoraks/jackets as a stretcher bed. The sleeves of the anoraks should be turned inside out before inserting the skis. Long poles or tree branches can also be used and climbing rope etc., used for the stretcher bed. The ends of the skis or poles can be taken through the stretcher bearer's rucksack straps to distribute the load (K Spence)

Below: The human pulley frame: here a rescuer is illustrated holding a sling and karabiner to enable a haulage/lowering rope to be kept clear of an edge, which could damage the rope or cause considerable friction. A pulley, or a karabiner with plastic pulley in place of a standard karabiner, makes this task easier (G Hunter)

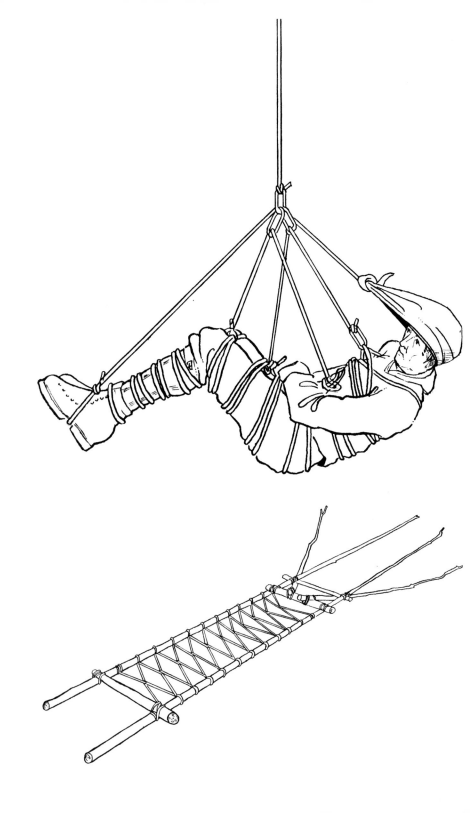

Opposite page, top: A rope basket being used for lowering a casualty with a head sling. Care should be taken that the head sling can't come off and it is better to make a further tie, with a triangular bandage, from the rear of the head sling to the top coils of the rope basket, behind the casualty's back. This technique is seldom used now and should only be resorted to in emergency. (G Hunter)

Opposite page, bottom: An improvised stretcher made from branches. The stretcher is pulled along at an angle on the rear branches which affords suspension (G Hunter)

Below: A climbing rope used for the construction of a rope basket. This is not suitable for evacuating a seriously injured person (G Hunter)

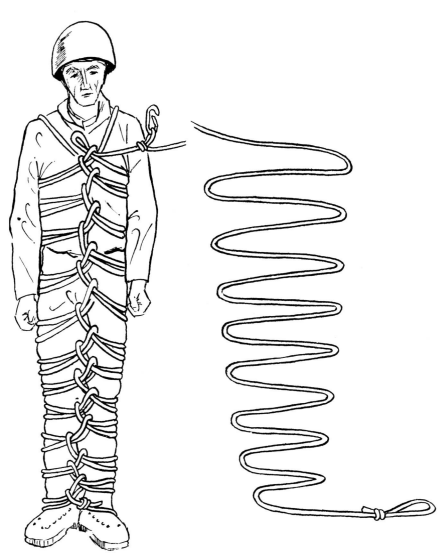

Top drawing: Older types of harness now obsolete. A simple rescuer's belt which can be made from 2 in/50 mm (approx.) wide nylon webbing. D rings can be used in place of a buckle and the end of the tape can be further secured by making a half hitch with the end behind the buckle. A further connection with line or tape can be made between the waist band A and the karabiner C for operations which may necessitate the rescuer hanging in space (K Spence)

Bottom drawings: Two further types of harness. A = the American type harness used for aid climbing. The legs go through the two loops L and L. The knot W and the loop formed go round the waist with W at the rear. B = the Whillans harness where C= a crotch strap and the climbing rope goes through the loop formed at the end of this strap and through B1 and B1 loops. The waist strap W is secured onto a buckle behind B1, right. A Swami belt is a long length of 25 mm wide nylon tape which winds round the waist and can be secured onto two D rings, which should be stitched to one end. An overhand knot with a crotch loop – similar to the American harness illustrated – can be made near the D ring end so that a sit harness is thus formed, with several turns round the waist. For rescue work the type of modified Swami belt was probably the most versatile as the tape can be put to other uses in emergency (K Spence)

Opposite page: The Troll two-piece harness used in conjunction with the chest harness for lowers and helicopter winching. Note the two methods of tying safety rope. For lowering/raising by helicopter winch the chest and lower harness should be interconnected with a tape sling to fulfil the same function as the rope in illustration. This type of harness can now be obtained with adjustable leg loops

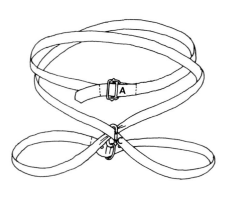

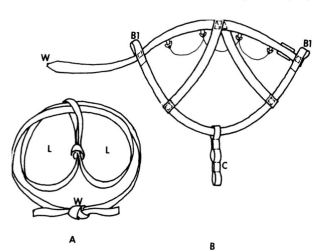

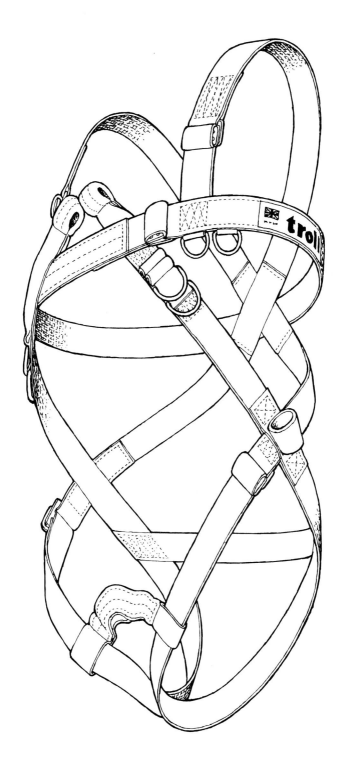

A casualty/body bag. This is a useful item for a rescue team for as well as being outer protection for the patients casualty bag, it can serve for evacuating a corpse down difficult terrain.

The area marked 'H' should be made from heavy canvas/cordura or ballistic cloth, 'F' fluorescent double flap of a lighter weight material. The bag laces up with nylon cord.

Electrically heated casualty bags are available. These should operate of low voltage 24v. for use in helicopters, or 12v/24v for generators. Heating strips are available which can be adapted.
(K. Spence)

Opposite page: the tragsitz. This is used for transporting casualties in a sitting position on the back of a rescuer. It can be used on the most difficult ground or for carrying an injured person down an easier slope. There are two rucksack-type carrying straps for the rescuer, 1 & 1. The triangular canvas section 2 is next to the rescuer's back, between him and the patient. A waist strap for the rescuer is marked, 3 & 3. The two canvas flaps 4 & 4 provide a seat for the casualty. The two hooks 5 are taken up to the two D rings at top of harness for securing the seat for the casualty. The shoulder straps, 6 & 6, are fitted to the casualty (these are sometimes detachable). For lowering, the rope end is secured to the suspension strap (7) which comes between the rescuer's legs and couples with the wire strop 8 and for free lowers a swivel should be used in conjunction with the karabiner or quick link. 9 indicates the rear part of the suspension strap (R Turner)

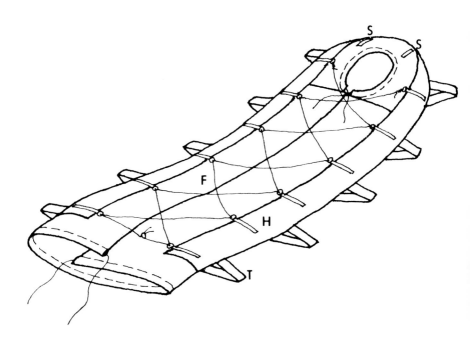

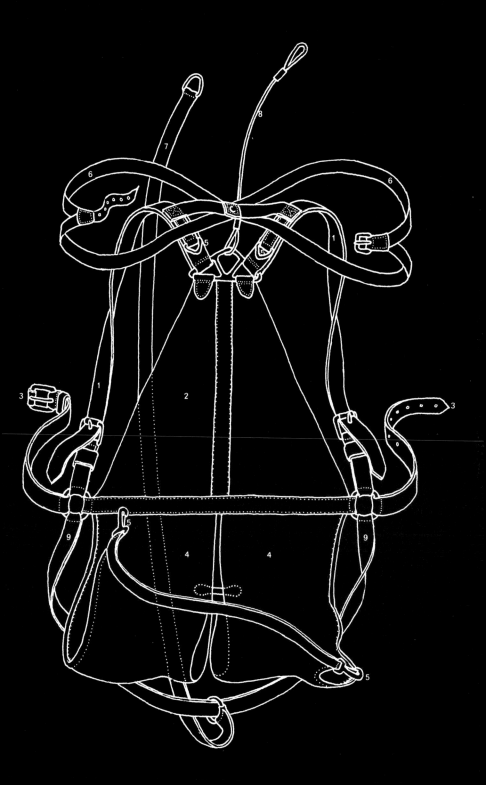

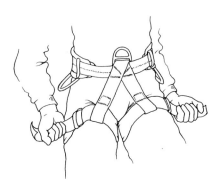
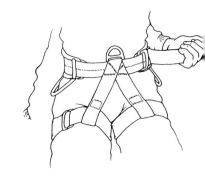

A modern body harness with quick-action waist and thigh straps. (E Donaldson)

Stretcher being prepared for a long snow lower, Japan. Note two climbers above stretcher also belaying stretcher as well as higher party out of sight (E Hameda, Japanese Alpine Club)

Right: A continuous snow lower. Fig A shows a stretcher being sledged down a snow slope from two belays (D). These can be deadmen, or rock belays. The belayers, 1 & 2, 1 & 2 use a figure of eight or a karabiner brake for lowering. When the rope is almost run out 5 & 5 insert their ice axes between the runner uprights and the stretcher frame, at either the front or rear of stretcher and 3 & 4, 3 & 4 take up new belay positions – see illustration (B).

Whilst this is being done, 1 & 2, 1 & 2 drop their rope ends and glissade, or climb down to catch up with the stretcher which, meantime, should have started down the next section. They then take up the positions vacated by 3 & 4, 3 & 4. On more difficult snow slopes a conventional lower should be used as in rock face evacuation. For descending bergschrunds etc., a simple cableway can be used utilising either rock belays or ice screws. For extra security, two rear lowering ropes can be attached to the stretcher as well as two front-ropes as ice screws cannot be relied upon for heavy loading. The rope cableway shouldn't be tensioned until the stretcher is clear of the lip of the schrund (K Spence)

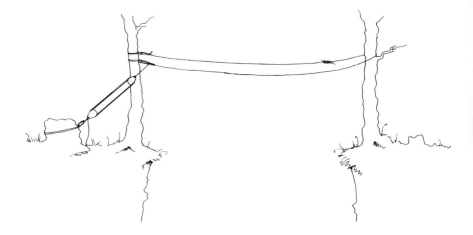

A cableway which can be retrieved from the active side (E Donaldson)

Horizontal rescue operation by Royal Oman Police and Fire Brigade (Dave Allport)

Above: Lifting a rescuer and patient from a cableway (Kootenay Highline). Span, 94 m, vertical lift almost 100 m (Arnor Larson)

Above right: A long cableway (Kootenay Highline System) being used across a large river canyon. Station to station distance, 475 m, inclination 7.32 degrees. Crossing time, approx. 20 minutes. All such operations should aim for a min. 10:1 Safety Factor on the cableway ropes (Arnor Larson)

Right: A close-up of the patient rig on the above cableway. Note the wide pulleys (Arnor Larson)

Opposite page: The Australian Larkin Rescue Frame: Top: The frame pivots on its base pole and ankles and offers a 2m projection at full extension. The four compression legs are each in two sections allowing full or half size modes. The unit has a SWL of 400 kg. Weight is 35 kg and it can fit on a stretcher.
Bottom: On a lift, when the stretcher is raised to the projection pulley, the rear frame is pulled down to ground level thereby swinging the stretcher inboard as with a davit, through the 'A' frame to the cliff top. The illustrations show the Larkin Rescue Frame in both short and extended modes (Stuart MacLeod)

Below: Royal Marines Rescue. Sennen Cove (Dave Allport)

Above: A 213 m Tyrolean traverse on a specially constructed Kevlar rope from the Old Man of Hoy to the Island of Hoy. For this cableway which was under considerable tension, a strain gauge was deployed

Right: There are various mechanical gauges suitable for monitoring cableway loadings which are slightly cheaper than the electronic versions. This Dillon unit for example has a range 10 kg – 500 kg (100 N–5000 N) (Dillon)

Far right: A compact electronic dynamometer which can be inserted between the active rope and the main anchor to monitor loading on cableway/hauling rig. A 'meter minder' should constantly monitor readings and relay these to the Rescue Controller (H. MacInnes)

Left: A horizontal lower using a Troll stretcher, Veedawoo National Park, Wyoming (Dave Allport)

Arriving at the accident scene

The Team Leader when reaching the accident locus has, with his colleagues, to assess the situation. Decide if the casualty has to be taken up or lowered down, or uplifted by helicopter, or attended until stabilised.

Rope/s must be taken down the cliff/gully, etc. to conduct the operation. This should be done with some thought, as throwing ropes down the face can possibly hit the casualty which, if he or she is in a confused state, may trigger other complications. Also it can tangle and if dropped in a rope bag, can dislodge loose rocks. Should it pile up on a ledge there is a danger of rope damage from those descending knocking rocks onto it. If the ropes cannot be lowered safely, without causing further hazards to the operation, it should be taken down by a rescuer using a rope pack and only with an in-line descender. The dedicated rope pack, or climbing sack, should be suspended from the abseiler's harness by a short sling, ensuring that the rope end is tied off to the pack for safety. Ropes should always be stowed in sacks in this fashion.

It is advisable for those abseiling down to the casualty to do this to one side if possible to avoid further injury from dislodged rock.

Lowering is easier than raising, and cableways are usually better for cliff evacuation than lowering down the face.

Make sure that all necessary equipment is taken to the scene of the rescue operation, enough to double-up ropes if required. A Prusik/rope clamp minder should be deployed to monitor these vulnerable links in the rescue chain and ensure there is no slack rope in the system which would allow excessive loading on the lowering/raising system. For peace of mind a dynamometer should be entered into the cableway rope rig. If this is of a lower load capacity than the estimated loading on the cableway ropes it can be utilised at the hauling side of the block and tackle and the mechanical advantage of the block and tackle allowed for. On long rope lowers it is often difficult to determine progress of the stretcher/barrow boy due to the weight of the rope/s plus friction. Should the rope temporarily snag, then release suddenly, the loading on rope/belay/lowering device can be excessive and dangerous.

Communication between the barrow boy and belayers/intermediate observer is vital and thought should go into the provision of a RT helmet unit specifically designed for such situations.

It goes without saying that deploying a lowering device which is not manufactured for long lowers is hazardous and a dedicated lowering/lifting system should be used. As well as the robust brake bars shown, it would be possible (with Prusik's or rope clamps built in as safety devices) to use a winch capstan as a friction lowering tool and its manually operated lifting capability could be utilised if required. A hinged jib with rope pulley attached, could be an 'extra' which would act as a tripod. Thereby making a versatile lowering/ lifting unit.

Helicopters

There are many types of helicopter in use throughout the world for rescue work. A machine which may be admirably suited for a difficult alpine rescue may fall short of the ideal on a protracted remote rescue where refuelling can present difficulty, or where large numbers of personnel must be transported for conducting a search.

There is no doubt today that the helicopter is the workhorse of rescue organisations and its deployment can save hours of back-breaking toil. The helicopter has come to stay, but its advent should be accepted with caution. There are certain conditions when helicopters cannot operate, such as dense cloud and severe winds, and a local rescue unit should not be run down or out of training just because for the last few months, or years, it hasn't been called on as helicopters were readily available.

A helicopter lift using an Alpine stretcher (F B Marsden)

Range and altitude

Some of the helicopters in current rescue service have a wide operational range. The Seaking, for example, used in regular mountain and sea rescue work in the United Kingdom, has a maximum endurance of 6 hours 30 minutes with a maximum speed of 241 kph. For helicopters with restricted endurance, fuel dumps can be established at key points in regular rescue areas. Though helicopter rescues have been successfully carried out up to altitudes of 6,100 m, few helicopters will operate at this altitude, though the Lama has flown to 12,500 m.

Winching

A large percentage of helicopter rescues involve winching operations. Winch cable lengths vary from 24 m to 91 m. With long cable lengths it is possible to develop a pendulum motion, but such long lowers are usually done with experienced winchmen. Though swivels are used at the ends of helicopter winch wires, it is still possible to spin. To counteract this it is best to lean back with legs extended and apart if possible.

Body harness

There are a variety of these in use from the simple underarm strop favoured by the RAF to the full harness as used in certain other European countries. It is essential to have the attachment point at approximately chest level to prevent 'tipping'. If a helicopter hook is being lowered to you at the scene of a rescue, or at a pick-up point, be careful to allow it to touch 'earth' before grasping it if at all possible as you can get a shock from the static built up in the helicopter. The helicopter winch wire should never be tied off on to the mountain, e.g. to a belay, etc., as the pilot at any time may have to

Right: A helicopter wind indicator using a tent pole section, threaded with shockcord. The streamers are of fluorescent material

Below: A helipad showing the area and clearance required by a big helicopter

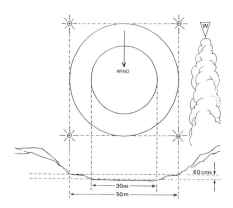

Below: The danger zones are marked with dotted lines: tail rotor, main rotor and exhaust. The exhaust, of course, varies with different types of helicopter. The helicopter should be approached only on a signal from the pilot and in the approx. line indicated by the arrow A to the door (K Spence)

Below centre: The danger of 'Blade Sailing' is shown in this drawing. The dotted lines indicate danger from the rotors and the exhaust (R Turner)

Bottom: Landing near sloping ground. The slope must not exceed 4 m in 10 m (R Turner)

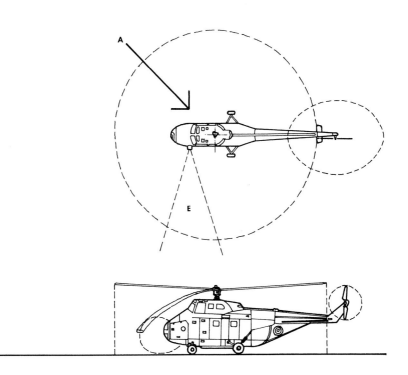

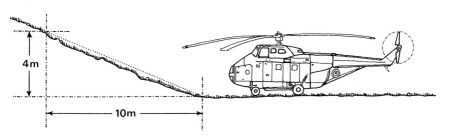

Below: Locator high-intensity helicopter searchlight. This illustration shows the 3.5 million peak beam candle-power searchlight with helicopter mounting. The beam is controlled remotely from within the helicopter. For example at a height of 300 m the unit is capable of illuminating the ground with an intensity hundreds of times greater than the full moon. Other models are suitable for vehicle mounting etc.

The BK 117 is a newcomer to the SAR scene and has exceptional high altitude ability (eurocopter)

take action which necessitates his repositioning the machine. There is a facility on the helicopter to cut the winch wire in absolute emergency. Extensions can be used on helicopter winch wires made up from 25 mm tape or from similar helical-wound stainless steel cable as used on the winch. Excellent extra swivels can be manufactured from automobile brake hubs (see illustration).

Other high-performance swivels can be made using mercury bearings. When skilled pilots are involved, rescues can be undertaken in which a winchman can pendulum from the end of the winch wire on to a face, or beneath an overhang, or employ some of the methods illustrated in the text. Some helicopters have the facility of automatic hover, which can be used over water as a rescue 'platform'. It is essential when deploying long winch lowers that adequate communication is available between the rescuer and the pilot/navigator. Winch extensions of over 150 m have been used successfully, but such operations obviously require a great deal of mutual understanding between the pilot and the rescuer/s. Before such an operation is attempted, it must be discussed with the pilot over the RT, and in the case of large helicopters remember that communication can be difficult in the downwash/engine noise.

Winching rescue dogs
Rescue dogs must have special harnesses for winching operations and when possible should be lowered with their handlers.

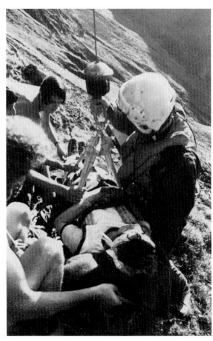

Winching stretchers

Stretchers in regular use for winching operations should have a detachable winching harness, made from either professionally stitched and tested tape, or from stainless steel cable with a diameter of not less than 4 mm. The stretcher anchor points should be at the four corners of the stretcher. The MacInnes Mk6 stretcher has a six-point attachment. The two central cables of the lifting harness have a good psychological effect on patients who are often, even in shock, apprehensive of helicopter winching. Stainless steel Quick Links offer a safe method of attaching the stretcher winching harness to the stretcher. Often the cables/tapes of the lifting harness are

A series of photographs showing an injured climber being put on a Neil Robertson stretcher and winched aboard an RAF helicopter (H MacInnes)

Left: Helicopter extension wire/tape swivel made from an automobile front hub. Casualty/winchman attachment is at opposite end from shackle. The ring on the side is used for guide rope to prevent pendulum motion

Right: An extended helicopter winch lift. The winchman is seen at the end of a 45 m climbing rope, attached to the end of the helicopter winch wire for a lower into the defile of a narrow gully to reach a seriously injured climber (H MacInnes)

Below: A Seaking helicopter arriving to pick up a rescue party and survivors in a partial clearing in white-out conditions in the Scottish Highlands. This helicopter is equipped for 'blind' flying. In exposed situations there is a danger from the excessive downwash created by such machines (H MacInnes)

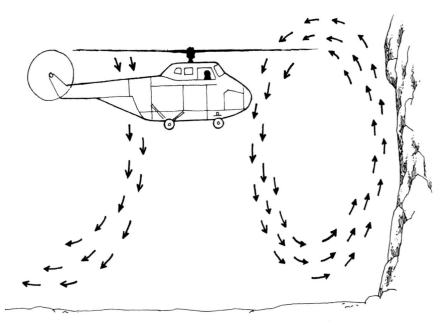

Above: The airflow pattern when close to a cliff or obstruction

Left: Using a Wessex helicopter to winch an injured climber (H MacInnes)

Overleaf: A Chinook helicopter being used to transport rescuers on a search. Mt. Evans in background (The Denver Post)

colour-coded and should be attached to their respectively coloured anchors on the stretcher to ensure that the stretcher is in proper trim when being hoisted. The stretcher winching harness can be used for horizontal cliff lowering. If a Neil Robertson stretcher is used for helicopter lifts, it should be fitted with a back board, to prevent crushing the casualty (see modification to Neil Robertson stretcher). Sometimes, with small helicopters, the stretcher is transported on top of the skids on a special mount but the patient must have adequate protection from the wind.

It is important that the length of the slings/wires on the stretcher lifting harness is suitable for use with the helicopter. Also, protruding stretcher handles, etc. can make it awkward to swing the stretcher inboard the aircraft. It is useful

to have an address label on your stretcher to ensure that you get the right one back should it be taken in the aircraft to hospital.

When lifting a patient the area should be cleared of all but a couple of rescue team members, who can assist the winchman with the lift operation. There is no point in endangering more people at the pick-up point than necessary and confusing the scene for the aircrew. Most rescue teams now have a talk back facility with the SAR helicopter. Voice-activated two-way communication helmets are also used. This equipment is invaluable for the barrow boy on a cliff, big wall evacuation and also for use with noisy power winches.

Some SAR units use a back-up system for safeguarding winchman and casualty during a hoisting operation (several

**Getting winchman into deep gulley using wire
winch rope extension and hand-held anti-spin
rope. A second rescuer is put into the gulley using
the same technique**

A   *Swivel*
B   *Extension wire*
C   *Winch wire*
D   *Guide rope*
E   *Patient*
F   *Winchman*

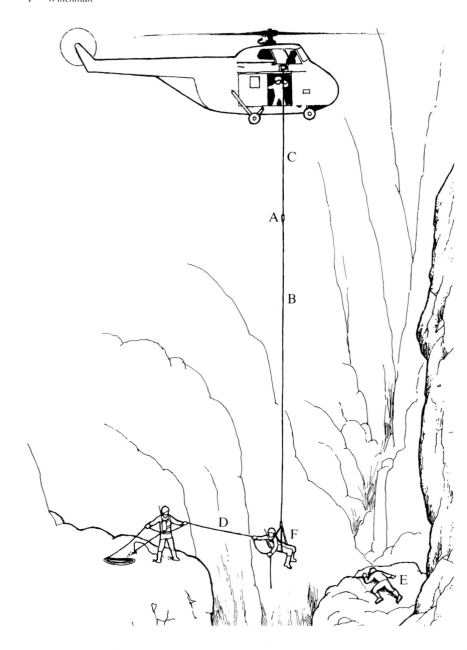

Taking patient from gulley using extension on winch wire

A   Swivel
B   Extension wire
C   Winch Wire
D   Guide rope
E   Patient
F   Winchman
G   Transfer ledge

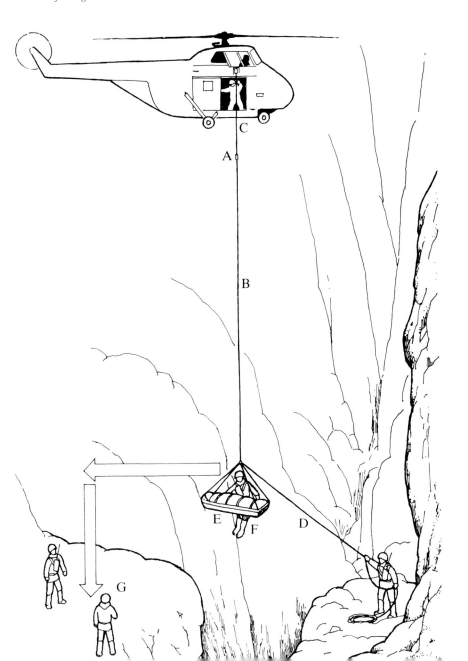

Method used to get extension rope down to rescuer at patient

N.B. Guide ropes MUST NOT be attached to a belay.

A   Winch wire
B   Swivel
C   Extension wire
D   Swivel clipped to guide rope with karabiner
E   Rescuer with patient belayed

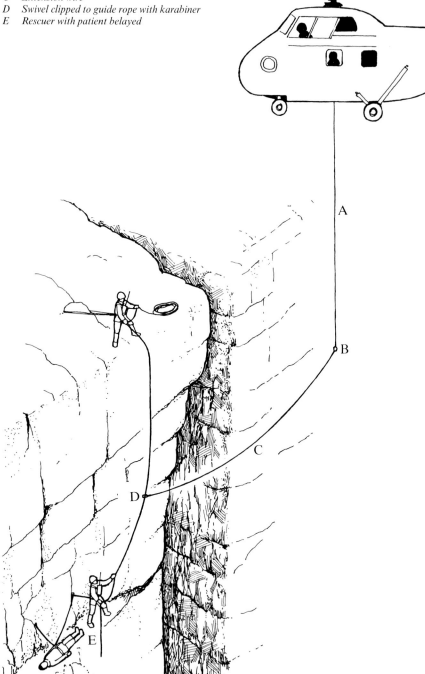

Flight path of casualty

The helicopter extension rope is attached to the stretcher which is then pulled out and up. The rescuer hand holds the guide rope. The patient is deposited at the top for transfer.

A   Winch wire
B   Swivel
C   Extension wire
D   Guide rope
E   Casualty on stretcher

175

Signals for use in marshalling helicopters
The marshaller must position himself facing the aircraft and in full view of the pilot.

Hover
Arms extended horizontally sideways, palms downward

Vertical movement upwards
Arms extended horizontally sideways beckoning upwards, with palms turned up. Speed of movement indicates rate of ascent

Vertical movement downwards
Arms extended horizontally sideways beckoning downwards with palms turned down. Speed of movement indicates rate of descent

Winch up
Left arm horizontal in front of body, fist clenched, right hand with palm turned upwards making upward motion

Spot turn
Left or right hand moving upward and backward, from a horizontal position, to indicate direction of tail movement. Other hand pointing to centre of spot turn

Winch down
Left arm horizontal in front of body, fist clenched, right hand with palm turned downwards making downward motion

Horizontal movement to starboard (right)
Left arm extended horizontally sideways in direction of movement and other arm swung in front of body in same direction, in a repeating movement

Horizontal movement to port (left)
Right arm extended horizontally sideways in direction of movement and other arm swung in front of body in same direction, in a repeating movement

Land
Arms crossed and extended downwards in front of the body

Above: The Kaman, SH-2G Super Seasprite helicopter has 5.3 hours flight duration at 1525 m and a service ceiling of over 5000 m (Kaman Corporation)

Left: In rugged regions, such as the Grand Canyon, SAR helicopters are a vital aid to evacuation of the injured (K. Phillips)

Below: This shows the technique of holding a wheel or skid of a helicopter against the crest of a ridge to enable a rescue party to enter or exit (L Gramminger)

Above: An S-61N helicopter used for SAR. This, like the Sea King, has a max. operating radius of 287 nm (530 km), (2 hrs 24 min) and has many facilities such as all-weather day-night approach capability and auto-hover. It is fitted with a hoist (winch) with 90 m of cable. This has a capacity of 272 kg at 0–46 ml/min. In common with such winches a cable cutting device, employing an explosive charge, is mounted at the base of the cable drum which the pilot can activate in a dire emergency (Bristow Helicopters Ltd)

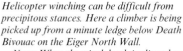

Helicopter winching can be difficult from precipitous stances. Here a climber is being picked up from a minute ledge below Death Bivouac on the Eiger North Wall.
Note: When the winch hook is clipped onto your harness, you mustn't have a 'fixed' attachment to the mountain. Use a sling from your harness through the belay karabiner with two turns and hold the end of the tape. Also, never grasp the swivel cable-hook with your bare hands as it is possible to receive a hefty static shock. Initially field the cable in the crook of your elbow before grabbing the hook.
(H. MacInnes)

people have died due to winch cable failures). A standard climbing belay is set-up in the fuselage, using 11mm kernmantle climbing rope which uses the cargo rings as anchors. The belayer deploys a friction device to secure the winchman/casualty. The winchman's end of the rope should be attached below the swivel at the end of the hoist cable and run up and back to a running belay to a suitable anchor to the rear of the cargo/winching door, at a point which will prevent the belay rope twisting with the winch cable. It is important that the belay rope is as long as the winch cable and that the end of it, in the aircraft, is tied off. This system requires practice, but has saved lives.

Helicopter call-out procedure

This of course varies in different parts of the world; some countries operate a helicopter rescue insurance scheme where the helicopter plus guide/doctor/winchman are flown directly to the accident scene and complete all but the more difficult evacuations themselves. Where helicopters operate as part of the general rescue organisation, it is essential that the pilot or his control are advised on: the type of accident/search; the prevailing weather; rescue control location and possible landing site and identification; a map reference of the incident locus; injuries; communications; any special information, e.g. the number of rescue parties involved, their line of approach or area of search, colour of clothing of injured/lost persons. Such information should be relayed again to the pilot when he approaches the rescue area by the rescue controller, as such information often gets inadvertently distorted through a basic fault in human nature.

Dark air

More rescues are now being enacted in the hours of darkness, but obviously there is an element of risk and such evacuations must be weighed up against the urgency of the situation. Some helicopters are equipped with facilities for 'blind flying', but adequate lighting is also essential for mountain rescue night use. Some fixed wing aircraft in coastal command work have night searchlights of 70 million candle-power. Such units can only be used for short durations due to the heat generated, e.g. one minute operation, three minutes cooling. For helicopters various compact, highly efficient, remotely controlled (by pilot) lights are available such as the Night Sun and the Locator. One of these is illustrated and has a high luminous output of 3.5 million peak beam candle-power. Such a lamp at 300 m is capable of illuminating the ground many hundred times more brightly than full moonlight. The special gimbal-mounted mechanism of the lamp's reflector allows the beam to be projected in any direction

Below: Evacuation of climber in the French Alps (A Contamine)

179

through the glass dome of the searchlight housing whilst the unit itself remains in a fixed position on the helicopter or fixed wing aircraft. The metal arc lamp used in such lamps gives more than twice the lumens per input watt as xenon or tungsten lamps and thereby draws the minimum current from the aircraft's power supply. The consumption of the Locator, for example, at any input supply of 12/14V DC is 35 amps. Such searchlights can also be used on base vehicles, etc.

Searches

Helicopters are used widely for search purposes, but they do have limitations. Unless the victim is wearing bright clothing, it can often be difficult to locate him, especially after a storm when the missing party can be covered in fresh snow. Also forest search is restricted by the forest canopy and, in the case of aircraft crashes, the plane can go through the canopy without necessarily leaving any sign of its passage.

Thermal imager

In countries where military/police helicopters are used for SAR, it may be possible to use a thermal imager. A thermal imager can detect thermal contrast – the difference between the intensities of infrared radiation emitted by an object and its background. It can penetrate a forest canopy to detect, for example, a crashed aeroplane or a human being.

Loud hailers

High output loud hailers can be used on helicopters and can be invaluable for giving instructions to ground parties and lost persons.

A keen lookout for tracks on snow, signal fires, mirror signals, and carrion birds or animals may also give some indication. There have been numerous examples of helicopters flying over injured or lost

Left: Using a net to evacuate a body in the Swiss Alps (Eiger north wall) (Alex, Grindelwald)

Below: 1, 2 and 3 illustrate various ways of lifting casualties. 1 is the sit-sling method, 2 the net, and 3 shows both the winchman and casualty being lifted (Pressbild)

Top: In order to evacuate injured climber a helicopter platform was built on a steep hillside so that machine could land, Banff National Park (B Engler)

Left: This photograph illustrates the helicopter winch and the harness used on some helicopters (Pressbild)

Above: It can be very dangerous flying a helicopter in mountainous regions. This photograph shows a crashed helicopter in the Caucasus (H MacInnes)

This photograph shows the winchman being lowered with a Neil Robertson stretcher (H MacInnes)

people without spotting them. It is essential that when a ground search is being conducted at the same time as an aerial one, the distribution of ground parties and their identification should be notified to the helicopter crew. The party to be rescued should if possible hold both arms up in a stationary extended V. Binoculars can be used by searchers in helicopters for checking on an object, Gyro binoculars are excellent for aerial searching, as the standard optical binocular is limited for continuous scanning by the vibration, which in any case limits useful magnification to about × 4. There are obvious advantages in having at least one local member of a

rescue team in a helicopter on searches to check on known danger spots.

Searching by helicopter is a difficult and tiring operation. It is very easy to fly too fast looking, but not seeing, and to imagine that an area has been searched when really it has only been glanced at. Low speed, low altitude and very conscious and deliberate use of the eyes are essential. A prolonged search in a helicopter induces a considerable 'laissez faire' attitude in those on board, so that without suitable personal and crew discipline the lookers cease to see and, probably worse, there is a great reluctance to turn the helicopter around and stop and investigate apparently insignificant

A close-up of a helicopter winching operation from close to the 'Fly' on the Eiger North Wall (H MacInnes)

signs of a casualty's possible presence. So try to allow each party of 'Observers' to be changed at ideally two-hourly intervals and ensure that they will look, see, and act to find casualties.

Night Vision Goggles

There are two popular night vision aids in use by aircrew today, the Thermal Imager, such as F.L.I.R. and the image intensifier, N.V.G., Night Vision Goggles. Both of these items are illustrated in this book. It is important when doing a pick-up with an aircrew using N.V.G. that all lights are extinguished, except the one at the casualty. Usually, once this location has been identified, the pilot will switch to the aircraft's floodlighting for the winching/or skid evacuation.

Helicopters and safety

Helicopters are well-named 'choppers' for obvious reasons. There have been countless accidents with people walking into tail rotors and, less frequently, by blade sailing of the main rotors. This can be caused through turbulence, and sometimes when shutting down and starting up, i.e. when the blades have little rotational speed. Keep away from the tail rotor at all times and only approach a helicopter with its engine running on a signal from the pilot or crew member. Always keep within the vision of the pilot or crew member. *Approach* with head down and any ice axes, avalanche probes, etc., stowed away where they won't get chopped off. An approach should be made directly to the door of the helicopter in vision of the pilot or crewman, as indicated. With larger helicopters a crew member will usually advise on the approach line and give a thumbs up sign

Extended helicopter winch lift

Using the pulley-winch principle for an extended helicopter winch lift by increasing the lifting distance using a long braided synthetic fibre rope. On the winch wire hook a jumar type clamp is attached, positioned upside down and secured both top and bottom. The braided rope is taken through the jumar. The rope end is lowered to the casualty, who ties on to it. The winch wire, with clamp attached, is lowered to its full extent and is then winched in. The jumar grips when pulled upwards. Inside the helicopter the braided rope is taken through a further securing rope clamp as the helicopter winch operates. When the winch is taken in to its full extent, it is again lowered and meantime the braided rope is secured by the clamp within the helicopter. This process is repeated until the casualty can be taken aboard. It is essential that only a braided synthetic fibre non stretch rope is used for this technique and that a swivel is used between the casualty and the end of the rope (K Spence)

W = Winch bracket
S = Winch swivel
J = Jumar clamp in reverse position
R = Braided synthetic fibre rescue rope

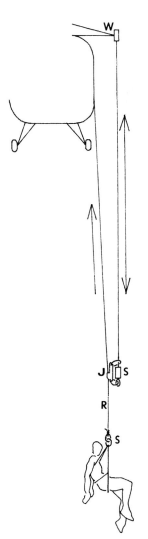

Above: This shows a helicopter being used to carry a bloodhound to the point where a missing person was last seen. The dog is carried in a harness on the end of the winch wire and the handler travels in the helicopter. 1 indicates dog and 2 indicates a Stokes litter stretcher. As bloodhounds are very heavy, they can upset the stability of a small helicopter when they jump out as the helicopter hovers. This technique is used in California (J Duff)

187

*Below: Evacuating a casualty in the French
Alps. Note how stretcher bearers are stooping
low to avoid danger from the helicopter rotor
'sailing' (A Contamine)*

*Right: Lifting a climber off the north wall of the
Grandes Jorasses, Pte. Walker (L Holliwell)*

*Opposite page, left: Combined operations in
the Scottish Highlands. Helicopters, search and
rescue dogs being used for large-scale search
operation (H MacInnes)*

*Opposite page, right: Helicopter being used for
taking rescue personnel to avalanche scene in
French Alps (A Contamine)*

*Above: The Steiner 7 × 50 Commander
Electronic binocular is microchip controlled and
bearings recorded. Can be used from -40 to +80
degrees. Formulated for distance and dimensional
measurement.*

*Fujinon Stabiscope, 12 × 50 & 16 × 40. These
gyro-stabilised binoculars can be used for
helicopter SAR.*

when it is safe. Avoid exhausts and air intakes. Don't approach from or disembark to higher ground, where there is less clearance for the rotors. Crampons should not be worn unless it is imperative to wear them at the intended landing point. Don't wear rucksacks, carry them and hand them in ahead of you.

Getting aboard on sloping ground

Kneel at the pick-up point and the pilot will position the helicopter accordingly. Should a crewman give a 'patting' sign, this will indicate that someone's head is too high. On no account enter or leave the aircraft without permission. *Rescue dogs* should be already in their harnesses and held by their handler/s. Don't allow them to move about the aircraft. *Don't* allow them to jump out, as in their enthusiasm they often disregard the height above the ground.

Operational limitations

As mentioned, weather can adversely affect a helicopter's performance and in certain conditions ground it. Heavy snow, high winds, low cloud and severe icing are all hazards which the helicopter pilot must face from time to time in the rescue situation. Though some of the larger helicopters are equipped for 'blind flying', doing so in a mountain environment is obviously a dangerous business. In low cloud conditions it is better for the rescue team to take the casualty below cloud level for pick-up. Some helicopters are fitted with special engine intake cowlings which enable them to fly in snowfall at temperatures in the region of -40°C. Hot air and altitude also affect performance, and in high ranges it may be necessary to descend with the casualty for considerable distances to enable pick-up to be completed. The pilot can usually give you an indication of his ceiling for a given situation. When it is not possible for a helicopter to reach the scene of an accident it can often be used to transport

rescuers to a point close by, which can save valuable time.

Turbulence, up-draughts and down-draughts can all have an adverse effect on helicopter performance.

Marshalling a helicopter requires practice and an understanding between the pilot and the ground marshal in dangerous locations. The international marshalling signals are illustrated in the text. Often in difficult mountain situations only part of a skid can be rested on a rock or cliff, and accurate marshalling will greatly assist the pilot. The marshal should be in front of and upwind of the landing/touch-down point, in direct view of the pilot, out of possible danger if an emergency take-off is necessary.

Strobe lights

These are excellent for indicating the point for pick-up to the helicopter pilot, and they can be used effectively even in sunlight. Further, a fluorescent wind marker on a light-alloy tubular tent pole will also help the pilot to judge air movement. Several rescue teams carry such streamers as part of their personal MR kit. In whiteout or uniform snow conditions it can be difficult for the pilot to obtain a 'fix' for hovering or landing. A rucksack, wind marker, etc., placed forward and upwind of the pick-up zone will greatly assist him. A rescue team member at the scene of an accident can usually talk a helicopter in to the locus, but in any case the normal signal of arms extended in a stationary open V will verify the point for the pilot. There is also a Clock Code for talking in a helicopter to the accident scene, which is especially useful on complicated faces where there are various search parties. If you consider the nose of the helicopter as 12 o'clock and the tail 6 o'clock, the procedure can be quite simple, e.g. 'Pick-up point 2 o'clock (which is to the pilot's right) low ½ mile'. The pilot would then re-position until he was at 12 o'clock and descend the

Ojos del Salado, 6885 m, the highest active volcano in the world, was the scene of a high altitude helicopter crash in 1984. A Lama helicopter crashed at 6710 m. The crashed aircraft had been spotted by a fixed-wing aircraft and the crew were able to relay the location to ground parties, who managed to pin-point the find by the description of a 'patch of snow, like a map of South America at 6710 m., with the Lama in the position of Buenos Aires,' (see circle in illustration). Aerial photographs taken a few days previously as a back-at-base aid, for experts on aerial photography, enabled the wreckage to be quickly identified.

Such photographs in remote regions can be of great value for the search operation. High quality video footage can also be an advantage for large-scale search operation in high altitude and wilderness regions as this can be studied in more conducive surroundings. (R Lyle)

required height. 'High' of course would indicate that the helicopter was below the pick-up point. By using a strobe this procedure can be avoided.

Some helicopters carry their own smoke, but a smoke flare displayed by the ground party upwind and to one side of the pick-up point can be of great assistance to the helicopter pilot in assessing the conditions.

Landing areas

The landing ground should be as flat as possible, away from power cables, trees, boulders, cliffs and hillsides. On ridges, cornices should be avoided and, on glaciers, snow bridges and seracs. Deep snow should be trampled down to give a firm base, an orange dye canister, similar to the type used in marine rescue, can be utilised for marking the site, and remember to give the pilot some 'fix' to windward of the pad. On steeper hillsides it is sometimes possible to excavate a landing ledge, at least for a wheel/skid, but remember, adequate air space is also required for the rotor and any such landing point will be used only at the discretion of the pilot. A trellis type landing platform can be manufactured in bush/forest country on slopes – see illustration – but this must be adequately strong for the purpose. At high altitude it is better if the helicopter can land on a glacier moraine mound or on a rognon, as take-off can often be hazardous in rarefied air.

At difficult drop-off points only step out of the aircraft when the pilot tells you. Never do it unless the pilot is aware of it – as he may have to take corrective action. When you step out or are winched down, always stay there until the helicopter moves away. It can be highly dangerous to move in 'tight' situations and it can also distract the pilot with smaller helicopters. If the helicopter doors are in place these should be closed when the last rescuer gets out, as should any lockers used for carrying equipment which has been off-loaded. When everyone is safely out the team leader/marshal should give a thumbs-up signal to the pilot indicating that everyone is out and he can now take off. Some rescue areas have floodlit landing pads, but emergency night landing illumination can be utilised, with torches encircling the landing zone shining inwards, or vehicle headlights/flashers. Don't forget to illuminate a wind marker.

A landing zone can be marked with an 'H' using flat stones, etc., but ensure that any object won't be disturbed by the downwash as it may enter the engine intake. This also applies on pick-up points on the mountain/outback where bivvy bags, cagoules, etc., can get blown. When being picked up from a belay on a face ensure that you or the casualty are off belay before clipping on to the winch wire. A sling attached to the waist/ stretcher and taken through a crab on the belay with two turns and held will ensure safety until launching time, yet will not be a 'fix' on to the mountain and thereby endanger everyone in the event of the pilot having to take emergency action. The helicopter winch wire must never be attached directly to a belay.

In some countries rescuers abseil from helicopters where a landing is difficult and the helicopter is not fitted with a hoist/winch. This practice is common for getting personnel through a forest canopy. The Sky Genie is an abseil device which is in common use, but it must be used with a special braided nylon rope. The standard figure of eight is also popular for this operation and indeed most of the tested abseiling devices will function well. It is important to use a self-equalising belay if the aircraft's deck rings are used for anchors. The rope should be in a dropbag and thrown out over the helicopters skid through a suitable gap, or taken down in rope bag attached on sling from rescuers harness. It is important that once the rope is down it should be checked for kinks etc. before a descent is made.

Manufacturer	Model	Variant	Engine/s	Personnel Load Capa…
Aerospatiale	Alouette 111	SA316	1	2 + 3
	Lama	SA315	1	2 + 3
	Ecureuil	B1	1	2 + 3
	Gazelle	SA341	1	1 + 4
	Puma	Super 332L	2	2 + 15
	Dauphin 2		2	1 + 9
Augusta	K2 109		2	1 + 7
Boeing	Chinook	CH47	2	4 + 44
Bell	Iroquois	UHID	1	5
	Jet Ranger	206B	1	5
	Long Ranger	L4	2	7
	206	LT	2	7
	412	EP	2	15
	222	UT	2	10
	407		1	7
	430		2	9
	212		2	15
E H Industries	EH101		3	2 + 30
Eurocopter	BK 117	C1	2	2 + 9
	AS355	N	2	2 + 4
	AS365	N2	2	2+11
	BO105	Super	2	2 + 4
	EC 135		2	2 + 6
	BKW117C1	MN	2	3 + 6
Kamov	Helix	KA27	2	3 + 16
Mil	Hip	M18	2	2 + 24
Kaman	SH-2G	Super Seasprite	2	
Mc Donnel Douglas	MD90*	Explorer*	2	8
Westland	Super Lynx		2	2 + 9
	Seaking	HAR 3	2	4 + 1
	Wessex	MK2	2	3 + 12
Sikorsky	S61N	MK2	2	4 + 19

*No tail rotor

eful iling	MR Stretcher Capability	Winch Length	Cruise Speed	Range
00 m	2	23 m	119 kt	340 nm
00 m	1	23 m	113 kt	278 nm
40 m	1	23 m	155 kt	295 nm
	1	23 m	120 kt	300 nm
		75 m	143 kt	345 nm
	3	75 m	140 kt	473 nm
00 m	2	75 m	140 kt	570 nm
00 m	2	46 m	168 kt	365 nm
70 m	24		148 kt	400 nm
00 m	6	75 m	118 kt	216 nm
04 m	1	33 m	100 kt	270 nm
00 m	1	33 m	92 kt	183 nm
00 m	1	33 m	92 kt	
41 m	4	33 m	110 kt	260 nm
		33 m	134 kt	544 nm
46 m	1	33 m	112 kt	226 nm
78 m	2	33 m	120 kt	260 nm
	4	33 m	118 kt	158 nm
	12	91 m	150 kt	570 nm
00 m	2	91 m	136 kt	300 nm
00 m	1	40 m	135 kt	180 nm
	2	33 m	158 kt	431 nm
00 m	2	33 m	132 kt	250 nm
00 m	2	33 m	141 kt	310 nm
00 m			247 kt	300 nm
			125 kt	420 nm
			122 kt	440 nm
22 m			141 kt	540 nm
	2	76 m	135 kt	320 nm
	3	61 m	136 kt	520 nm
50 m	4	75 m	110 kt	600 nm
	5	75 m	100 kt	270 nm
	5	91 m	120 kt	500 nm

Note: 1 nautical mile (nm) = 1·8532 km
1 knot (kt) = 1·8532 km/hr

Rope clamps and their application for rescue work

Ascending a fixed rope using jumar clamps (H MacInnes)

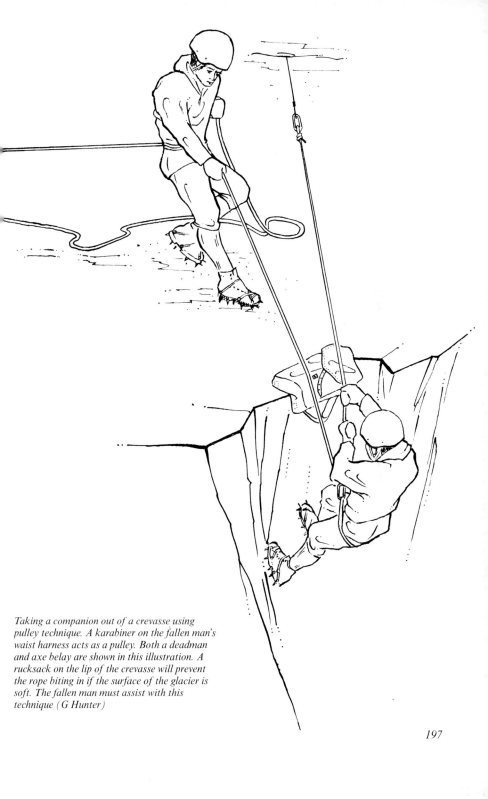

Taking a companion out of a crevasse using pulley technique. A karabiner on the fallen man's waist harness acts as a pulley. Both a deadman and axe belay are shown in this illustration. A rucksack on the lip of the crevasse will prevent the rope biting in if the surface of the glacier is soft. The fallen man must assist with this technique (G Hunter)

197

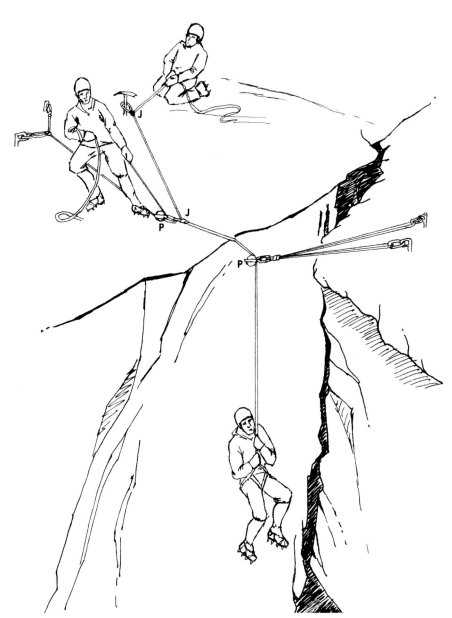

This crevasse rescue technique employs two jumar-type rope clamps (or Prusik knots) and two pulleys P. One man, or two, haul the victim's rope in via pulley and jumar clamp (J). The victim's rope is locked as it comes in by the clamp or Prusik knot at the ice axe belay. The haulage pulley and clamp can be taken back to near the edge of the crevasse again if a further 'bite' is required (E Grieve)

A and B show two different methods of rescue from a crevasse. The rucksack in A, a karabiner, keeps the rope in tension thereby making movement of the lower Prusik knot easier. Three Prusik knots (P) are used for this method. Figure B shows the movement of the knots being done by the climber on the surface of the glacier, with the ropes anchored to a deadman belay. The fallen man has the two ropes going through a chest loop and one is attached with a loop to his foot. It is necessary that he assists in raising himself by pulling on the anchored rope, thereby taking weight off the other rope when he moves up. This enables the top man to take in the slack and re-adjust the knot. These techniques can also be used on rock faces, but proper use of rope clamps is much faster (G Hunter)

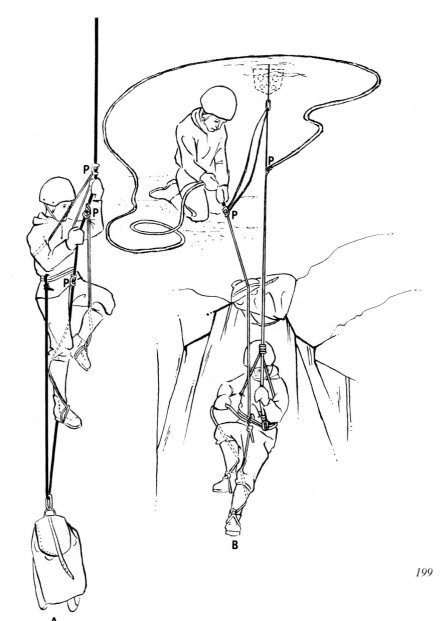

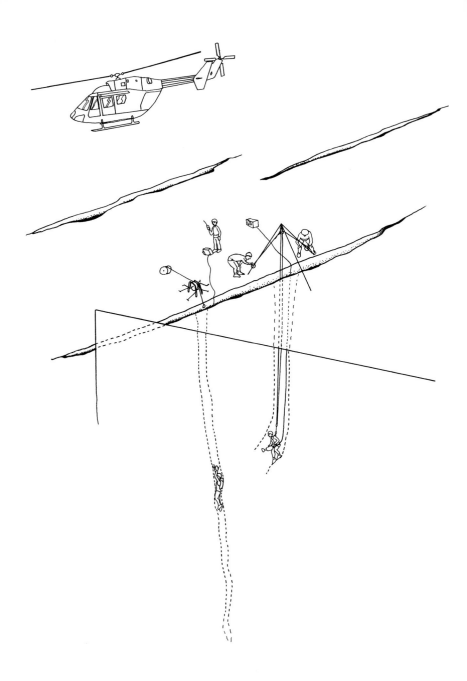

Crevasse Rescue

The tripod is now a popular and efficient tool of the rescue team for raising people out of crevasses. Some of these have a winch mounted on a leg, others have two separate winches which can be used for raising or lowering a rescuer, with a separate rope/winch for the casualty. In areas where the crevasse is an everyday chore, teams have portable hot-air blowers which can pipe hot air to assist in melting ice round the victim to facilitate extraction (nb. It can be dangerous to have the victim exposed to this heat and a medical advisor should be consulted who is versed in hypothermia).

In the unlikely situation where the victim is easily accessed a chain saw can be deployed, but it goes without saying that extreme caution for both the operator and the victim is paramount, not only from the possibility of a 'chain saw massacre', but also from carbon monoxide emissions.

Backpack de-icing units are available for spraying round a wedged casualty and kango hammers, operated by compressed air from a compressor at the surface (transported by helicopter) can be used to facilitate the extrication of a victim. This should be done to one side, obviously, and at a point where the ice chippings fall into the crevasse. See illustration. A remote camera is often useful for those on the

This Petzl harness is well suited for crevasse rescue work having an attachment point above the head of the rescuer/victim which allows more freedom in the confines of the crevasse. (Petzl)

Left: Showing a possible method of reaching a casualty in a crevasse too narrow to facilitate a normal winch extraction. Using a pneumatic chisel a wider tunnel is made by enlarging the crevasse. Ice chippings fall into the crevasse and don't impede tunnel progress. The rescuer/chisel operator wears a dry suit and top-anchoring harness and can have a two-way communications helmet. He is belayed with a top rope from the tripod winch and takes a further rope for the casualty. The casualty's situation can be monitored using a CCD closed circuit tv camera which has been lowered down, with the monitor on glacier surface. Helicopter back-up can ferry further equipment as required. NB Generator/compressor engines should be modified for altitude (E Donaldson)

surface to monitor the possibly seriously injured victim and also to read medical monitoring equipment which can be attached to the victim and also to direct the evacuation.

It is sometimes possible, in forested regions, to span the crevasse with timber or a ladder to facilitate the rescue and possibly for mounting a winch. Also, timber can be lashed in the form of a rope ladder over the lip of the crevasse to act as an edge roller. It is common for a trapped person to suffer from rib or lung injuries and care must be exercised in the winching operation. A harness, like the one illustrated above can be excellent for a lifting operation if it can be put on the victim!

The telescopic tripod is now a popular item for crevasse rescue. It can also be used in various configurations for cableway/lowering systems. They can have either one or two winches mounted on the legs. (P Moores)

A similar type of harness is useful for the rescuers using the top rope attachment, especially in tight crevasses. Dry suits of a bright colour are recommended where crevasse rescue is a common occurrence and reinforcing patches can be attached to knee and elbow points. Dry suits allow normal clothing underneath and climbing boots can be worn. An advantage, too, is a two-way talk-back waterproof helmet unit, as communication can often be difficult.

Anchors

The importance of good anchors cannot be over emphasised. There have been many serious incidents and fatalities on both rescues and rescue training exercises due to faulty anchors.

Never rely on a single anchor point. Even if a boulder is huge and has been used on many previous occasions, grit or small pebbles may have made it 'mobile' due to a flood, melt water or frost. If it is partially buried it can also be suspect, back it up!

Have at least two separate equalised systems. Use a Load Distributing Anchor or as it is sometimes called, a Self Equalising Anchor.

Ensure that all abrasive edges are padded, and that tree trunks are not damaged. Trees may appear massive, but may have shallow root systems.

Anchor tension and load:

When the angle is 0 degrees, 50 per cent of the load is on each leg
When the angle is 145 degrees, 166 per cent of the load is on each leg
It is vital that the angle should be less than 90 degrees, always try to have it over 45 degrees (see p. 331).

Man-made anchors can sometimes be backed up with natural anchors, eg.

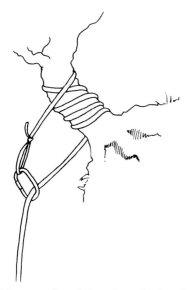

A friction anchor which can be easily released. If used on a rock bollard make sure any sharp edges are padded with a rucksack or anorak. (E Donaldson)

pegs/chocks/camming devices and tree/s/solid boulders/chockstones etc. The recipe for ensuring a post-rescue drink at the pub is:

No slack in the system and bomb-proof belays.

Changeovers:

Changing from abseiling to jumaring entails maintaining two points of attachment whilst doing so. If a spare rope clamp is not available, use a Prusik knot. Don't undo your harness karabiner. It is best to have two harness screwgate crabs, one for ascending and one for abseiling.

The Brake Bar:

This is a popular piece of gear for high-angled rescue work. Friction can be adjusted and there is good heat dissipation. However, their use requires practice and this should be done other

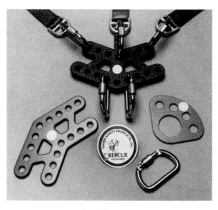

SSP Rigging Anchor Plates.

Adjustable Anchor Straps. These can also be used for stretcher/litter harnesses. These have a proof load of 22·27 kN.

Figure of Eight anchor

Opposite page, photograph: A climber hanging on the end of a rope after a fall. In situations such as these, when limited manpower is available, one of the rescue techniques described should be adopted as soon as possible (L Gramminger)

Right: An experimental crevasse clamp-frame being used in the Alps for casualty evacuation (L Gramminger)

Opposite page, drawing: Many climbers have died hanging on the end of a climbing rope after a fall. If a good harness is used the fallen climber has a much better chance of surviving. Such a situation leaves the belayer in a very serious situation, for he will be unable to haul his colleague to safety and indeed even a rescue party can have difficulty. This technique evolved by the author employs a rope clamp, which is put onto the taut rope in reverse and, provided the rope is hanging free, this can slip down the taut rope when weighted by a rucksack etc. Another rope should be attached to the clamp and the fallen climber pulled in from the side, or winched up at an angle. Should the belayer manage to tie-off the taut rope directly to his belay using a Prusik knot and sling, this will enable him to untie from his rope and render assistance in the above way, or by employing one of the pulley techniques illustrated in the text (K Spence)
J = rope clamp. R = rucksack etc. P = Prusik knot. (K Spence)

Right: A Clog Expedition rope clamp with a function similar to the jumar

Bottom left: Using a jumar for holding and feeding a rope through for rescue work. The rope clamp is secured both at front and at the rear to enable the rope to be taken through the clamp without holding onto the clamp. Q = quick links for securing jumar (H MacInnes)

Bottom right: Two types of rope clamps. A jumar on the left and a clogger clamp on the right. The clogger has a rescue modification as this clamp is subject to rope creep in certain conditions. Two 6 mm bolts are inserted through the extension plate, which is attached to the clogger by a countersunk setscrew, which allows free movement of the cam lever. The two bolts (1 and 2) can move freely in their holes thereby allowing easy threading of the rope through the clamp. The extra friction given by the bolts avoids rope creep and the rope should also be taken through a karabiner or link marked N. When using the jumar clamp for traversing, the rope from the jumar cam lever should also go through a karabiner at the base of the jumar. Rope clamps should not be used on rescue rigs subject to high loading such as cableways or security for stretcher lowers, they can cause rope damage and even failure of the rope. As an alternative you can

use tandem 8 mm, 3-wrap nylon kernmantle Prusiks as 'clamps/ratchets' on active rescue ropes. It is always safer to appoint someone as a P.M., a Prusik Minder, to ensure that the knots are snugly formed and not loose on the master rope. (H MacInnes)

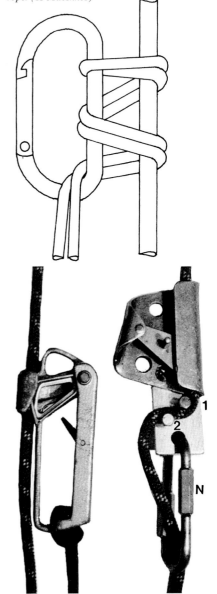

Opposite page: The karabiner knot. This friction knot can be used in place of a rope clamp or Prusik knot. It is more convenient to use a screwgate karabiner for this technique (R Turner)

Below left: The Bachmann knot

Below right: The Klemheist knot tied with a karabiner

Bottom left: The Penberthy knot tied with a length of rope which is then joined

Bottom right: The Kreuzklem knot

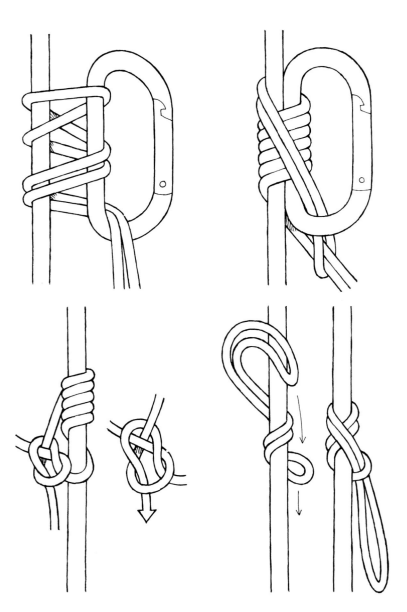

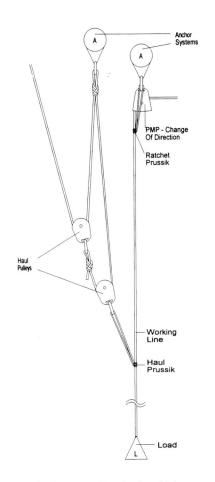

Anchor
Systems

A

A

Simple   Hauling System

Anchor
System

A

PMP - Change
Of Direction

PMP

Ratchet
Prussik

Ratchet
Prussik

Haul
Pulleys

Haul
Pulley

Working
Line

Haul
Prussik

Haul
Prussik

Load

Load

L

L

A 4:1 haul rig, using 'Ratchet Prusik's.'

*A basic hauling system using 'Ratchet Prusik's'
in place of Jumars/Gibbs etc. (K. Phillips)*

*Rope Bags. These are necessary to protect rescue
ropes and for storage. The bags should have a
record card attached to monitor age and wear.*

than in a life and death situation.

The anchor eye of the Rack should be welded to prevent unwrapping under load. Various materials are used for friction bars and certain metals are better suited for this function. For example titanium bars are the lightest/strongest and dissipate heat well. Stainless steel weighs more, doesn't wear so quickly, but uses less friction. Aluminium provides more friction but wears faster and also discolours the rope. Considerable heat is generated in a lower and with a 366 kg load a temperature of 300°C is reached with aluminium bars, but only 120° with titanium/stainless steel.

Either one rope or two can be threaded through the rack and the rope should run as shown in the diagram so that it/they run evenly over the bars.

Always use a minimum of four bars.
A. First start with all bars in operation until the rescuer/s/stretcher are over the edge of the cliff.
B. Descent speed is controlled by the number of bars used and by sliding bars closer together to increase friction, or by pulling them apart to reduce friction.

Knot passing, Raising; using the hauling system as illustrated.
1. Attach system's hauling Prusik below knot.
2. Haul until knot reaches ratchet Prusik.
3. Well past the knot, in front of the ratchet Prusik, insert temporary Prusik to an extension sling from a LRH attached to anchor.
4. Take up load on temporary Prusik.
5. Extend sling of the ratchet pulley to enable it to be re-inserted beyond knot.
6. Remove temporary Prusik once hauling re-commences.
7. Commence raising until knot reaches second pulley.
8. Allow safety ratchet Prusik to take load.
9. Remove pulley at reattach beyond knot.
nb. If a double haul system is deployed the knot pass-over is simplified.
Knot passing, Lowering: With the knot at

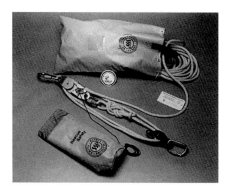

The Smith Safety Products Res-Q-Master double block pulley designed for 16 mm ropes. The locking cam can be released under load

SSP Prusik Minding Pulley. The pulley side plates will automatically slide the Prusik without attention

least 4 m behind the lowering device, lock the device off.

Attach tandem Prusik's/rope clamps on a spare rope with a spare lowering device from the master anchor.

Release the load by unlocking the master lowering device and transfer load to the secondary lowering device.

Now lower until knot is well past master lowering device then lock off secondary lowering device.

Re-connect master lowering device and transfer load to master lowering device. (See also p. 214)

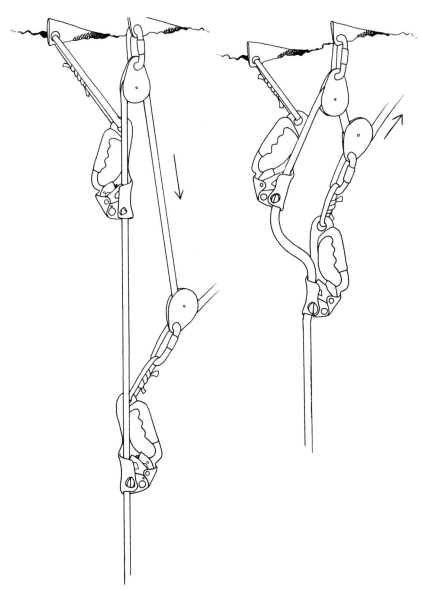

This illustration shows a simple pulley system
giving 2–1 theoretical gain. The top rope clamp is
used as a 'ratchet' and the bottom clamp moved
down after each hauling bite. If used for man-
hauling always use a further safety rope. Under
UIAA recommendations, all ascenders now have
a min breaking load of 4kN. (E Donaldson)

Right: A system of using jumar clamps for ascending a fixed rope. A = fixed rope. The rescuer is attached to the end of this rope (it forms a loop below him as he ascends). The end part of this same rope is marked B on the drawing. It is attached to the karabiner of the lower jumar clamp with a figure of eight knot and the end is then tied to the rescuer's waist loop. This ensures that the rescuer cannot slide off the end of the rope. S = a sling from the waist harness to the top jumar. A tape etrier correctly adjusted is attached to each jumar. The rescuer can climb very fast using this technique, but the slings etc., must be adjusted correctly and should be kept already made up if much jumaring is required in any particular area. The foot etrier attachment can be seen in the following drawings. Tying onto the end of the rope shouldn't be done in areas where faces are broken and rough as the following loop of rope can snag. However, it is better to put a large knot on the end unless one is starting ascending from the ground. If the end of the rope is left hanging, a separate short sling must be used from the waist loop to the lower jumar for safety (A McKeith)

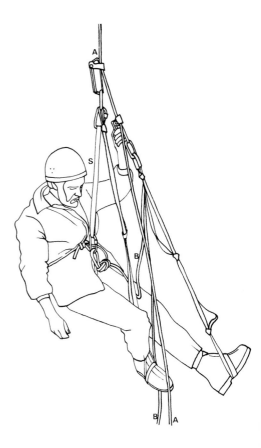

Below left: Place the foot in the lowest loop of the aid-sling right up against the knot and twist the lower part of that loop

Below right: Then place the lower part of the loop over the boot in such a way that it locks itself and pull it tight

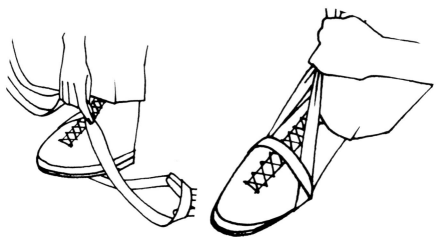

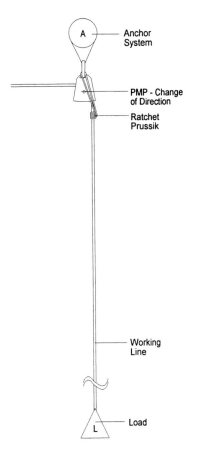

A — Anchor System

PMP - Change of Direction

Ratchet Prussik

Working Line

L — Load

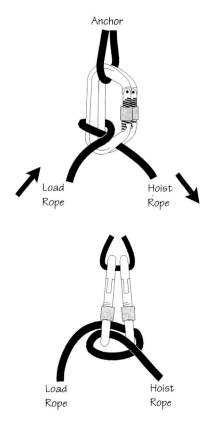

Anchor

Load Rope

Hoist Rope

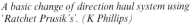

Load Rope

Hoist Rope

The Garda knot, a one way system. (K Phillips)

A basic change of direction haul system using 'Ratchet Prusik's'. (K Phillips)

Right: Two types of rope clamp: the Gibbs above, and below the fixed position lever rope clamp, which can be attached to a winch frame. The tubular pin on which the cam lever pivots can be replaced with a Pip-pin or similar high-tensile self-locking pin. Top right is a figure of eight lowering device made from tubular steel, with small holes on the crest for air cooling. This is both light and strong, and keeps cool for long lowers. It should be noted that many rope clamps seriously weaken the rope and some should not be deployed for heavy or shock loading

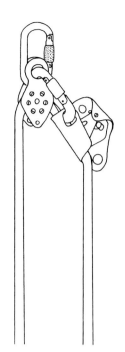

A ratchet pulley. Never have slack on the active side of the pulley. (E Donaldson)

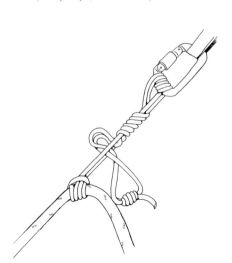

A load releasing hitch used in conjunction with a Prusik knot. (E Donaldson)

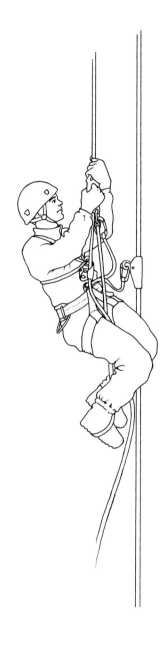

Jumaring using a Gibbs, or other type of sliding clamp on a safety rope. (E Donaldson)

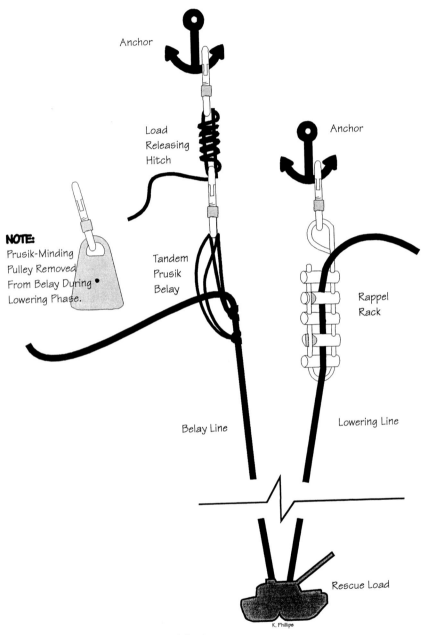

Anchor

Load
Releasing
Hitch

Anchor

NOTE:
Prusik-Minding
Pulley Removed
From Belay During
Lowering Phase.

Tandem
Prusik
Belay

Rappel
Rack

Belay Line

Lowering Line

Rescue Load

K. Phillips

A lowering system for cliff rescue. (K Phillips)

DO NOT GIRTH HITCH
ANCHOR POINT ATTACHMENTS !

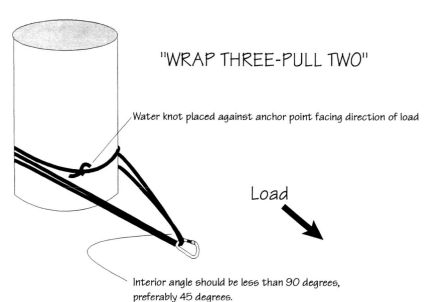

"WRAP THREE-PULL TWO"

Water knot placed against anchor point facing direction of load

Load

Interior angle should be less than 90 degrees,
preferably 45 degrees.

'Wrap three-pull two' This is a good rule for tree/bollard belays. (K Phillips)

Lightning

It is dangerous to shelter in a cave, which may in fact be an area of high conductivity due to moisture and/or minerals. Ensure that the body doesn't cause a 'short circuit' by not leaning back against a rock face or by standing under a projecting rock (G Hunter)

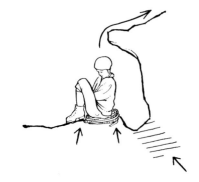

Lightning

Lightning can present a considerable hazard to the task of the mountain rescuer. On most rescues a certain amount of metal equipment must be carried, and during electrical disturbances great care should be exercised on exposed ridges etc.

Even in fine weather an electrical field exists in the atmosphere in the form of negative and positive carriers of electricity which move evenly and slowly. In thundery weather the electrical charges are much more dense, and during such conditions they are not distributed evenly. Some areas are predominantly charged positive, others negative; this creates large electric fields and eventually leads to breakdown and a discharge.

Climbing parties and rescue teams can be exposed to extreme danger during an electrical storm.
(Meteorological office national library.)

A lightning flash is not a single spark. The main flash is immediately preceded by a smaller spark (the leader). The leader has ionised the air and the full discharge follows at 100 times higher speed down this conducting channel. There are also flashes which spring from cloud to cloud, or from cloud to mountain summit, which discharge with thunder. These are partial flashes.

St Elmo's fire, ball lightning, ice axe buzzing etc.

These phenomena seem to be mainly connected with induction.

Precautions

During a severe electrical disturbance it is safer for the rescue party to halt, cache all ironmongery a short way off and unrope. Coiled climbing rope, especially if wet, should be taken off, if the person carrying it is himself dry. Wet snow and rock conduct well but old snow or glacier ice are bad conductors and it is safer to stay on such a surface. It is safer to move about as the air above one's head doesn't so readily become ionised creating a lightning 'channel' along which a discharge can occur. The point to remember is that lightning always seeks a projecting, well-conducting object with a good earth connection. Lightning will therefore mostly strike on rocks containing iron. Moisture is an important factor and will obviously provide a good conductor. Lightning doesn't always strike the highest summits and pinnacles, but often the weathered boundary layers of two geological strata. Such layers often contain moisture and iron. Avoid sheltering in caves or crevices in rock. In the construction of emergency shelters these things should be considered and an adequate lightning conductor should be installed ensuring that it leads to a good ground earth.

Location Equipment

Night vision equipment

Long range viewer CU 15

The CU 15 embodies a catadioptric system of high aperture which collects light from a target and brings it to a focus on the photocathode of a three stage image intensifier tube. The resultant electron beam is focused onto the fluorescent screen of the image intensifier tube and the visual image is viewed through a convenient magnifying eyepiece.

The viewer is located on a mounting which provides movement in elevation and azimuth and can have tripod, or other type of support. The objective and eyepiece are separately focused onto the intensifier cathode and screen respectively. The high power objective has a focusing range of 50 m to infinity, which is controlled from a small lever on the front plate of the instrument. The low power objective is pre-set at a range of 800 m.

The optical system, which is of dual magnification, has a highly corrected cassegrain

system with a meniscus lens front element for high power, and a telephoto lens for low power, both of which work in conjunction with a 7½ × eyepiece.

Power for the intensifier tube is contained within the training handle and replacement batteries can be fitted without redesiccating the instrument. (Barr & Stroud Ltd)

	HP	LP
Magnification	5·907 ×	1·2 ×
Angular field	7°	35° 20.
Overall length	586·7 mm	
Weight of viewer with mount	25·4 kg (approx.)	29·5 kg

The function of the image intensifier long range viewer type CU 15 is to provide an observer with a visual image of objects at low light levels, the maximum range depending on scene illumination

Passive night miniviewer

The Barr & Stroud miniature night vision system has been developed to provide an extremely portable unit for various night surveillance applications. The viewer is self-contained and will operate very satisfactorily down to starlight conditions without any illumination other than natural night sky radiation. Weight is 1·45 kg.

The system is based on a three-stage cascade tube with an 18 mm photo-cathode and fully encapsulated EHT supply unit which, with its 2·7V battery, will give up to one week's normal use. (© Barr & Stroud Ltd)

Magnification	4 ×
Field of view:	10°
Objective aperture:	f1·9–50 mm diameter
Endurance:	40 hours continuous
Man detection range:	220 m

A glass fibre coffin for transporting mutilated or decomposed corpses. Such a coffin is virtually airtight

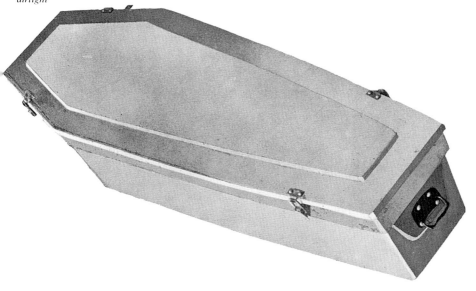

A view of a helicopter winching operation taken in darkness through a large image intensifier where the crew are operating with NVG. This photograph was taken from over one mile (1.6 km) away and 2,000 ft (610 m) above. (H MacInnes)

Pocketscope
Passive night vision device

Night vision equipment: The Pocketscope is an excellent instrument for night searches, being both light and efficient. It has a very fast objective lens which collects the small amount of light reflected from the night sky by the scene. This forms an image on the front end (photocathode) of an image intensifier tube. Electrons which are emitted by the photocathode are then accelerated through a high voltage, and form an image up to 60,000 times brighter on the rear end (screen) of the tube. The image is then viewed through an eyepiece which provides necessary magnification.

This type of night viewer supersedes the earlier models which deployed a cascade of three electron-optical tubes arranged in series. Second generation devices like the Pocketscope are based on a single microchannel tube. Earlier instruments may be available through government surplus.

Field of view:	15°
Overall magnification:	2×
Range performance:	Recognition of a standing man as being a man at 250 m in clear starlight (10^{-3}ux), assuming 40 per cent target contrast and 15 per cent reflectivity.
Focus range:	0·8 m to infinity
Weight:	900 g (1·09 kg including zeroing box)
Overall size:	203 mm × 76 mm
Image intensifier tube:	Mullard XX 1306 18 mm micro channel plate with P20 phosphor
Objective lens:	68 mm f/1·17 (catadioptric)
Eye relief:	25 mm
Exit pupil:	15 mm dia.
Power supply:	Mallory type TR 132N 2·7 volt. Average life 40 hrs continuous operation
Stray light protection:	Rubber shutter eyeguard

Above: The IR18. An early thermal imager made by Barr & Stroud. It has the advantage over other night vision equipment as it can penetrate foliage, smoke etc. It has great potential for forest search for crashed aircraft and can be used from a helicopter (Barr & Stroud)

Left: A transistorised loud hailer, which can be used for listening as well as speaking. There is also a hoot button for attracting attention. Such an instrument is used regularly by rescue teams for communicating with injured climbers high on faces or for large scale rescue operations, e.g. avalanches (H MacInnes)

The KVH DataScope is a 5 × 30 monocular digital compass/rangefinder which can give instant bearing and range (L Gramminger)

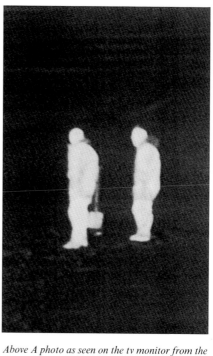

Opposite page: A thermal imager mounted on a tripod for an avalanche search experiment. The tv monitor is located in a tent (H MacInnes)

Above A photo as seen on the tv monitor from the thermal imager. 'Hot' objects stand out white, for example the shovel which was used for digging the grave in which a volunteer lies. The underlayer of snow is at a higher temperature than the surface. From these experiments it appears that the thermal imager detects pockets of warm air (filtering through the avalanche boulders to the surface) from a buried victim (Barr & Stroud)

This illustrates the Forward Looking Infra Red unit mounted on a SAR helicopter, (FLIR). It is a popular and efficient method of locating heat sources such as survivors, casualties or recently crashed aircraft. It is of particular value where a distress beacon is not being used or has been damaged (Bristow Helicopters Ltd)

The 'Lite Sight' manufactured by Pilkington Optronics is one of the new generation of night sights developed for military use. This thermal imager has considerable potential as a mountain rescue tool. It is lightweight (13kg) and self-contained. A video output is available in PAL or NTSC format
(Pilkington Optronics)

The EEV Nite Watch Plus is a lightweight (330 g) image intensifier with over 20,000 times light magnification with interchangeable lenses

Above: D.S. Developments of England built-in helmet waterproof communication system operating on 49.830 MHz with an approx. range of 400 m. It can be interfaced with VHF radio. Similar equipment is used by winchmen on SAR helicopters

Below: N.V.G.; Night Vision Goggles as used by SAR helicopter crews. When a SAR helicopter is assisting in a night evacuation/search, it is important for ground parties to extinguish lights when requested by the aircrew if N.V.G. are being used. One headlamp is sufficient for the helicopter to home in on the casualty/rescue team. Always liaise with the pilot and Base for instructions from the pilot (REGA)

Forest Penetrator. This is a useful item of equipment for rescue in heavily wooded regions. On the right you see the unit closed for lowering through the forest canopy and on the left, ready to lift (E Donaldson)

Searchlights and lighting

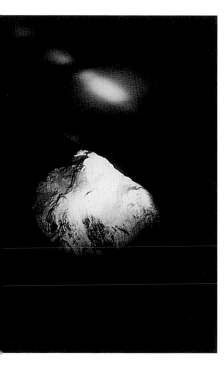

Searchlights illuminating the summit of Buachaille Etive Mor in the Scottish Highlands (D. Taylor)

Searchlights/floodlights

These are among the most important items for successful and speedy rescue evacuations during the hours of darkness. Any rescue team which operates at night should give lighting details its full attention.

There are three main requirements for artificial lights:
a) Personal headlamps, lanterns etc. for team members.
b) Searchlights for searching and evacuation.
c) Floodlights for major accidents such as large avalanche searches.

Headlamps

At the present time we are on the threshold of a battery 'revolution' and during the next few years many new batteries will be available, which will outdate the existing types.

However, we must deal with what is available within the often very limited budget of rescue teams.

Headlamps should always be taken in each team member's pack (irrespective of the time of day) as often delays, or even further rescues, can occur which can mean a night evacuation. At least one or more spare batteries should be taken in winter months.

Lithium cells are used for headlamps for expedition and rescue work, but there are various points about their use which should be noted by rescue teams. The battery has an outstanding performance, especially at low temperatures. However, the case is in fact a pressure vessel

Searchlights, radio communications, radio links and signalling equipment

Night evacuation. Using two quartz halogen searchlights for casualty evacuation. One searchlight is used for picking the descent route and the other for illuminating the ground round stretcher party. Note that ropes are 'V'd' out for maximum control and this will also prevent any stones dislodged by the rope-anchor men from falling on stretcher party (G Hunter)

Searchlights can be a great asset to night rescue. Here we see a 7kv, 1 billion candlepower unit with a range of 25 km. This searchlight can light a mountain and is 6 times more powerful than a lighthouse

(pressure up to 2700 kPa (400 psi)). Such pressure can be reached if the battery is overheated or short-circuited, and the cell will then audibly vent and will release high-pressure sulphur dioxide. The quantity of toxic material is small and will dissipate rapidly unless confined. Special precautions apply to multi-cell applications.

Rechargeable headlamps

There are many of these available, usually of the miners' variety, giving a long life with two wiring circuits, one to give a small, low output, but adequate light for general work, and the other a more intense beam. The miner's-type lamp is expensive and heavier than the simple headlamp with an expendable battery, but for long-term use these can prove much cheaper than dry battery headlamps.

Suitable charging facilities must be available, and in the case of a prolonged search away from base some suitable charging generator must be used if main power is not to hand.

Portable searchlights

To date, for rescue work, the best searchlights employ a quartz iodine or halogen bulb. These bulbs give a very intense light and are more economical than the standard tungsten filament bulb.

A car spotlight, or fog driving lamp offer the two best alternatives, or a

Top: Miners headlamps were once popular with MR Teams. They have a long operating life and a two bulb headlamp, a normal and main beam. Approx 16 hours duration

Below: A multi-charger for miners'-type headlamps, built into a rescue mobile base truck

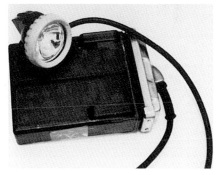

variable beam lamp can be used. The consumption of the standard IQ bulb is approx. 5 amp, therefore one should aim at using a battery of at least 20 amp.hrs duration of the lightest possible weight.

Other quartz halogen or iodine projector bulbs are available at 24 V with a higher output.

A portable searchlight can be made using an unspillable car type battery (see illustration) in conjunction with a quartz halogen bulb. A non-reversible connector should be used to ensure that the charger output cannot be connected the wrong way round.

In mountain regions where there is considerable night search and rescue, two searchlights at least will be necessary for the team.

The weight of the unit together with lamp and rucksack should not exceed 11 kg. Though the range of a good quartz halogen lamp is in the region of 600 m approx., maximum searching distance is seldom more than 100 m approx. unless the search victims are wearing fluorescent clothing.

Care should be taken that the searchlight is not used unnecessarily, to conserve power. Switching off at intervals will give the battery time to recover and will improve the long-term use of the lamp on an actual rescue.

Despite their weight in the present form, such searchlights are essential for night search and evacuation. No rescue team should be without at least one. Nickel-cadmium batteries are available which give excellent performance, though they are initially more expensive.

One reliable person should be put in charge of the searchlights to ensure that they are kept fully charged and ready for use.

Incandescent, tethered helium balloons which contain floodlights, can be useful for disaster locations, in the absence of high winds/helicopter downwash.

Military type searchlights

These can be useful for illuminating a face from below, or across a valley, and for lighting the access route to the location of an accident.

There are various forms of high-intensity lighting, such as the HC-130 Flare Ship, but with this there is fire risk. From aircraft, 'Night Suns' can be used with great effect, also the nine million candle-power Carolina Moon. Mounted on some coastal command aircraft is a 70 million candle-power searchlight. This generates so much heat that it can only be used for one minute duration followed by five minutes shut-off.

Motorised searchlights

A compact, low voltage generator can be mounted on a packframe for night work. Care should be taken, when using low voltage quartz halogen bulbs, that the running speed of the engine is suitably adjusted to avoid 'blowing' the bulbs.

Searchlights illuminating a section of Buachaille Etive Mor in the Scottish Highlands (D. Taylor)

It is safer to have the fuel tank of this unit separated from the engine when mounting it on a packframe and to have a non-leak safety fuel cap incorporated in case the person carrying it falls. Spare fuel should be carried by other team members.

The above-mentioned unit and others of a similar high output weight ratio tend to be very noisy. For search work they can be troublesome due to the noise. It would be impossible to hear cries or shouts of an injured person in close proximity to the generator.

Two searchlights (quartz halogen 12 V 50 W) can be operated from the unit, and it is advantageous to have a very wide beam, or even a halogen bulb mounted without a reflector on the carrier frame for a spreading light round the unit. This can be especially useful if the person carrying

Top: A small portable generator which can be used for flood-lighting accident areas. Provision is also made for low voltage battery charging (Honda Co)

Below: A strobe signal light. The unit is very compact – 114 mm long. It operates at 50 flashes per minute and lasts 9–14 hours. A spare battery is seen alongside. This marker is excellent for marking landing sites etc. The light output is in excess of 100,000 lumens per flash (J Duff)

A lightweight generator mounted on a military type pack frame. Two 12 v quartz halogen lights are being used. 1 = the main searchlight with switch incorporated in the handle. 2 = a quartz halogen bulb mounted onto the alloy weather protection plate for lighting the area behind and to the sides of the unit. 3 = a compartment for rescuers' equipment, searchlight etc. (H MacInnes)

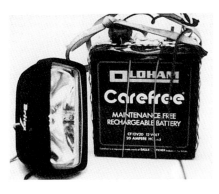

Portable searchlight utilising an unspillable battery and a quartz halogen lamp. The plug must be irreversible to prevent charger being connected wrongly

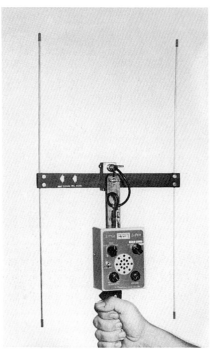

Direction finders

This equipment is used mainly for locating crashed aircraft. For example, the L-Tronics DF equipment is designed to operate in frequency ranges from 100 to 300 MHz and will track AM, FM, pulsed signals and random noise. Light, portable units are available for hand use, with the DF antenna folding flat for transport

Radio distress beacon. The Locat is one of the most advanced of its kind with a shelf life of ten years. The operation is simple and it transmits up to 36 hours. Operating temperature –20°C to +60°C. It operates on frequencies 121·5 or 243 MHz

the unit walks to one side of the stretcher party, thereby giving both general light and a powerful beam for picking the way ahead.

Floodlights

The portable generator unit can also be used as a floodlight with a suitable lamp or such lighting plants as the Honda models give quieter (four-stroke engine) operation. There are several types available for such work, but they must be as portable as possible and reasonably long connecting wires should be available for these, as often a good location for the generator is some distance from the site of the accident. Ensure that the correct cable lengths and size are used to avoid voltage drop. Use only waterproof connectors.

Other means of lighting

Illuminating flares can be very useful, both parachute and fixed, but care should be taken so that the smoke from these does not interfere with the rescue/search operation.
Portable gas lanterns were once used for night search work, they tend to be heavier than lightweight electrical equipment. Care should be taken with the mantles and spare ones should always be carried together with matches in a waterproof container. Propane gas is better for low temperature work.
Pressure lanterns These afford a very good source of light at an economical weight, and are still used in some regions. Again care should be taken with the mantles and they can give trouble in winds over force 6.

The Sea Marshall Personal Locator which has a range of 6–8 km from a search aircraft flying at 152m, and over 16 km at 600 m.

Signals from Locators have been picked up by commercial aircraft from injured climbers as well as from sailors but such location devices are used mainly for maritime distress situations and at the time of writing, only to a limited extent by walkers/climbers.

They operate on an International SAR distress frequency of 121.5 MHz and provide a homing capability for rescue in all weathers and visibility. Some also transmit longitude and latitude from a built-in GPS unit. Hand held directional location receivers are available for searching by ground SAR teams.

Radio communications

There is a wide variety of radio equipment available today. The problems usually are, which is the best for a Team's specific requirements and how much will it cost?

In the interests of efficiency and life saving it is desirable that each Team member has his/her own personal walkie-talkie which is kept at home together with spare batteries and charger.

Base stations and repeaters should come under the maintenance blanket of a qualified 'Team friendly' radio engineer with day-to-day supervision by the Team's own radio officer.

Due to the extremes of SAR work, radios are expected to perform in the most extreme conditions, from humid rain forests to sub-zero temperatures. The choice of frequencies will be dictated by your country/county, and not always is the best mountain frequency allocated due to international pressures for emergency frequency slots.

There are several basic requirements for a mountain rescue walkie-talkie. It should be lightweight, waterproof if possible (even in dry regions there can be heavy rains). Preferably, it should have several legal operating frequencies. For example, as well as a common Team/police frequency, a helicopter channel is vital for good communications. The operating controls should be both robust and easy to use (with gloves) when enclosed in their protective case, and the transmit button shouldn't be proud of the case which could result in accidental transmissions, which could cause havoc to your Team's radio network. Most modern walkie-talkies of a quality suitable for SAR have re-chargeable nickel-cadmium batteries. However some Teams still use transceivers with dry batteries. It is essential that these are replaced regularly as they have a limited shelf life, and that sufficient spares are taken on a call-out. It is important to carry spare batteries and to keep your personal walkie-talkie insulated from the elements as both extreme heat and cold can have detrimental effects. Spare batteries enclosed in a sealed waterproof bag (avoid condensation) will prevent accidental discharge to damp or metal objects in the rucksack. It is important in humid regions to keep terminals/contacts clean and dry.

Most walkie-talkies used on mountain rescue operate on VHF (Very High Frequency) which is basically line of sight, though sometimes hillsides and cliffs act as 'reflectors' and contact can occasionally be made 'round corners'. By slowly rotating the walkie-talkie on a horizontal plane whilst transmitting it is sometimes possible to bounce the signal, thereby making contact with base who will advise the point of greatest signal strength.

Transmission uses almost twenty times more power than receiving and this should be borne in mind when sending messages: be brief, but speak slowly and clearly and don't transmit unless you have to! Sometimes it is not possible to transmit an audio signal but by pressing the transmit button a prearranged number of times some basic communication can be established. For example, three presses could indicate, 'Sorry I'm not transmitting, but I can hear you. . . . .'

Most modern transceivers have scan facilities, by which other frequencies can be scanned to alert you of traffic on the scanned frequency. In some countries, where it is permissible, a location frequency can be crystalled into the set to allow aircraft and ground parties to pin-point your position. This is a useful facility in poor visibility or to allow a helicopter to home in on your position.

Repeaters/Radio Links

Many SAR units use repeaters to relay signals to otherwise blind-spots. These can be activated by Rescue Control or by telephone. If triggered by a radio signal from Rescue Control a further frequency is usually required unless a delay and repeat system is deployed. Such installations should be discussed with your radio engineer in conjunction with the relevant authorities. Repeater stations can be powered by mains power, preferably, solar power, propane gas, or batteries.

Many repeater stations are in remote and exposed locations. It is advisable in regions of high snowfall to have shovels in an elevated position for digging out, and repeater shelters fitted with adequate door and keyhole seals to prevent spindrift from entering. There are available now, 'stand alone repeaters'. These can be operated by remote control from base and are placed in position at the start of the search operation either by helicopter or by man-pack.

Where a human radio link is used, some form of shelter is desirable for the operator who, by nature of the terrain,

Above right: Walkie-talkie Test Transmission Instrument: This is a field-strength meter to indicate the effective output of a walkie-talkie. The unit requires no power other than that produced by the walkie-talkie.

Right: A useful State of Charge instrument for testing walkie-talkie batteries (H MacInnes)

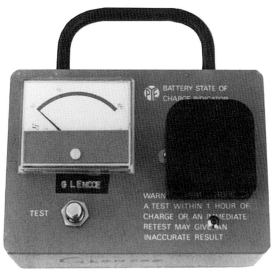

Phonetic alphabet

A – Alpha	H – Hotel	O – Oscar	V – Victor
B – Bravo	I – India	P – Papa	W – Whisky
C – Charlie	J – Juliet	Q – Quebec	X – X-ray
D – Delta	K – Kilo	R – Romeo	Y – Yankee
E – Echo	L – Lima	S – Sierra	Z – Zulu
F – Foxtrot	M – Mike	T – Tango	
G – Golf	N – November	U – Uniform	

Pronunciation of numerals

Number	Spoken as	Numeral	Spoken as
0	Ze-ro	5	Fife
1	Wun	6	Six
2	Too	7	Sev-ven
3	Thuh-ree	8	Ate
4	Fo-wer	9	Nine-er

may be forced to establish his base at an exposed position such as a ridge dividing two valley systems which have to be searched.

Aerials

The choice of these for both repeater stations and fixed base units should be addressed carefully as atmospheric icing can present problems and heater units may have to be developed. High winds too can present problems. Base and mobile stations can utilise telescopic aerials, some of which operate by compressed air and can be elevated to 12–15 m.

For long-range communications many of the military attachments for SAR use short-wave communication to remain in contact with their HQ. VHF radios have a very limited use for cave rescue and special long-wave transceivers are available for such rescue operations. On large scale rescues fixed wing aircraft and helicopters can be used as radio links.

Radio Procedure

It is vital to use proper radio procedure otherwise time can be wasted and messages misunderstood. Some Teams record all RT conversations; a useful de-briefing tool!

Remember the ABC code: ACCURACY / BREVITY / CLARITY. Always use your callsign and, in the case of a large scale search and rescue, be familiar with the call-signs of other teams participating.

Questions over the air should be asked individually, otherwise confusion may result. Use the commonly used procedural words such as 'Over', 'Out', 'Wait', 'Radio Check', etc. These terms vary in different countries, but the Phonetic Alphabet is International.

Communications (pyrotechnics)

Various forms of flares can be used for communication, especially in reasonable weather, either by night or by day. There are many different types available from mini flares to large parachute rockets.

Message	Flare	Light, Sound or Semaphore
1) Help wanted here	Red	Alpine: Six long flashes/notes in quick succession repeated after a minute's interval
2) Message understood	(from party on hill) White	Alpine: A series of three long flashes/notes repeated at one minute intervals
3) Position of Base	White (or yellow)	Steady white or yellow light or car headlights (if possible, pointed upwards)
4) Recall to Base A thunderflash or maroon may be used to attract attention.	Green (used only at base)	A succession of notes on horn, bell or whistle. A succession of white or yellow lights switched on and off. A succession of thunderflashes.

Flares represent an expensive form of communication, but in the absence of radios they afford a good means of signalling provided a prearranged code is adhered to.

The signals mentioned below offer a relatively simple method of communication:

In the absence of walkie-talkies for raising or lowering on a rope, the following code is standard:

1 Whistle or flash	Stop
2 Whistles or flashes	Pull up
3 Whistles or flashes	Slack off or lower

An air-operated (electric) fog horn or mechanical siren can also be used as a recall signal for parties on a search. This has been used successfully in several areas.

Further flares can be used for rescue work such as the 4 star white rocket of 100,000 candle-power. This rocket goes up to a height of 370 m. There is also a rocket parachute illuminating flare of 100,000 candle-power which has a duration of 28–30 seconds which goes to the same height. Care must be exercised in high-risk fire regions when using flares.

Smoke generators

These can be successfully used for signalling when a prearranged code has been established. They are more often used for indicating wind direction for helicopters and small aircraft used in rescue work.

Signal mirrors, signal lamps

If properly trained in the use of signal mirrors (heliographs), a rescue team can find these of considerable use in climates offering sufficient sunshine to merit their use. A lost/injured party may also use such a signal medium (especially good for signalling to aircraft). Aldis-type signal lamps can be excellent for signal work, but cannot compare with good RT equipment.

The strobe as illustrated is probably the best available flasher unit for signalling aircraft, teams, etc.

Rescue Teams

The ultimate DIY rescue: Doug Scott crawls, with two broken legs to base camp from close to the summit of the Ogre, Himalayas (Clive Rowland)

Climbing/expedition restrictions

The closing of areas by authorities should be carefully considered and only implemented as a last resort. However, environmental, political and hazardous elements sometimes necessitates curtailment of access. In certain parts of the world it is now mandatory for expeditions and climbing parties to provide some means of self-rescue if necessary and it is also quite common to pay a deposit (which is reimbursed if there is no accident) to defray the cost of any SAR operation mounted by the host government/national park, etc.

In Russia, climbers have to undergo a medical examination before embarking on a serious climb and must also give a 'control time', i.e. give an estimated ETA for return to base. Also, a panel of Masters of Sport assesses if the proposed route is suitable in the prevailing conditions. Should there be more than one party wishing to climb a given route, the parties are staggered to a 24-hour departure differential. In the event of a party exceeding their 'control time', a rescue party is immediately alerted. However, during the climb, communication is usually maintained by the climbing party/s and Base via radio, or sometimes daily flares indicating progress or distress. Dangerous icefalls and faces with abnormal stonefall due to 'dry' conditions are frequently off-limits.

In other parts of the world permission must be obtained for climbing peaks outwith the high ranges. This is the case in some National Parks where climbers must adhere to local rules, declare the number

High Altitude Rescue: Recovering a body from the north face of Mount Everest, MacInnes Superlite stretcher (P Moores)

in the party, and have the necessary equipment and experience. There are also stipulations regarding roping up on glaciers, etc. In drought country, or on big wall climbs, there may be rules on a minimum supply of spring water (which contains necessary minerals not found in melt water).

Regulations usually make good sense despite sometimes being frustrating for the participants.

Rescue teams sometimes supply information on climbing, weather, and avalanche conditions on a local basis, though this is normally catered for by specific authorities. In many countries an avalanche forecast is broadcast as well as a specific mountain weather forecast and 'climb/ski lines' exist as a phone-in service for mountaineers and skiers.

It may be advantageous for rescue teams to establish permanent belays in accident black spots. In the case of bolts/pitons, these should be of stainless steel and of an adequate strength. In areas subjected to salt air or spray care should

be taken to avoid corrosion of fixed metallic inserts (see p. 98).

Caches

Rescue equipment/stretchers caches in remote accident blackspots can be an advantage, but again care should be taken regarding storage and that ropes and other 'vermin desirable gear' is not damaged. In regions of heavy snowfall, fix a shovel above the cache.

High altitude rescue

This is more common today and can present great logistical problems for both rescuers and rescued.

One of the main problems facing rescuers is acclimatisation, and self-rescue on the part of the climbing party is the best procedure if this is possible. Several high altitude rescues have in fact been

mounted by rescue teams based in Europe, but if possible it is best to deploy members from other expeditions climbing in the region.

In the Himalayas, Alaska and South America, helicopters and fixed-wing aircraft, operated by the military and Park authorities, have now considerable experience in high altitude evacuations.

Not only should the Team member be a capable climber, he must also be well versed and qualified in first-aid. Also a thorough working knowledge of the mechanics of modern face rescue is vital if a Team operates in precipitous or cliff terrain.

Balloons

Though balloons have been used with varying degrees of success for locating avalanche victims, the use of hot air/helium balloons for patient evacuation is fraught with problems, wind being the main difficulty.

Team leader

He or she as well as being an experienced mountaineer, must be able to deploy the Team to its best advantage and be well versed in all aspects of SAR techniques. It is important to have good relations with all other emergency services that may be called in to assist from time to time, as in the case of a large scale search.

Personal equipment is largely a matter of choice and won't be dealt with here in

Above left: The first portable telescopic pressure chamber designed by the author for use at Pherichi, near Everest base camp for pulmonary and cerebral oedema victims, now superseded by the kevlar pressure bag (H MacInnes)

Above: A modern portable pressure chamber, the 'Gamow Bag' set up on Mt. Everest during the 1990 climb. This is an essential tool of any high altitude rescue group (Portable Hyperbarics Inc.)

Right above: Participation on a large scale air disaster can have a profound psychological effect on SAR personnel and may necessitate counselling at a later date (Daily Record)

Right below: An SAR dog takes a brief break at the Lockerbie air disaster (Daily Record)

detail. In 'busy' rescue areas subject to severe winter or snow and ice conditions full mountaineering equipment is required as well as the other essential 'tools' of the trade, e.g. avalanche bleeper, bivvy bag, walkie-talkie, avalanche probe, etc. Personal cliff rescue gear such as ascender, descender, pegs, chocks, personal first-aid, and flares should also be issued on a personal basis.

Press

Inevitably there is public interest in any serious mountain accident, and if the incident is protracted with fatalities there will be an influx of reporters and tv crews. Often, they set up satellite links close to the rescue base. It is usually better to give periodic press releases, otherwise reporters will use their imagination, and a factual account of the incident and progress, without divulging the names of the

casualties and survivors will in the end produce more balanced reporting. The police or other law enforcement agencies can release names once relatives or next to kin have been informed. This lets the Base Controller and Team Leader off the hook.

The press, radio and tv can be used to advantage when information is required from the public about missing persons, and many teams rely on public donations for their survival. Publicity always helps with donations.

Relatives: Often next-of-kin and friends or relatives arrive at Rescue Control during the search operation. Care should be taken that they are not within earshot of radio equipment where they may be upset upon overhearing certain communications.

Left: Mt. Kinabalu (4,103 m) in Malaysia was the location of a major rescue operation in 1994, where several servicemen were overdue from the 1830 m descent of Low's Gully, in foreground. To assist and descend the gully a detachment of RAF personnel were sent, over almost 10,000 km. from the UK. Such long range rescue operations require careful planning for as well as taking the right technical equipment, such things as vaccinations, cash or credit cards for local purchases are necessities which can be overlooked and in the case of higher mountains, acclimatisation of Team members (RAF Kinloss)

Below: The scene of a double fatality 1985 in Crazy Jug Canyon, USA. As the Piper Cub didn't have a locator (ELT) there was a delay of two weeks finding the aircraft (Martin Anderson)

The rescue team

The primary function of a rescue team is to save life, and evacuate the injured. In various parts of the world the local mountain rescue teams are formed from mountain guides, military personnel, police, rangers or local volunteers. Many countries have full-time professional rescue team members and staff. We are concerned here mainly with the formation of local volunteer rescue team members, as the official teams are integrated with government, military or local authorities.

The first essential for a member of a mountain rescue team is that he should be a competent mountaineer. Obviously, he can help the injured party to a greater extent if he himself is experienced and can move over difficult terrain without consciously thinking about it. Next, it is most important that he should have (or acquire as quickly as possible) knowledge of the mechanics of rescue work and the principles of evacuating a patient by the simplest and most effective means from a

given position. Naturally, such knowledge comes largely with experience, but the basic techniques of stretcher lowering, etc., can be acquired in several training sessions.

First aid

Most MR teams now have trained paramedics in their ranks, but each team member must be capable of dealing with the wide variety of injuries found on mountain accidents. As well as each team member obtaining a first-aid certificate the rescue team should try to enlist the help of a sympathetic doctor, who has experience of mountain accidents, to further their knowledge of diagnosis of injuries and of first aid. Often the ordinary rescue team member has to face decisions and take action regarding the life of an injured climber or walker which could be difficult enough for a doctor. It is essential therefore that as wide a knowledge as possible of first aid should be acquired by each member.

The rescue team: individual equipment

Rescue team members, especially those who go on regular call-outs, should keep their personal equipment at home. This is in the interest of efficiency and of consideration to the accident victim, as time will be saved in reaching the accident locus.

For less active team members, equipment kept with the communal gear will, if the need arises, allow such items to be loaned to other rescuers when required.

Team members should be equipped, especially in high mountain regions, as for mountaineering. Such equipment will have a basis of essential items such as:

Mountaineering boots.

Crampons, 10 or 12 point type with quick release bindings.

Snow gaiters.

Loop stitch stockings.

Climbing breeches, or **long climbing trousers**.

Overtrousers, with zip bottom and velcro overlap, for ease in putting on over boots or crampons. These, as well as a cagoule, should be of fluorescent or bright colour, 113 gms weight. A breathable material is of great advantage for overclothing as well as for bivvy bags.

Underclothing, thermal vest and long johns.

Down duvet jacket, hip length with hood. Both the duvet and the cagoule jacket should preferably be fitted with a front full-length zip for ventilation etc., and be equipped with pockets. Synthetic fibre pile is in certain areas more convenient than down clothing as it absorbs little moisture.

For wire rope handling, gloves are necessary; these should be kept with wire rope equipment rather than have several pairs issued.

Standard woollen mitts – the dachstein type are probably best for general work.

Overgloves, for bad weather conditions, will also be required and carried as spares. A strip of artificial fur or nylon pile stitched to the back of the overgloves can be useful for wiping goggles clear.

Suitable headgear both for cold and for protection from stonefall is essential.

The helmet, hard hat, etc. should be up to the highest possible standard and must not restrict hearing ability, essential in rescue work.

Sun glasses, should be issued for SAR for use in bright snow conditions and goggles if working with helicopters in sand/blizzard conditions. The type with a single transparent plastic lens is the best, and if this is fastened by press studs (for easy replacement of different lenses etc.) the end press studs can be left loose to allow free movement of air and reduce the risk of fogging.

Face masks. These are only required in the worst blizzards at low temperatures and should be so constructed that they do not cause one's breath to fog the goggles.

Rucksacks. The most popular type is the medium/large frameless mountaineering pack and again the colour should preferably be orange for easy location.

A larger Himalayan type can be used for first aid, casualty bag etc. and all sacks should be fitted with bivouac extensions.

Below: Bringing down the bodies from a crashed Fokker Friendship aircraft at 3000 m. (RAF)

Bottom: At the wreckage of the crashed Fokker Friendship aircraft, Turkey (RAF Kinloss M.R.)

Bivouac sacks. If there is an extension to the rucksack, this plus a cagoule will generally suffice. Otherwise a large polythene bag of 500 gauge transparent plastic makes an inexpensive bivvy sack. This should be approx. 2 × 1·2 m approx. It should have holes in it to allow the passage of air, as asphyxiation is otherwise possible. A bivouac sack of woven ('breathable') material is the best.

Ice axe. For rescue work the tubular metal or carbon shafted axe is by far the safest. Often ice axes are under severe strain on rescues and only the strongest ice axes or north wall hammers should be used. It can be useful to have several longer axes in each team.

Piton hammer. This should preferably be of the all-metal type as it can be used in conjunction with karabiners as a lowering brake etc. The model with a short spike is useful for excavating belays round rock bollards.

Dropped pick ice tools are essential if any technical ice climbing is anticipated.

Slings, karabiners, pitons, etc. Sufficient hardware should be issued to each team member and again it must be stressed that individuals must have a good apprenticeship in climbing as this is the only way they will have a sound knowledge of inserting pitons, using slings, etc. Ice screws and deadmen can be issued as required. Only steel karabiners should be used for rescue work, as even a short lower can damage an alloy karabiner. Screwgate karabiners should be used when possible, or quick links, which are stronger.

High quality heat-treated pitons should be used for rescue work as these have much higher tensile strength.

Slings. Nylon tape slings should be inspected frequently, as even slight damage can seriously affect the strength of the sling and in such circumstances they should be discarded.

Wire slings and chocks. In many instances these are stronger and quicker to utilise than pitons, especially for vertical cracks. Chocks are better fitted with wire slings for rescue work. Whenever possible, a full range should be allocated to each team member, or at least to those usually involved in the more technical aspects of a difficult rescue evacuation.

Rope clamps. These can be a great aid to the mountain rescuer. Not only do they offer a quick, safe method of reaching the accident scene after a rope has been fixed, but they can be used for all aspects of rescue rigging work and can be quickly attached to and detached from ropes when need be. There are various types on the market, but none of these current ones should be subjected to great strain. Several models are illustrated on pages 293–295.

Whistle

Headlamp

First aid. Personal first-aid kits should be made up as suggested by the local team medical adviser. Usually it·is well worth carrying extra food such as glucose tablets, high calorie drinks, etc., for emergency use, or for administering to exhausted accident victims, etc.

Mini flares. The small mini flare pack, with a selection of different coloured flares, should be taken by each team member, especially if there is a shortage of RT sets, or in case these should fail to operate in a 'blind' area, etc.

Map and compass. Maps of a large scale should be carried by as many team members as possible. The use of map and compass should of course have been mastered by the team member, even before he joined the rescue group, as all climbers should have a sound knowledge of navigation. Even the expert map reader can be fooled by an excess of iron in the area and care should be taken in unknown regions regarding this. Such places, however, are usually well known. Metal objects such as ice axes and piton hammers can affect the compass if in close proximity, as can photoelectric exposure meters. G.P.S. is useful for remote search areas or in severe weather/darkness.

Avalanche transceivers. These should be issued as personal equipment.

Crashed aircraft

There are numerous hazards attached to crashed aircraft. If the aircraft's distress beacon is operating locating the crash site is simplified, but often in the initial stages of the call-out there can be many unknown factors: how many people are involved, the type of aircraft, the severity of the incident and its location. All vital questions, but sometimes unknown in the initial stages of the emergency.

Saving life is the obvious priority. If you approach from uphill and downwind this will lessen the danger from toxic fumes. Do not smoke anywhere near the crash site and don't enter areas of smoke unless you have to for casualties who require assistance. Should no survivors be visible, organise a line search, but don't move any of the wreckage unless someone is underneath. Special care should be exercised in the case of military aircraft: fire, smoke, ejection seats, explosives, ammunition, missiles, ruptured fuel tanks and dangerous cargo can each add to the hazards of rescue. Mark the position of important items for expert investigation later. Some aircraft carry explosive-operated fire-extinguishers and compressed gases. Try not to inhale dust and fine splinters which can be created on impact by carbon-fibre composites. Look further afield for aircrew, who may have ejected, and possibly for other sections of the aircraft.

River crossing

Avalanches and river crossing present two of the greatest problems to the mountain rescuer. In certain parts of the world rivers must be crossed to arrive at the scene of an accident, sometimes several times on the one evacuation. Some rivers and creeks are subject to freak floods, usually through the forces of nature, but occasionally when water is released from a dam up river. Heavy thaws and excessive rain over country which is already saturated and cannot accept more moisture are particularly apt to cause sudden rises in water level. Some rivers in gorges rise by more than 20 m.

The catchment area influences the problem, as does the floor or bed of the river. If the river bed is made up from large boulders, some submerged, some visible, the current will vary to a considerable degree in different places. In some cases the banks and bed are of shingle and gravel; sometimes the river can be both deep and slow flowing. Only experience will enable you to pick the optimum place for a crossing. A ford which was passable one day may be impassable the next. It is often to one's advantage to study a possible crossing place from a suitable elevation, and polaroid glasses can be of use for this. A stick thrown in will enable you to determine the speed and current more accurately. The best crossing place is where there is a bed of smooth, firm shingle and gravel. Sand, mud (possibly quicksands), logs and snags are best avoided, as are large boulders. Look out for slow-moving smooth water, especially where the river widens. Also where the

gradient of the river changes there is often a shingle bar running diagonally across above the start of the decline which can offer a suitable shallow ford. The place where a river splits up into several branches often presents possibilities for a crossing; each branch should be treated as an individual problem, and remember that it may be necessary to retreat should a dangerous crossing be encountered. Where the river runs through an S-bend it is checked and between the bends often

affords a possible ford. Remember that on the 'active' curve of a bend the river is deeper.

It is also possible to cross by swimming provided the current is not strong and the water not too cold. Buoyancy aids can be used in the form of one's rucksack, with the contents enclosed in plastic bags and with the bivvy extension securely tied, but waistbands should not be fastened in case the pack has to be jettisoned. Though a 'ford' may be marked on a map,

River crossing practice in the USSR. It is safer to practise this technique in rivers of moderate proportions (H MacInnes)

conditions can change, as can the weather. Always treat river crossing with caution as in some countries more people are killed crossing rivers than on the mountains.

The colour code: If rivers which are normally clear are murky, discoloured and fast flowing, this may indicate rainfall or thaw at the headwaters; try to seek some alternative means of crossing other than fording. Remember that glacial streams and rivers will tend to fall overnight. Boots should be left on for river crossing, though socks can be taken off. Shorts or long-johns reduce drag (the latter also keep you warmer crossing glacial streams). Snow gaiters will help prevent shingle getting into boots.

The use of a rope: The use of a rope for river crossing is for safety, not as an aid, though a certain amount of strain can be put on it when crossing, as shown in the diagrams. For this type of crossing the rope must be twice the width of the ford. On no account should the rope be tied off at the bank; the belayer/s should be able to move down the bank/s to help the person crossing ashore, should he have difficulty and lose his footing. The rope must not be tied to the belayer, and the person crossing should have it secured as high as possible on his chest. The strain on the belayer/s when the man crossing loses his footing can be considerable, and he must be taken to the most convenient bank when there is

a rope to each side. This is done in a pendulum motion with the belayer/s moving down the bank/s as indicated. In the case of a serious crossing some form of hand signals should be established for emergency if walkie-talkies are not available. In the event of not enough rope being available for this two-man belay system, line or cord can be used from one bank. It should borne in mind that thinner rope offers less current resistance. Also, if the rope can be held above the water it will assist the person crossing. On serious crossings rucksacks should be hauled across.

Where the river bed is boulder-strewn, a prop in the form of a sapling can be used slightly ahead and upstream. It can also be used as a depth tester. The prop should be utilised in the following way: you put it in ahead of you, upstream, and then move round it, on the downstream side, leaning against it and taking short shuffling steps. Only move the pole on when you feel secure in your footing. It is sound policy when crossing deep fords to keep sideways-on to the current.

In the event of a river being too strong for one man to cross, several rescuers, by using a sapling as a connecting bar, can unite their strength and thereby make a safe crossing. This is shown in the drawing below. It is necessary for the strongest man to be upstream with the weakest members in the middle. The top man should control the group and progress must be made with short, shuffling steps.

Most rescue teams in areas subject to rapid river rise are well acquainted with the difficulties of river crossing, however it

Using the combined strength of a party, interlinked with a sapling, to cross a river (Terry Brown)

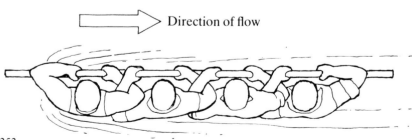

Direction of flow

A sequence for river crossing as pioneered in New Zealand where river crossing is a major hazard. (Terry Brown)

The five illustrations on these and the following page depict a common whitewater situation where a backpacker/canoeist is stranded on a boulder or rock islet. A SAR helicopter is an obvious rescue choice, however one may not be available, or perhaps non-operational in a narrow gorge.

Various rescue systems can be used, some of which are illustrated elsewhere in this book, which could be adapted for such an emergency. However, the technique shown here, with variations to suit terrain and circumstances, can be deployed.

For this operation a light rope or line must be taken over the river. Various means can be deployed to do this from model radio controlled aircraft in the case of wide ravines/canyons, to line guns and mortars, or even throw-lines in a narrow section of river. The technique illustrated uses a double-rope cableway in the interest of security. This is hauled across the river by means of the light rope/line. Wide suspension pulleys must be used on the double-rope cableway.

NB pulleys with double sheaves can become inoperable due to the cableway ropes twisting under load.

1. Several team members cross the river by a suitable route, ford, etc. and a haul line is fired or thrown to them. To this the stretcher haul rope is attached. To the other end the two non-stretch cableway ropes are tied. These are pulled across. If high ground, a cliff or a tree is available at the operational end (in the illustrations, on the right), the cableway pulley should be anchored as high as required to expedite the crossing by keeping the stretcher and barrow boy clear of the water. The other end of the cableway should be anchored. The cableway can be tensioned in various ways, eg. block and tackle, hand winch, manpower. Two double Prusiks can be used to attach the winch to the cableway ropes for tensioning. Further security can be obtained with Prusiks on these ropes, anchored close to the winch belay. This will also allow additional 'bites'

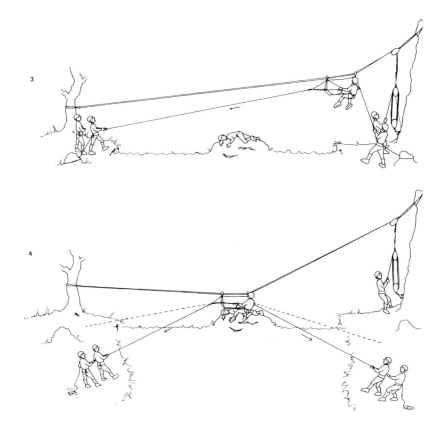

to be taken on the cableway ropes by sliding the winch Prusiks up the two ropes towards the cableway anchor pulley.

2. The stretcher is attached to the cableway using two wide pulleys and the two respective stretcher haul ropes are attached to either end of the stretcher. (The line which was used for pulling the ropes across the river can now be utilised for taking the end of the haul rope back across to the stretcher). A rescuer is belayed to the stretcher/pulley rig in a comfortable position to accompany the stretcher.

3. With rescuers belaying the stretcher ropes on each side of the river, the cableway is tensioned and the stretcher pulled to the casualty, aided by gravity. NB. Only two rescuers are shown tensioning the cableway for clarity.

4. Upon travelling the requisite distance to the boulder/islet, the stretcher and rescuer can be lowered. In the likely event that no belays are available on a direct line across the islet, the stretcher can be manoeuvered into position by tensioning the stretcher haul ropes either up or downstream as required.

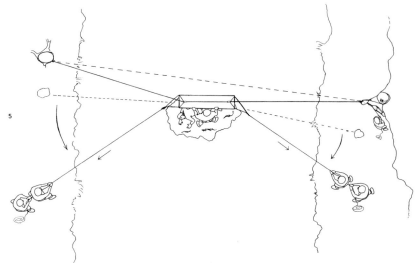

5

should be emphasised that care must be taken in crossing swollen rivers, especially with heavy rescue equipment, and if there is any danger a simple cableway should be established and the equipment ferried across on this. In some situations, such as on large rivers in remote regions, the stretcher may have to be floated across a river on a makeshift raft with belay ropes anchored both sides. River crossing can be particularly dangerous at night, when it is often difficult to keep one's balance, and those crossing should have extra illumination from the belay party on the bank when possible. The use of a rope by someone crossing a swollen river can be highly dangerous you can be dragged under by a taut, anchored rope. The use of a prop against the current in the form of a companion or a pole can be of great assistance.

Whitewater

Though rescue in whitewater is a specialised subject, a mountain rescue team may become involved in assisting in such an operation and in certain parts of the world river crossing is part and parcel of SAR. In New Zealand for example,

5. This is a plan view of the final part of the operation where the casualty can be evacuated to either bank, once the cableway is re-tensioned.

Opposite: GCES rescue Hance Rapids

Above: The stretcher and paramedic cross to rock islet on the double rope cableway (B McDermott)

Left: With the rescuers on the rock with the casualty, the stretcher is lowered for the evacuation – see sequence of drawings (B McDermott)

Opposite : Water recovery operation at base of waterfall in narrow canyon. The rescuer is lowered from the cableway (Kootenay Highline System). Note dry suit, flotation, white water helmet, knife etc. on rescuer (Arnor Larson)

there are a considerable number of drownings each year due to river crossing.

Several of the techniques for cliff rescue are applicable to river work (see illustrations pp.130–137).

The helicopter is the best tool for river SAR and auto-hover capability is an advantage for searching pools. The best time to do this is around noon, when there are fewer shadows. Also, polaroid glasses are of assistance. At an accident scene. where the helicopter cannot gain access to the victim, it can be used for ferrying rescuers to the far bank and if required 'tow' over cableway ropes. Protracted search can be assisted using a sub-aqua infra-red video camera, with a monitor on the bank or rescue craft. Some SAR dogs are trained for underwater search.

Whitewater search is much akin to avalanche search and grid pattern searches are used. There is also a system using a 15 m cord on a reel which has a weight and swivel on the end. This is placed in the centre of the search grid and the divers swim in a circle holding it. The line is increased in length for further sweeps. This system can have its centre in a boat and the occupants can increase the cord length when advised by a tug on the line by the diver/s. A similar technique can also be used with the weight on the bank and successive sweeps are then 180 degrees. Marker buoys can indicate water searched. Poles or pikes are used like avalanche poles, but by having a hook on the end, bodies can be retreived. A simple instrument can be made by lashing a dropped-pick ice axe to a length of lancewood or suitable sapling.

Definitions of river features are useful for whitewater SAR:

Rapids are a section of rough, turbulent water and are formed by river gradient, type and number of obstacles, width of channel, flow rate and volume.

Tongues, are waves created by water flowing over underwater rocks and they form smooth V-shaped waves, usually at the start of rapids.

Haystacks, or *Standing waves* are generated by water flowing over fixed obstructions and usually indicate the deepest and fastest pitches.

Reversals, Holes, Hydraulics are names given to one of the most dangerous features, formed by water moving over a submerged object such as a rock. The water curls up and back on itself. Large 'holes', which are generally behind steep rocks, can hold a body or even a boat in suspension. They can usually be identified by flotsam circling in one spot. Such 'holes' are common beneath waterfalls or where water falls the fastest over a barrier. Often they are too dangerous to search.

Strainer. This is an object such as a tree that combs the water and can arrest a victim.

Eddies are sections of calm water, usually moving in a circular motion and found downstream of obstructions.

Entrapment as the name implies the pinning of the victim in the water.

It is worth bearing in mind in whitewater rescue, as with avalanche search, that time is of the essence. For example, a victim immersed in water of 4.5°C becomes unconscious in 30 minutes!

Polypropylene (floating) ropes are useful for river rescue, and loud-hailers are often more effective than walkie-talkies. Stretchers or litters should have positive buoyancy as well as PFD's (positive buoyancy devices) for the rescuers. Line guns are useful for establishing cableways, or for establishing belays on each bank.

Bridges downstream are excellent lookout points for victims and a rough estimation of the possible distance travelled by the victim/s can be calculated by working out the flow rate of the water using a twig over a given distance and multiplying this by the time elapsed since the accident.

The search

The search can be one of the most frustrating aspects of rescue work and in some areas is a major recurring problem. Where such call-outs take place on a regular basis it will be possible for a rescue organiser to establish a mode of action pertinent to the region. It is not practicable here to lay down definite rules for search work as the factors to be considered differ widely from area to area. The search technique for missing persons in deserts or flatlands is different from that for high mountain country. There are obviously many variables in terrain and hazards, but the actual organisation of a search operation still has much in common for all regions.

Rescue controller or organiser

This should be someone who knows the search area or has wide experience of the type of terrain and of search and rescue work. It is essential that he or she can control possibly large groups of rescuers in what may be both difficult and dangerous country and be able to deploy them to the best advantage. It is also vital that the rescue controller has a good liaison with associate groups, who may be requested to assist. The rescue controller should not necessarily be the highest ranking military officer, sheriff, policeman, etc., unless he is also suitably qualified as indicated above. During a search the rescue controller should stay at Base Control and elect a deputy who can take over in the event of a prolonged operation.

Common sense and the optimum deployment of personnel and equipment are the prime tools of the rescue organiser.

Relevant points

Lost? First try to establish if the person is indeed missing and has not 'gone somewhere else'. Many searches have been mounted when the 'victim' has, for instance, returned home, without informing anyone.
Weather. Is important, as a large percentage of those lost and subsequently found, suffer from exposure. Obviously in severe weather a missing, ill-equipped party could be in dire danger if not located quickly.
Age, experience and ailments. These give pointers to the possible action of the missing person/s as does physical condition.
Equipment and food. If the missing party is well equipped with bivouac gear, adequate clothing, map, compass, food, water (in hot climates), etc., it will obviously influence the triggering of a search operation and more time could probably be allowed for them to turn up.
Terrain. The type of country dictates the mode of search.

The missing person/s

If the base of the missing person/s can be located – tent, hut, vehicle, etc. – some clues may be found as to how the party is equipped and possibly a note giving the planned route. In many countries car ownership can be established in minutes through police computers and, if necessary, relations and friends can be contacted. If the companions of a missing person are available they should be closely questioned by the rescue controller or someone familiar with the area. Aerial photographs can often help, and flying survivors by helicopter over the area will often refresh their memory if they are hazy as to their movements subsequent to losing their colleague/s. Obtain and

A large scale search:

1 Rescue control, with road, telephone and RT communications to all parties and helicopters. Reserve personnel should be kept here for immediate emergency use. They can be transported rapidly by helicopter.
1a Rescue control sub-units, under the direction of rescue control. This is often only possible by telephone/radio links or by links from aircraft in high mountain regions. Often such units are on the other side of a mountain range.

2 Link station. This can be either a permanent station or a portable one. Aircraft can be used in emergency.

3 Main search groups carrying out a fine search. These groups should have as many walkie-talkies as possible and they should be distributed in such a way as to give messages to all members when need be.

d Search and rescue dogs being used for rapid search of most likely areas.

da Avalanche dog/search and rescue dog searching avalanche.

p Avalanche probing party.

s Ski parties making rapid search over remote areas.

When weather conditions permit, the helicopter can be used for transporting equipment and personnel to various locations and to help in search work. The noise from helicopters does not put dogs off work (R Turner)

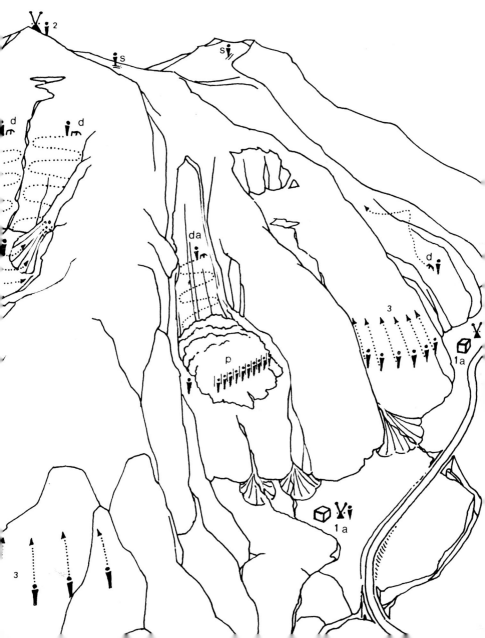

document from the missing person's friends all pertinent information such as colour of anorak, pullover and shirt. The date when a woman went missing can sometimes be established, if there is no more direct evidence, by a check at base, vehicle, tent, etc., for dated contraceptive pills. An appeal to the public too can often elicit results in respect to missing persons. It can be useful to tape-record all information from survivors and indeed subsequent progress.

Weather

The rescue controller should obtain up-to-date weather reports to enable him to plan the operation. Climatic and ground conditions will dictate how a search will be conducted. Storms, high winds, heavy snowfalls, blizzards, excessive heat are all factors influencing a given search. A lost skier may travel miles, and the parameters of a search for cross-country skiers must obviously be extended to take their degree of mobility into account. The wind has a decisive influence on lost and exhausted persons, as has slope inclination. A party caught in heavy snowfall without snowshoes or skis will be restricted in their movements, as may also a party lost after a strenuous day. People caught in winter blizzards often dig snowholes. Once inside these, they may not hear the calls of rescuers. The author knows of one case where the rescuers actually fell through the roof of a snowhole on top of a sleeping 'lost' person!

Experience and age

Experience is an important point to consider. Obviously an experienced bushman or mountaineer is less likely to get lost than a novice, therefore due deliberation must be given to the possibility of his having sustained injury.

The behaviour pattern of children lost in a wilderness situation is similar to that of adults, but they usually suffer less from stress.

Medical history, if available, may also give some useful indications to a person's physical capabilities, e.g. he/she may suffer from a weak ankle, coronary trouble, diabetes, etc. This could have a direct bearing on their possible distance of travel. It should be remembered, however, that an exposed person can behave irrationally, for instance, he/she may discard essential clothing and throw away items of equipment. As suggested, it is always better to try to establish the colour of people's undergarments, shirts, etc., with such behaviour in mind. People lost in desert regions can also behave irrationally as they sometimes suffer from heat exhaustion and dehydration.

Equipment and food

Both are vital to the lost person. If a mountaineer has adequate bivouac equipment he can endure a prolonged storm, provided his clothing is dry and he has enough food to give the necessary calories to produce heat. It is sometimes possible to assess the amount of food and equipment the lost person has with him from a colleague and by checking the remaining food and equipment left at base. As mentioned, the colour of items of clothing is very important, and the actual clothes the missing person could be wearing may be deduced from the prevailing conditions: e.g. anorak and overtrousers in bad weather, shirt and perhaps shorts in warm weather.

Terrain

The type of country greatly influences the method of search. Natural features such as watersheds, escarpments, rivers, etc., provide good search boundaries and should be incorporated in preliminary perimeter checks when planning search procedure.

Forest presents one of the more frustrating search areas, though a helicopter equipped with a thermal imager may possibly locate people and objects through foliage – especially crashed aircraft. A precipitous ridge can pose search problems, as there may be hazards, gullies, etc., perhaps on both sides, where an injured person could remain hidden.

There may be a concentrated search within the general search area; for example, a fresh avalanche in which the missing party could be trapped. This could also apply to rockfalls, collapsed seracs and flash floods, which might even have carried the victim out of the designated search area.

Desert search can pose unusual problems, for in some of the great deserts survivors of, say, a plane crash may travel at night to avoid excessive heat, though they should in fact stay at the site of the accident. During the day visibility can be so bad as to invalidate normal forms of signalling (signal mirrors, etc.) Cold, too, can be severe at night in some desert countries and mirages can both exhaust the survivors, who travel towards the imaginary safety of an oasis, etc., and frustrate rescue parties.

Desert survivors may dig holes in the sand in which to sleep and keep cool during the day. Also the walls of wadis and creeks often have caves in which survivors may take shelter. Knowing how to make a simple solar still can save life.

Psychological aspects

All known evidence should be considered, and from it the possible action of the missing person is deduced: (a) consider the known evidence and (b) deduce the probable action of the missing person/s.

Though largely hypothetical, the psychological aspects of a search are of great value to the rescue controller. Unless the missing person/s are affected by hypothermia or shock, there is often a degree of logic in their actions. For example, they will usually go with the wind and downhill, unless they know that safety is relatively close to hand to windward or upwards; or they may

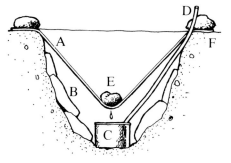

A solar still

A *Plastic sheet*

B *Cactus slices*

C *Water collector*

D *Plastic tube*

E *Rock*

F *Ground surface*

The diagram shows the side elevation of a solar still. It should be a little over 1 m in diameter and ½ m deep. The plastic sheet should be of the 'wettable' type so that water will cling to it and run down to the bottom and drip into the container (which should be large enough to collect all the drips). Sunshine heats the area beneath the plastic, vaporising the moisture in the soil and plant material. When the air beneath the plastic becomes saturated, water vapour condenses and runs down the plastic and drips into the container.

It takes about one hour for the still to function. It will then continue to operate throughout daylight hours and into early evening. Dampish soil will yield approx. 2 l of water a day. Polluted/saline/brackish water can be made palatable by pouring into the soil of the still. A plastic tube can be used for extracting the water. In very dry soil or sand, cactus slices or other vegetation should be used to line the still and obtain the above amount of water.

bivouac. Usually, too, channels of least resistance are taken, e.g. firebreaks, watercourses, paths, game trails, etc. It pays to check these and natural boundaries/hazards first.

The pattern of weather, as mentioned, can also play its part, as a change can create an alteration in the plans of the missing person. The rescue organiser must consider this from a study of the weather at the time the party went missing. What would he expect them to do in the circumstances, allowing for the other factors previously mentioned?

To give an example of psychological detection, I will recount a case where we found a car parked in a well-known climbing area. No one had been seen at the vehicle for two days and there was no tent nearby. Enquiries through police established that the occupants were two climbers on holiday, but nothing was known of their plans. From the equipment left in the car we came to the conclusion that they were highly competent rock climbers, with well worn, yet sound equipment. From the gear they left it appeared that they had possibly gone off to do a climb, but not a serious one, as one rope and considerable hardware remained, but no guide book was to be found. We then established that on the day that the car was left at this spot the weather was blustery with a south-west wind and light rain, which in this particular area makes the rock greasy. For climbers of the 'apparent' experience of the two missing men, a hard route would probably have been avoided, yet an easier one, perhaps close to the road and sheltered from the south-west, could have been attractive to them.

It was resolved to make a preliminary check of the easier routes which fell into this category. In other words, we proposed to conduct an investigation of highly probable hazards. We found the two men, both dead, at the base of the first route we checked. This is only one case in dozens where psychology and logical thinking

have played an important role. The same technique can be applied to other searches where there is a lack of positive information.

Search pattern

From this chapter it will be obvious to the reader that the search should be 'tailor made' for a given area. Rain forests are easier to search than dense bush country, but man-made forest and jungle remain the most difficult of search problems, especially in remote regions. The indigenous people of the area can be of great value in such a search as they are acquainted with trails, local hazards, swamps, etc. Often a systematic block search has to be instigated in the event of no response to perimeter or hazard checks. Periodic calls to the lost person should be made, and what these should be must be agreed upon at the start of the search to avoid confusion between search groups. Loud hailers can be used from the air or on the ground where it may just be possible to impart some useful information to the lost person. For example, if the ground is sloping with a river at the bottom one could tell the lost person to head downhill to the river and try to reach some open point where he could be spotted, or tell him to follow a valley down/up hill, or in the direction the helicopter/plane is flying to where there are clearings. With ingenuity there is usually some way of imparting useful information and instructions.

One does not always know where a lost person was last seen, but if this information is available it can be of value to the rescue organiser.

Search and rescue dogs/Avalanche dogs

The use of dogs for search work cannot be too strongly stressed. In various countries dogs are used for both summer and winter search work. In other countries they are used purely for avalanche work. They should be permitted to search an area

Right: The traverse sweep search. This is a useful means of searching when more than one side of a mountain has to be covered. The search party should be formed as in this illustration, as this will prevent any stone fall from a searcher above injuring a man below. If the search party starts by making a rough search uphill in a likely area, with members dropping off to their required level at intervals, further ground will be covered. Again natural traverse lines should be taken and the bottom of cliffs and likely areas given particular attention. An observer in radio contact, at a suitable vantage point on the face of an adjoining mountain, or at the base of the mountain, with binoculars, can keep in contact with the sweep and advise on the positioning of the searchers (D Craig)

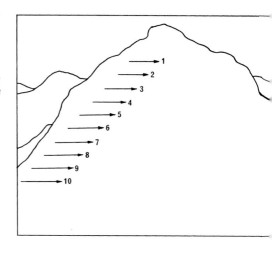

Below: A sweep search conducted uphill. Often the sweep has to be broken up into natural boundaries such as buttresses, and gullies and regions where a person could possibly have fallen, or got into trouble, should be gone over with extra thoroughness. The ground above schrunds and waterfalls which fall behind and under the snow cover should be searched for tell-tale signs of a fallen climber. In cases of people missing in storms, the lee side of boulders and any natural shelter should be carefully examined (D Craig)

Below: An overlapping sweep search. This is used for a concentrated search of a likely area. The area searched should be carefully marked. Should the victim not be found with this method, a further overlapping sweep can be conducted at right angles. Spacing will depend on the number of searchers available (D Craig)

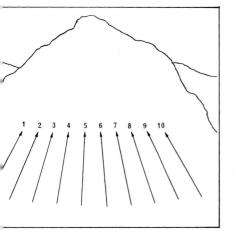

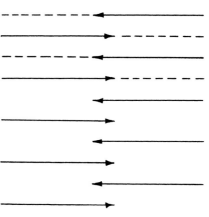

Signals for fixed-wing aircraft

Need medical assistance   *Our receiver is operating*   *Use drop message*

Affirmative (Yes)   *Negative (No)*   *All OK – do not wait*

quickly, or at least move in ahead of the main search group/s before the scent is confused. Remember that dogs work equally well at night, when normal search parties are handicapped. Night-vision equipment should also be considered for the search if it is mounted in the hours of darkness.

Tracking

Experienced trackers can be of great assistance in locating missing people. Even the inexperienced rescuer should keep a constant look-out for prints, especially in muddy areas or on snow, e.g. river banks can often give good clues at places of crossing. Log-jams, too, often offer a good means of crossing rivers and prints should be looked for in the vicinity, as well as in mud round water holes.

Knowledge of the size of the missing person's feet and footwear can be of value where snow cover, or areas which may hold prints, are being searched.

Signal fires/Mirror signals

Rescuers searching bush scrub country should be on the constant look-out for

such signals by the missing party. In some circumstances fires can be used by the search party for signalling, though these are not usually very successful, except for the most simple signal.

Binoculars

Binoculars are not used widely enough for rescue work. Their proper use can save many hours of tedious work. By selecting carefully a prominent point from where a search area can be observed, a systematic search can be conducted from different angles so that any 'blind' ground is covered. People used to looking for game, etc. – shepherds, rangers, hunters – should be employed for this task as their eyes are 'tuned' to this type of search. Many of these individuals have their own favourite vision aid such as a telescope, but 7×50 binoculars with coated lenses make the ideal search instrument.

Binoculars fitted with a reticule scale, which provide direct measurement of objects provided their distance is known, can be of particular use when you want to pinpoint an object to someone alongside with similar binoculars. They can also be used for estimating the scale of an

Do not attempt to land here

Land here

Can proceed shortly – wait if practicable

Need mechanical help or parts

Pick us up – plane abandoned

avalanche, etc., when used with an accurate map. There are surplus military binoculars with built-in reticules graduated in mils. An artillery mil is 1/6400 of a circle. An infantry mil is the angle subtended by 1 m at 1000 m distance. 100 artillery mils equal 98·2 infantry mils. Reticules can be of either kind.

A careful and systematic study of the area must be undertaken and, as mentioned, gone over again from other vantage points.

Binoculars with big objective lenses such as the 7 × 50 are also excellent for night vision and can enable reasonably good appraisal of search areas on a starry night.

In certain circumstances large tripod-mounted telescopes can be of advantage for searching and for communicating to rescue teams the best means of access to accident scenes.

Binoculars with large objective lenses should be chosen for rescue search work, despite their extra bulk. The numbers stamped on binoculars, e.g. 7 × 50, mean that the instrument has a magnification of ×7 and an objective lens of 50 mm. A large objective lens gathers more light and is therefore better for searching in poor

lighting conditions. On the other hand, don't buy binoculars with powerful magnifications unless you intend to use them on a tripod. A numerical rating has been evolved for these larger binoculars called the 'twilight performance'. This is calculated by multiplying the objective lens by the magnification and taking the square root of the product: 6 × 30 = 180; √180 = 13·4.

When should a large-scale search be started?

This of course varies in different circumstances and in different parts of the world. For example, a competent party of three or four can be missing in the bush or in remote mountainous regions for a considerable time without causing concern. A party of two presents a greater problem, for disaster could, in fact, easily affect them both.

In a party of four there is not such a great chance that all the group will be involved in a mishap and usually at least one can return for assistance.

In some particularly popular regions a full-scale search can be mounted within 12 hours of a party failing to return, and before this time several small search parties may have been out. Not only does it depend on the terrain and the weather conditions, but also on the 'known record' of the party. Each individual case must be judged on the evidence available.

In more compact mountainous regions the problem can be even more difficult, from the point of view of analysis of 'evidence', than in a remote area, where parties are less likely to change their objective and are usually better equipped.

Helicopters

The helicopter is an essential search 'tool' and should be deployed as soon as possible on any search operation. Not only can it check hazards with the minimum of delay, but by transporting searchers to a high point, where they can then work downhill, valuable time can be saved. The effectiveness of a downhill search operation when helicopter transport is available cannot be overemphasised. See chapter on Helicopters.

Large scale search

When the most likely zones have been searched to no avail, the search must be spread over a wider area and likely places gone over again. It is too easy to observe in the case of one missing person that he must have 'done a bunk'. In most cases of missing solo climbers and walkers they are dead or injured, and the morale of the search party should not be allowed to wane by the suggestion that 'he wanted to disappear'. This has happened in countless cases of missing solo walkers or climbers and needless to say it is a dangerous and irresponsible attitude.

The staging and operation of a large-scale search is like a military manoeuvre. Orders to the various search groups must be clear and concise. Communications should be as good as possible in the circumstances and the leaders in the field must be highly competent, preferably with local knowledge, or at least one member in each search group should have local knowledge.

Sweep search

It is usually better for the search party to move forward in line and they should be spaced not more than 45 m apart except on the easiest ground, e.g. moorland with few peat hags or boulders which could afford shelter to the missing persons. The more experienced personnel should be at each end and at the centre.

Fine search

In the case of an extensive search of a likely area, parties can start from opposite ends of the search area so that they pass between the members of the opposite search party near the middle of the search area. If this is to no avail, then another double fine search should be conducted at right angles to the previous one.

The spacing of the parties will depend on the ground to be searched and the number of people available.

Concentration

A search often transpires into a pleasant outing, with rescuers chatting together, when they should be giving their full attention to searching. The group leader must stress to his party the importance of keeping properly spaced and devoting full attention to the search. It is very easy to pass a body, or an unconscious person, lying among boulders, or even on open ground, unless they are wearing bright clothing. With a fresh fall of snow it is even more difficult finding a dead or unconscious person.

Communications

It is desirable for all search personnel to have their own walkie-talkies. If this isn't possible, those without should be flanked with those so equipped. Many of the modern walkie-talkies are VHF and rely mainly on line-of-sight communication. It is possible, however, to 'bounce' the signal off rock faces, etc., and surprising results can often be obtained from isolated corries and hanging valleys. If you are unable to establish contact try various places nearby, or if you are moving keep trying to make contact. If reception is weak the signal can sometimes be improved by rotating slowly, with the aerial kept horizontal, until the best position is found.

Always carry spare radio batteries in an inside pocket and see that they are either new or fully charged and dry.

Search briefing

This can be a very important part of search procedure and great care should be taken in allocating suitable search areas to personnel particularly qualified for specific tasks, e.g. experienced mountaineers to search difficult faces, etc., and local men in areas they know best.

The rescue controller should always be available for suggestions from other experienced rescue team members and from men with local knowledge. It is on such information, together with the information available about the missing persons, that he should base his plan of action, and even this should be flexible in case of further information and/or clues regarding the possible location of the missing persons.

Liaison with group leaders in adjoining areas who are taking part in the search is important to ensure that communications are adequate and that search work is not duplicated. Often such group leaders in other valleys cannot attend the briefing and full details must be relayed to them from rescue control.

In the case of protracted searches in high mountain or outback country, where search groups may have to camp out, three or four is usually a good self-contained group as they can all use one tent and the party is large enough to deal with mishaps within their own party.

The rescue controller should advise on the type of search to be conducted, where dogs will be used and which outlying rescue groups should have vehicle or helicopter transport to their areas of operation.

The rescue controller should ask each group leader for the individual names of his group and their call sign, and ensure that the group leader has checked that his party is properly equipped.

Further briefings/de-briefings must be held until the search is completed, and the rescue controller must have previously alerted other sources of manpower, rescue teams, etc., to assist.

As many of the rescue/search party as possible should attend the briefing, provided discipline can be maintained. All questions should be kept to the end of the briefing.

For outlying search areas the rescue controller will obtain either RT communication from the various groups or word by telephone or, as a last resort, by skier/runner. The various group leaders should have clearly marked the area searched, either on their maps or, in the event of a finer search, by markers, cairns, etc. In the case of a large search area, it is unlikely that the less important terrain will be searched again, so the exact coverage of search is very important and should be recorded.

A large-scale map should be used for the briefing, with the various search areas clearly marked, so that the group leader can study and copy on to his own map the areas he has to cover. Even better, prepared briefing maps can be issued to team leaders by control. On such maps can be delineated the search areas (photo-copying is an excellent method to communicate this). Also a system of wall-mapping with facilities for marking or sticking on movement indicators etc. for illustrating the search operation is useful.

Only after the most thorough search of the whole area should the search be abandoned. There have been innumerable cases of people surviving incredible hardships and injuries for long periods in severe weather conditions.

There have also been many instances of parties avalanched or lost in the winter months and being subsequently covered in snow. It is sometimes to everyone's advantage, when all possibilities have been exhausted, to call off the search until a thaw and, in the case of higher mountains, until spring, for the recovery of bodies. Rescue dogs have been instrumental in locating bodies after a period of thaw, when previously the bodies had been encased in ice, offering no scent.

In some parts of the world, in busy mountain rescue areas, permanent RT repeaters are established. These are often remotely controlled. Radio links (see section on Radio links) either at fixed points of known good reception or from aircraft must be taken into account by the rescue controller, especially in the case of a large-scale search, for it is imperative that radio communication is maintained whenever possible.

A mobile or public service telephone should be to hand. Mobile 'phones are used regularly by hill walkers and climbers in emergency, and helicopters or rescue teams can be directed to casualties or cragfast climbers. In remote regions it may be necessary for the rescue hill party, or helicopter, to relay by radio to a point where a telephone is available to enable the emergency telephone message to be received. In this way it is often possible to 'home in' on the injured party. Team reinforcements should be advised to stand-by in case of the need for ambulances, as this can help their organisations to plan accordingly.

RT equipment should be allocated so that all parties and individuals can be recalled if need be. Both a recall time and a recall signal (flares, sirens, maroons) should be understood by all.

Search groups should be told to make maximum use of the daylight hours, and whenever possible each group should carry its own first-aid equipment, glucose, spare clothing, etc., for the use of anyone located; this is in addition to their normal team equipment.

Stretchers, casualty bags, extra equipment, etc., should be kept at key points, where they can be transported in the speediest way possible to the accident scene. Enough personnel stationed with this equipment should be available for its rapid deployment.

Computers Computers have a role in SAR and can be invaluable for correlating information. They can also be used for logging data for later use and for producing a 'SAR Information Sheet' for personnel. Some teams use them for search logistics.

Contingency arrangements It is advisable for all agencies involved in MR for a given area to pre-plan operations and define the areas of responsibility.

Manpower The rescue controller should not necessarily be influenced by any restriction on manpower by authorities; after all, life may be at stake.

De-briefing on large-scale search

If search groups return to rescue control each day, in the case of a protracted search, it is essential that group leaders at least attend a de-briefing. Usually the rescue controller gets reports over the RT from the various group leaders throughout the day and when they are returning to base, so he will have a detailed picture of the progress of the search.

Psychic help

Mediums, clairvoyants and diviners have been called from time to time to assist in difficult searches, where other, more conventional means have failed. Though interesting, and sometimes positive, results have been obtained, such 'aids' should not be relied upon.

The author conducting a search for a missing climber, Everest Icefall (D Scott)

*Using a flat-bottomed rescue sledge for
ski-avalanche evacuation in Czechoslovakia
(Horska Sluzba)*

Ski rescue

Opposite page, top: Evacuating an injured skier using an improvised ski stretcher. The skier in front has ski sticks attached flexibly to the front of the stretcher and the other two skiers help to hold the stretcher with lengths of line attached to rear of stretcher (L Gramminger)

Opposite page, middle: Using an Akja stretcher for ski injury patient (L Gramminger)

Opposite page, bottom: Evacuating an injured skier at speed using an Akja stretcher (L Gramminger)

Left: An emergency stretcher made with a ski-coupler. The injured man's ski sticks act as a brace for keeping him upright and the two sticks at the front are for the skier who guides the stretcher (L Gramminger)

277

Below: Transporting an Akja stretcher to the scene of an accident. The stretcher is usually carried in two sections (G Hunter)

Right: This stretcher is similar to that illustrated on page 280. However, in this arrangement a further pair of skis are used, to which the poles are lashed for handles. The tops of the patient's skis are tied to the stretcher bearer's skis about the half-way point. The temporary stretcher runs on the rear ends of the four skis, thereby taking some of the weight off the stretcher bearer and affording him more freedom of movement. If further help is at hand, two ropes can be used at the rear (Austrian Alpine Club)

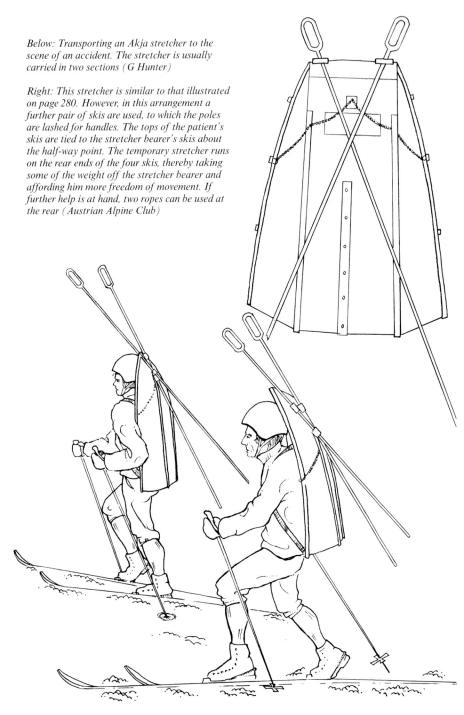

Right: Evacuating an avalanche victim on a helper sledge in Norway. The brackets etc., for adapting the injured person's skis are very light and the ski sticks are also used for the sides of this temporary stretcher. A slight modification of this design is used for dog sledging work and for packing in rescue equipment, supplies etc. The container bag for the sledge modification can be used as a sail for use on open snowfields, or as a wind shelter in an emergency (Norwegian Red Cross)

Below: The Akja stretcher. The top illustration shows it fitted with a transport wheel. The lower illustration shows it fitted with the traction bridge for leg injuries. This stretcher is used mainly for ski rescue work and two skiers can easily move downhill with a casualty aboard with reasonable speed. Various types of handles are available and the stretcher comes to pieces for easy transport. The weight is approx. 12–15 kg. The Akja can travel over the snow equally well in either direction as the hull shape is similar both ends. The chain is used for braking on descent (K Spence)

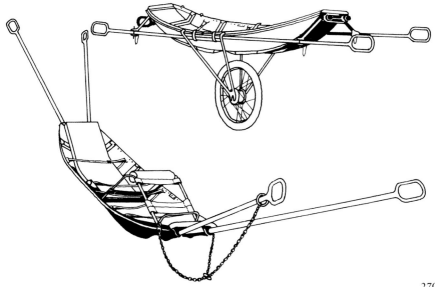

A simple emergency stretcher made up from the injured person's skis, with the poles lashed (baskets upwards) for handles to the skis. Two simple spacer clamps are used and an avalanche cord lashed across the skis as the stretcher bed (Austrian Alpine Club)

Below: Changing direction on a new traverse line using the Akja stretcher (G Hunter)

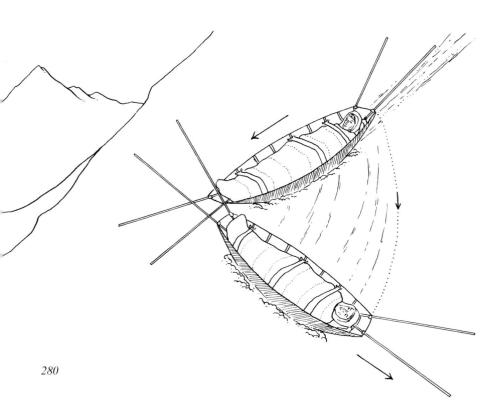

Synthetic fibre ropes

Nylon, polyester and nylon-sheathed Kevlar are the ropes mainly used in mountain rescue. The ropes are either 'dynamic', capable of stretching to absorb energy, or 'static' non-stretch ropes favoured by most MR teams. 'Perlon' is a European trade name for a Type 6 nylon dynamic climbing rope.

Rescue ropes vary in length from 60 m to 300 m and common diameters are from 11 mm to 16 mm. Polyester ropes have an anti-abrasion advantage over nylon ropes; neither are much effected by water absorption.

Kernmantle constructed rope is commonly used in MR work today. It has a core, the kern, and a sheath, the mantle. The core comprises of parallel fibres and the sheath holds this together. The primary load bearing is taken by the core. This type of rope construction has an advantage over the three strand laid rope in abrasion resistance and it doesn't twist and tangle so readily.

Block Creel construction refers to the continuous filament construction of the rope – without splices – a more expensive method of rope construction. Teams should check the rope's performance and strength information supplied by the manufacturer. There is a further simple check, not normally used. Check the weights of comparable diameter ropes. As nylon fibres are usually fairly similar strength-wise, a stronger rope requires more fibre.

The recommended working load for braided rope is 15–20 per cent of the tensile strength of new rope. Percentages vary with the diameter and type of rope.

Comparative sunlight and weather resistance of commercial ropes
(Data obtained from specimens of 12 mm diameter ropes exposed outdoors in Florida)
(D Craig)

© *Du Pont de Nemours & Co Inc., Wilmington, Delaware, USA*

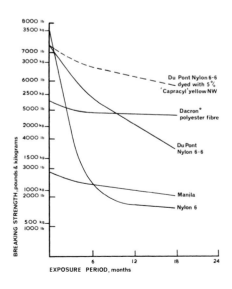

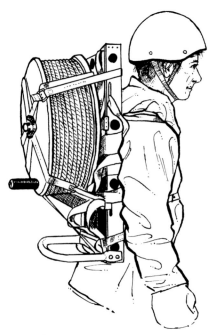

The static strengths of knots and splices where 1 indicates the knots used for joining two ropes, and 2 knots used for attachment. The figures give a percentage of the ultimate breaking load of the rope

1 Joining Ropes	%
Standard short splice	80–90
Fisherman's knot (double or single)	60–65
Sheet bend	60
Reef	55–60

Thus, a rope rated at 10 kN could fail at 5·5 kN because of the knots used.

2 Attachment	
Eye splice	85–95
Tarbuck	80–90
Bowline	70–75
Alpine butterfly	70
Figure of eight	70

282

Knots in common use in rescue work

A *(1 & 2) Tarbuck knot, useful for an adjustable belay loop*
B *Double fisherman's knot. This is used for joining two ropes of equal thickness*
C *Reef knot. Used for joining ropes of equal thickness*
D *Sheet bend. For joining two ropes of unequal thickness*
E *(1 & 2) The bowline knot. For a waist tie or end loop. Always secure the tail end of the rope with a half hitch or overhand knot*
F *(1 & 2) Bowline-on-a-bite. This is used as a middleman loop or for securing a double rope round a belay etc*
G *Fisherman's bend. This knot can be used for tying off onto a thicker rope or for tying a rope end to a stretcher*
H *Clove hitch. Used for attaching a rope to a horizontal axe belay; also as a secondary security knot for stretcher attachment etc.*
I *(1, 2 & 3) Prusik knot. A rope of smaller diameter than the main rope must be used for this knot. It is used as a sliding-locking knot for ascending fixed ropes etc.*
J *Alpine butterfly knot. This is a further middleman's knot*
K *Figure of eight knot. This knot is frequently used for tying off a doubled rope to a belay etc.*
L *The tape knot. This knot is in common use for tying tape slings. It is basically an overhand knot with each end running in opposite directions. As this knot tends to creep, the ends should be secured with some form of adhesive tape as stitching the ends in place can weaken the tape (K Spence)*
M *An overhand knot*

On long rope lowers it is often difficult to determine progress of the stretcher/barrow boy due to the sheer weight of the rope/s. Should the rope temporarily snag then release suddenly, the loading on rope/belay / lowering device can be excessive and dangerous. Communication between the barrow boy and belayers/intermediate observer is vital and thought should go into the provision of a dedicated helmet RT unit specifically designed for such situations.

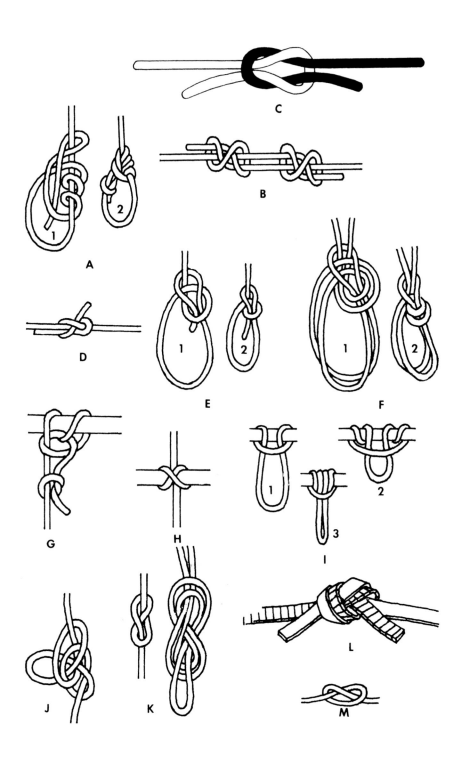

Abrasion, stone fall, crampon points all damage rope and it is important to be vigilant of these factors especially on night rescues. Also contact with acids/solvents and excessive uv can have detrimental effects. Vermin too can cause serious damage where ropes are stored in remote caches and they should be regularly inspected.

Rescue ropes should have a usage and date tag on one end, and be stored and carried in dedicated rope bags or spools. It is essential to use edge rollers or some form of abrasion protection for rescue ropes, especially when under load.

Coloured ropes are an advantage for rope management, but don't use coloured 'magic markers': some makes can damage the rope. Coloured ropes should be ordered from the manufacturers.

Kevlar 'speleo' rescue rope was developed for caving and has several advantages. A popular diameter of Kevlar rope for rescue work is the 11 mm type which is constructed with two braided nylon sheaths over a Kevlar core. This gives a very low working extension, but good energy absorption at peak loading (see graph). In the Bridon Fibres Viking Super Speleo rope, for example, the Kevlar element is designed to have a breaking strength of about 9·81 kN, whilst the nylon element has a minimum breaking strength of approx. 14·7 kN. Kevlar rope tends to be stiffer and care should be exercised when forming knots. As there is very little stretch in the fibre, try to ensure that the diameter on which it is secured, belays/pulleys, etc. is as large as possible.

Viking Super Speleo 11 mm rope. This has double nylon sheath construction over a kevlar core. It gives a good low extension, but also energy absorption at peak loading. The kevlar element has a breaking strength of approx. 10 kN (1000 kg) and the nylon sheaths a min. breaking load of 15 kN (1500 kg). Various manufacturers make rope suitable for rescue work with low extension characteristics. (Bridon Ltd)

Ultimate breaking load @ 16Kn load.
23% extension

Ultimate load on Kevlar element

Force in Kn

16
14
12
10
8
6
4
2

4   8   12 16 20 24 28 32
Percentage extension

Lowering devices

Below: SMC Rope washer. The unit connects with a normal water supply (SMC)

Bottom: Rescue ropes in storage/carrying bags. Ensure that the history of the ropes is recorded on the end tag (B McDermott)

Below right: Useful blocks for mountain rescue. On the left is a double block and on the right a single and becket. Both are fitted with an oval eye. Total weight of the two blocks is 700 g. Breaking strain 35·6 kN (3600 kg). These blocks are quite adequate for all the techniques described in the text, but larger diameter pulleys are more efficient. The blocks illustrated are fitted with swivels, which prevent rope twist when using them for winching. Rivets can be replaced with HT bolts and wing nuts to enable the sheaves to be swivelled for easy rope insertion (H MacInnes)

There are various lowering devices available for synthetic fibre rope, which are in general use for mountain rescue today. Probably the most popular over the years has been the figure of 8. This has its origins in the docklands of Britain where it was evolved by the stevedores. Now it has been superseded by such devices as the Rappel rack, Petzl 'Stop' and similar products. Many of these are illustrated in this book. For lowering using wire rope, the Austrian brake block is the most popular. Lowering, as well as hauling can also be done using winches, but not with the same degree of control.

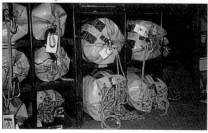

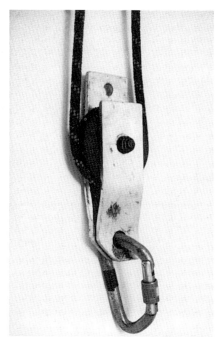

A rescue pulley using a tufnol sheave, with the aluminium alloy cheeks able to rotate on spindle for ease of use. Note upper crab hole for certain operations

Brake plate developed by Rocky Mountain Rescue Group. It can be used for lowering with single or double rope. In this photograph a second rope is being threaded. The degree of friction can be selected by the number of 'diagonal threads' used. For allowing knots to pass, a second plate can be attached using lower karabiner hole (Riverside MR, California)

Left: The start of a 200 m. lower, Turkey (B McDermott)

Right: Sometimes manpower has to be resorted to for direct hauls, South Australia Rescue (S MacLeod)

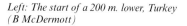

287

An ice bollard makes an excellent belay for lowering (G Hunter)

A simple self-adjusting belay where a single sling is inter-threaded through the load karabiner (centre)

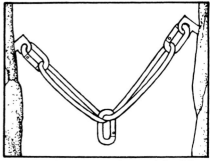

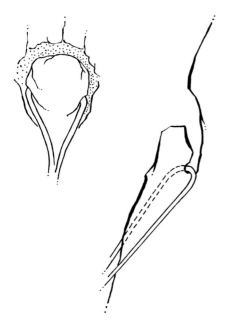

Below: A self-equalising multi-point belay. When it is impossible to get one really sound belay at a given point, several inferior belays can be used to best advantage in a rig such as that illustrated. Care should be taken however that the direction of loading is correct for each peg, chock or natural belay when used in this way. A figure of eight lowering device is shown in the right hand illustration connected to a quick link. The figure of eight is still used for rescue lowers in some areas, but they are not recommended for heavy loading, they can be doubled-up for extra friction. (K Spence)

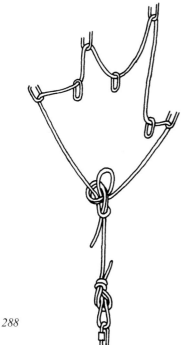

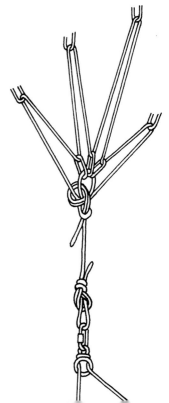

Above: A horizontal lower, Ben Nevis.
(B McDermott)

Below: Manpower haul, NE face Ben Nevis. If enough team members are available this is usually the fastest method of raising a casualty
(B McDermott)

289

The sequence of assembly of a karabiner brake control rope above

The sequence of assembly of a karabiner brake, control from below. Note, the active rope must not run over karabiner gate

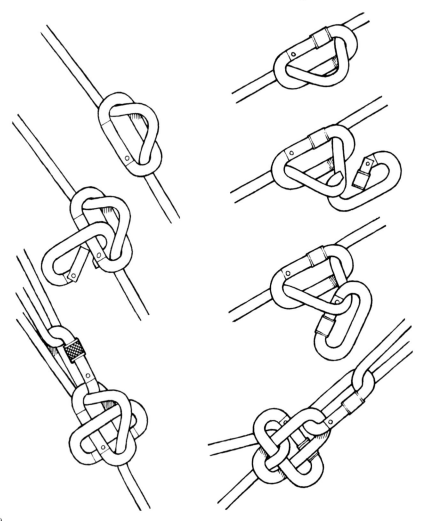

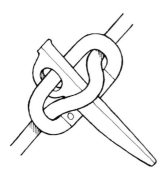

Using a rock peg as a brake bar

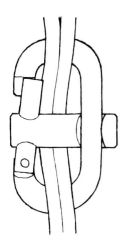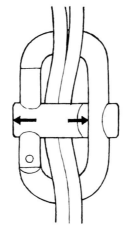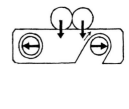

A karabiner brake bar and method of using it

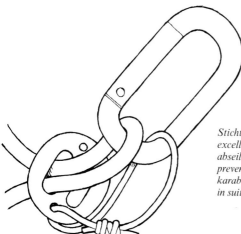

Sticht plate: This friction belaying device is excellent for safeguarding a leader, or even for abseiling. The cord (or sometimes a spring) prevents the plate from moving away from the karabiner. It is possible to make, or obtain, these in suitable sizes for MR ropes

Top drawings: Ice axe belays. The left belay illustrates use of a clove hitch to prevent the rope riding up the shaft which would increase the leverage under load. The right hand illustration shows a figure of eight tie, which is both quick and effective. For rescue work such belays are only recommended if the axe has to be hammered into the snow. Do not used wooden shafted axes for stretcher belays (R Turner)

Bottom drawings: On the left is a karabiner brake set-up for lowering. Note that the transverse karabiners have their gates on the non-active side of the rope. Also, the peg belay is doubled back to a further anchor (K Spence)

Bottom right: A simpler lowering device for snow lowers, where there is not much strain on the system. It is preferable for one belayer to hold the ice axe/peg hammer and another to control the lowering rope (E Donaldson)

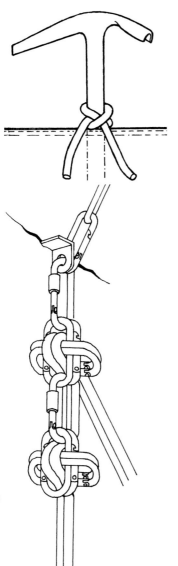

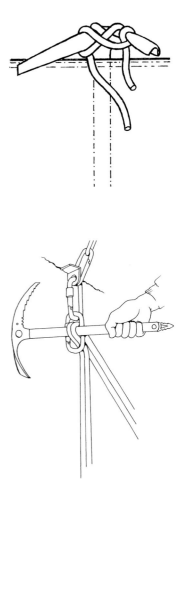

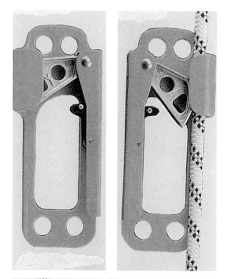

Above: A Petzl descender which has moveable bars for adjusting friction (Petzl)

Ascenders

Top right: SRT Ascenders (Sydney) are amongst the strongest manufactured and are suited for MR operations as the maximum working load is 8·8 kN (900 kg)

Centre right: SRT Ascenders. The SRT rescue stop has a max load of 7·8 kN (800 kg). It accepts two sizes of rope; 11mm – 13 mm & 16 mm – 19·3 mm

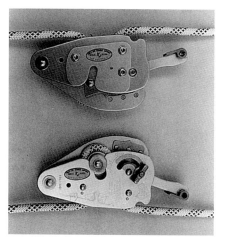

Bottom right: No worries two way stop. It accepts rope sizes 10–13 mm and the safe working load is 300 kN (300 kg). Made by SRT Sydney, Australia

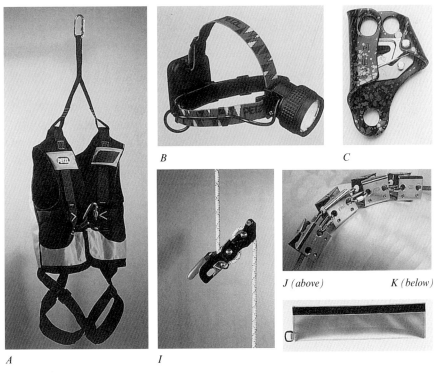

B

C

J (above)

K (below)

A

I

A   A harness suitable for lowering cragfast people. It is simple to put on.
B   A modern self-contained headlamp in common use with rescue teams. It has a quartz halogen bulb; some have dual bulbs, one for normal use, one more powerful. The beam can be zoomed. (Petzl)
C   Petzl basic ascender, BO8.
UIAA and EN Standards stipulate that ascenders must operate up to 4 kN. The figures given below are for static loads on 11 mm rope.
D   Ascension Ascender, BO7L 4 kN.
E   Ascender, BO7R 4 kN.
F   Croll Ascender, BO6, a chest-mounted ascender useful for ascending fixed rope to gain access to a difficult rescue location. 6 kN.
G   The Grigri used for belaying a lead climber or belaying a second.
H   The Shunt. This device allows one to lock onto a single rope or two identical ropes. Double 11mm rope slippage is 7·5 kN.
I   The Petzl Stop. A single rope autolock descender. If the handle is let go on descent the device will automatically brake to minimal speed.
J   One of several edge rollers available.
K   A protective rope sleeve for reducing abrasion over edges.
L   The Rescucender ascender and a compact rope swivel. (H. MacInnes)
M   Top left: the SRT fall arrester. The other three items are ascenders, all made by SRT, Sydney

294

D   E   F   G   H

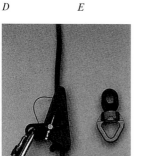

L (left)

M (above)

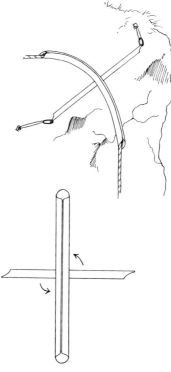

A simple, cheap edge protector, can be made from a short section of alkathene tubing of approx. 20mm ID. A channel should be cut in a straight line over its length and chamfered each end to facilitate entering the rope. An alloy bar about 50mm wide is centrally attached to the tube by a single countersunk setscrew, which acts as a pivot. This has a lug at each end with a karabiner hole for belaying. The unit folds in line for carrying in a rucksack (E Donaldson)

Above: Light-weight swivel sheaved pulley and figure of eight made by Russ Anderson, Sierra Madre, California

The AMS Systems Engineering 'Rescue Path' which has an application for rescuing people trapped on dangerous ice, swamp etc. The unit is inflated from a compressed air cylinder

Tracked vehicles

Using a tracked vehicle for transporting a rescue team to the scene of an accident, Czechoslovakia (Horska Sluzba)

Small snow runabouts

These can be very useful for easy evacuations, especially in ski areas and in wide rolling country. Properly handled they can cope with quite rough terrain, but again the patient's comfort should be considered in such situations as a 'rough ride' could have serious consequences in the case of the critically injured victim.

Four- (and more) wheel drive vehicles

Most rescue teams are equipped with some form of four-wheel drive vehicle, both for general transport work and bush/mountain access and evacuation. Their value cannot be overstressed and there are too many types available to list here. Most models are excellent for their particular job.

Tracked vehicles such as Kassbohrer snow terrain machines can be used for rescues and transport in very deep powder snow conditions

Below: In the Giant Mountains, Czechoslovakia. The small snow runabout is used for towing a flat-bottomed ski rescue stretcher (Horska Sluzba)

Right: The gnat three-wheel cross country vehicle. This machine can be used for ferrying equipment over rough ground. It is fitted with extra low pressure tyres giving a large area of contact with the ground or snow (A MacMillan)

A capstan or drum winch is a useful 'extra' on any rescue vehicle and can prove invaluable for winching the truck out of a bog or sand. It should be remembered that the spare wheel, or a log, etc. buried in the ground or sand, in a trench, will make a good 'deadman' belay.

There are also six- and eight-wheel drive 'Argocats' which offer a compact unit with considerable drive power for rough terrain.

Tracked vehicles

For traversing rough country, there is little to beat a tracked vehicle. Many of the ex-army tracked vehicles are in regular use today for rescue work all over the world, though the modern tracked transporter is better suited for SAR work.

Most of the industrial countries of the world produce suitable tracked vehicles for rescue work, but what is just as important as the type of machine is the type of country in which it will operate.

These vehicles have their limits and only well-known access routes should be chosen (and the route permanently marked when necessary), as a broken track on a remote glacier moraine can involve a more complicated 'rescue' of the vehicle than the actual 'human' operation. The captial cost of such a machine, and the means of transporting it to a given roadhead, should be carefully evaluated against other necessary rescue equipment, which may be of more use.

The advisability of transporting a critically injured person by this means should be left to the decision of a doctor, as the ride can be extremely rough. It may in fact be better to wait until the patient has recuperated before such a journey is contemplated, or to carry him by stretcher/helicopter.

Avalanches and tracked vehicles

Because one is in the 'apparent security'
of a tracked machine, the danger of
avalanches and mountainous country
should not be forgotten and the choice of
a route over potentially dangerous ground
should be carefully studied. In the event of
two or more machines being used on, say,
a dangerous glacier, they can be 'roped' up
as a precaution against large covered
crevasses. This technique is employed
successfully in Polar regions.

Winches

Winches

Winching a patient up a face can be a tedious business and should be avoided if possible. Sometimes it is necessary, however, and the best use must be made of the available equipment and manpower.

As I have mentioned elsewhere, a rescue party can haul a crag-bound climber up bodily without mechanical aids, other than grips for the wire rope, to which slings or a haulage rope should be attached. The wire rope will, of course, have to be taken through a securing device as it comes in. Very often this is the quickest way to get someone up if there are enough people available for hauling. Of course, synthetic fibre ropes can be used for this purpose and are easier to handle, but care must be taken to avoid excessive abrasion over sharp edges.

Types of winches

There are several types of winch in use for rescue work today. Each country seems to have its own ideas on the subject and indeed even different areas within a country have had several fields of development.

Capstan type

This type of winch relies upon the friction of the rope round a rotating capstan. Capstan winches are used for both wire rope and for synthetic fibre rope. When using a winch with wire rope, there is often a tendency for the wire to 'spiral' after it has been round the capstan, and this can be a definite disadvantage. Usually wire-rope winches for rescue work are of the capstan type mounted horizontally with the operating handle to one side. Normally, they are provided with a high and low speed, and some models have winding handles on each side of the winch.

Another disadvantage of this type of winch is the difficulty of finding a suitable area for setting it up, especially in snow, where some form of load-spreading (such as skis etc.) may have to be used as a base to prevent the winch frame from sinking. An area of at least 2 m × 1 m is essential.

Someone should stand behind the winch capstan to keep tension on the wire and to help feed it through. It is also better for at least one further man to ensure that the wound-in cable does not get in too much of a mess, and if possible to respool it on the carrying drums.

Synthetic fibre rope capstan winch

There are several yachting winches, mainly made from aluminium alloy, which are suitable for rescue work. These are often double-geared and fitted with a ratchet in both gears. Some types operate high-speed one direction and low-speed when the handle is contra-rotated. They can be best mounted on a rectangular frame of square section alloy (see illustration), which can be very light, and can be operated on either a horizontal plane or a vertical one.

Again, someone must stand behind (or to the side if a pulley/runner is used) to take the rope through a Prusik ratchet.

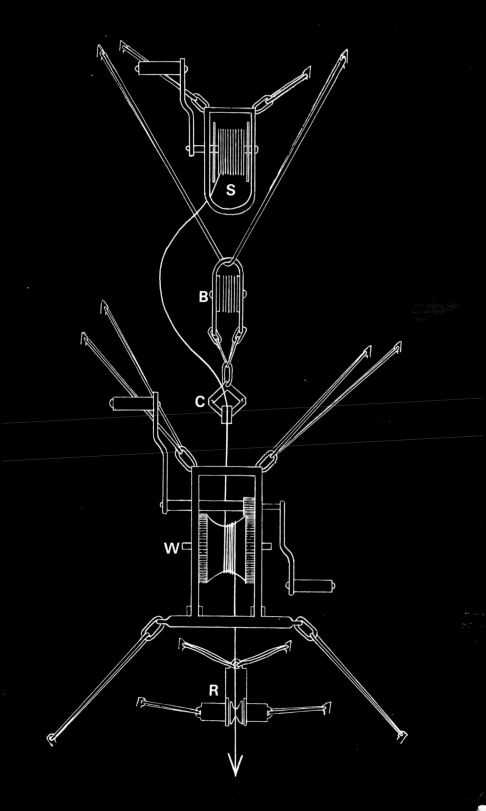

A small power winch mounted on a standard packframe. The winch is powered by a two-stroke engine driving through gears to a capstan (USA). There are many types of home-made winches. Some successful ones have been converted from chain saws (J Duff)

Bottom: A Sears T Roebuck winch converted for mountain rescue (USA). The edge tripod can be seen mounted on the packframe above the winch (J Duff)

This 'Mini winch' is available commercially in the USA. It is powered by a small two-stroke engine. The fountain pen in the foreground gives the scale (J Duff)

Bottom: An American hydraulic winch. In its present form this winch is obviously too complicated for general rescue work (J Duff)

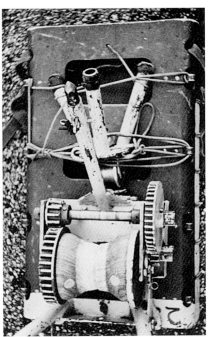

The American Prepco hoist which is mentioned in the text. With a few modifications this could possibly be a useful winch for mountain rescue work. It is shown here in its standard commercial form with short cable and hook (R Sachs)

Bottom: An American home-made winch which takes all the wire on the winch drum (J Duff)

A very lightweight lever-rachet type winch which is used in Russia. This operates on the capstan principle and the two anchor rings can clearly be seen. The three parallel rods are for locking the rope when necessary (H MacInnes)

Prepco hoist – Forza model

Though this winch has not been used much for mountain rescue work, it shows considerable promise. Like the Simpul Sport winch described, it can be attached directly on to the belay and is held in position by the tension on the haulage cable. It operates on the capstan/drum principle, but has the disadvantage of having to have the rope end threaded through a guide hole on the winch casing (though this could probably be modified). There would also be difficulty in feeding joining terminals round guides, etc. Of course, any difficulty in getting the rope joining terminals through the winch (if the winch is modified) could easily be overcome by having two or more lengths of belay slings for the winch and initially the winch slung on the shortest one. The haulage rope can be held by a rope clamp, and the winch could then be taken off the wire rope and moved below the terminal,

A winching operation for body recovery, Cape Royal, North Rim, Grand Canyon (K Phillips)

using a longer-sling, and reconnected for use.

This winch can be fitted with a disc brake and can free-wheel in both directions. It also has a built-in load protection and dual rachet pawls. The crank handle, as with some of the other winches, is either telescopic or has various points for attachment over its length, depending on the leverage required.

Simpul Sport winch

This is probably the simplest winch available as well as the lightest (next to block and tackle). It is an excellent winch for tensioning cableways and for short winch operations. It operates on a double-clamp, double-acting lever principle and it can be used with various thicknesses of wire rope as well as with synthetic fibre rope. When synthetic fibre rope is used, ensure that someone keeps the rope in tension behind the winch. Practice is required to lower successfully using this winch, and it should not be used in this mode for any great distance. Ensure that the haulage cable is further secured beyond the winch, round a brake drum or with a Russian clamp.

One of the main disadvantages of winches which are used on the tensioned haulage cable is movement of the winch when operating the handle or lever. To avoid loss of energy in this way a special frame can be made for the Simpul which allows one's feet to be kept on the frame whilst operating the lever, if used on the ground.

Block and tackle

Modern, low-friction block and tackle can provide one of the lightest, fastest and most versatile methods of cable tensioning and raising crag-bound climbers. The tackle can be used in conjunction with tandem or double-tandem Prusiks, and if two separate blocks and tackle are used, preferably from separate belays (to avoid

The Tirfor Evak 500 has its origins in the earlier Simpul-Sport hand winch. The Evak 500 has a lifting capacity of 4·9 kN (500 kg) and weighs 6 kg. The handle folds for transport and there is a shear pin to prevent overloading. The unit is designed for use only with static textile rope. Lowering is expedited by means of the integral lowering drum (Tirfor Ltd)

A lever-type capstan winch of Swiss design mounted on short skis for easier transport. Greater leverage can be obtained by increasing the length of the handle (L Gramminger)

Opposite page: One man using a block and tackle to haul up a crag-bound climber. The wire rope is being locked off on a brake block. The operator of the brake block must feed the wire rope round the brake block to safeguard the operation and to allow the man operating the block and tackle to move the wire rope clamp up for another 'bite' once he has pulled the blocks close together (G Hunter)

tangling), a rapid lifting rig can be thus formed. Whenever possible have the blocks rigged in the way shown in the illustration (pages 208–213) as this will give greater mechanical efficiency than if the block haulage rope were pulled from the belay end (i.e. if the block and tackle were rigged round the other way). Again, always have a 'back-stop' man to safeguard the rope and lock it as it comes in. The larger the diameter of the sheaves, the less frictional loss there is.

As this is probably the cheapest, lightest and most efficient way of lifting a casualty, the various techniques should be practised by the team. The blocks have various other uses, e.g. tensioning a cableway, pulleys for suspending a stretcher on a cableway, etc. Use a standard climbing rope or low-extension rope for reefing the block and tackle.

When using this system for winching, try to have one end at least of the block and tackle free of the ground as this will prevent the block and rope clamps fouling the surface.

Power-operated winches

In regions where long winching operations take place, some form of power winch is useful. Usually these are 'home-made', though the Prepco hoist can be supplied with a power attachment.

A small power capstan winch is probably the most efficient for such operations, since the ratio does not vary as it does with a drum winch (when the amount of wire on the drum increases the diameter), though a hydraulic model

Using a Poma wire rope winch on the Frendo Spur, Chamonix. The winch can be used for operations up to 300 m using 5 mm steel cable (A Charlet)

Left: Using a wire rope winch for crevasse rescue (P Moores)

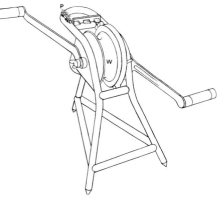

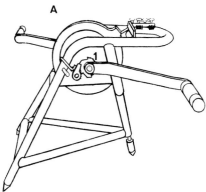

A

An Austrian hand rescue winch (see also below).
This is a double-handled winch incorporating an
internal planet gear. Several turns of the wire
rope are taken round the drum W, and for
changing cable etc., the rope can be locked at the
pins P. Rescuers can also be lowered from the
winch, using the drum W as a brake block. The
average raising speed for a casualty is in the
region of 4 m per min, with a 105 kg man as
casualty

A   The same winch as above: 1 = the rachet for
    locking the drum. The winch can be anchored
    by slings attached to the frame.
B   A wire rope swivel.
C   An Austrian brake block. This is a friction
    lowering device used for lowering with wire
    rope.
D   A wire rope coupling piece. This is used for
    joining two wire ropes together. It can run
    over the brake block.
E   A simple rescue pulley. The cheeks of the
    pulley are made from flat sheet and can move
    independently of each other when not secured
    through the belay hole by a karabiner etc.
    This makes it easier for attaching to ropes.
F   A rope clamp. The wire rope is gripped
    between the jaws at W and the
    haulage/holding sling is attached at the hole
    at other end (D Craig)

B   D

C 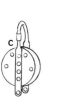   E   F

W

This winching system evolved by the author deploys a synthetic rope block and tackle for use in conjunction with a wire hauling rope, using Russian-type clamps. Alternatively, it can be used with low-stretch, synthetic fibre rope using jumar type rope clamps, or preferably tandem Prusik's.

C = rope clamp or Prusik knot. R = rescuer at cliff edge as observer, who has a good view of the stretcher/casualty. E = edge roller, B = backstop belayer of haul rope, using a rope clamp/Austrian brake block or tandem Prusik's for security.

The inset shows the rigging of rope clamps where K denotes the haul rope clamp attachment sling, or in the case of wire rope, a swaged wire sling of unequal leg lengths. If jumar-type clamps are used for this system with synthetic fibre rope, it is advisable to use another safety rope for belaying the party being hoisted.

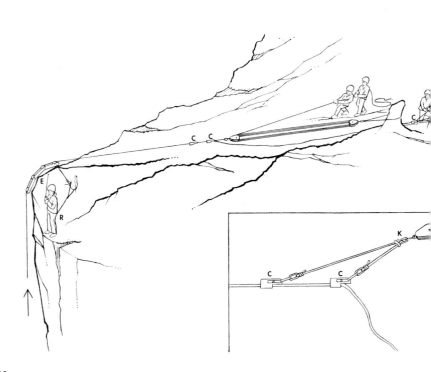

This is the same system, but using two blocks and tackle. A is the 'Prusik-minder', a rescuer who re-positions the clamps/Prusik's after each haul with the block and tackle. The haul operation can be done from different angles with a CDP (change of direction pulley). The speed of lifting a 76 kg man up a vertical face is about 18 m per min. It is important to have the blocks proud of the ground to prevent friction and abrasion.

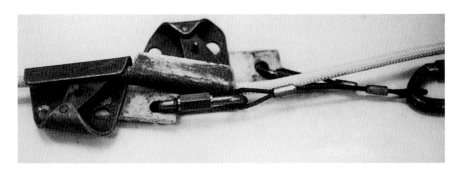

Opposite page, top: Adapted cloggers seldom used now used for the winching system described, with extension lugs for quick links. Note swaged wire sling made for this rig. The rope is 11 mm Viking Super Speleo low extension rope

Opposite page, centre: A7BHP winch designed by the author for large cliff work. It is normally transported by helicopter, weight 37 kg. It is capable of lifting two people vertically at approx. 80 m/min. Either steel wire rope or synthetic fibre rope can be used. Note locking device behind capstan. A further one-way rope clamp is attached to front of winch to allow rope changes. When using powerful (and noisy) winches such as this, RT communication should be available to the operator by using headphones with walkie-talkie

Opposite page, bottom: A power winch by Roheico of Gribsvad, Denmark. It has a single line vertical deadweight lift of 13·2 kN (1350 kg) Weight 11·9 kg. The capstan has a reverse-lock mechanism and takes 11 mm haulage rope

Below: A self-contained line throwing unit made by Pains-Wessex Schermuly. The line is projected by rocket, located in centre of container, with the line enclosed in the 'moat' surrounding it. The Speedline has a capacity of 275 m of ready-flaked line. The unit can project a line at least 230 m in calm weather. It can be used for getting a line and rope to a party on a cliff etc. Care should be taken when firing it in windy conditions and one must allow for drift

An Olini power winch

A two-speed yachting capstan alloy winch converted for mountain rescue use. This can be used in either a horizontal or vertical position. 1 indicates a pulley to the right of the operator's right leg and the rope goes from the pulley to a jumar-type clamp operated by a rescuer out of sight. 2 marks the rope going off at right angles to the jumar clamp (H MacInnes)

There are various low voltage winches on the market, some are mounted on 4 wheel drive vehicles. The Capstan type is probably the most versatile for MR work and certain models can be powered from a generator. Winches designed for yachting offer a wide range of possibilities and the one illustrated by Lewmar Marine Ltd as well as having a low voltage capability can also be operated, two speed, manually.
(Lewmar Marine)

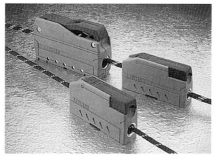

The Lewmar 'Superlock' is a rope 'ratchet' which boasts full holding power regardless of line type. This can be used as a continuous line back-up for a capstan winch, mounted behind the capstan. The model for 10–12 mm synthetic fibre rope has a holding load of 6·7 kN (700 kg) (Lewmar Marine)

would obviate this as it could cover a very wide range of ratios. Several power winches are illustrated in the text.

Electric winches

There are several small low-voltage electric winches available on the commercial market and no doubt some of these could be adapted for rescue work. At the present time, unfortunately, a suitable power supply in the form of storage batteries is just too heavy, but should a power source be available (e.g. hotels, observatories, cable car stations etc. on summits) a small electric capstan winch would be excellent for mountain rescue work. It is possible, however, to use an electric winch in conjunction with a generator.

Fortunately, one does not often have to use winches to evacuate injured climbers, and the value of such equipment must be judged by each team on a cost/use/weight basis.

The argument that no accident has happened on a certain wall or crag is of course no indication that such an event could not occur, and it is one of the purposes of the team to anticipate such danger and to be prepared to deal with such an emergency. Regrettably, it is often only after a number of serious accidents have happened that some preventive action is taken or better means of rescue provided.

Rescue teams should be equipped for any eventuality which could occur on their patch.

Wind, tables and chart

Wind can be a great hazard to a successful rescue operation and it has a considerable cooling effect on a normally clothed person. This can be even further influenced by rain and wet clothing. To use the graph, follow the known temperature line to the point where it intersects with the wind speed line and read directly down for effective chilling temperature. Graph based on table by courtesy of Museum of Science, Boston (I Kamlish).

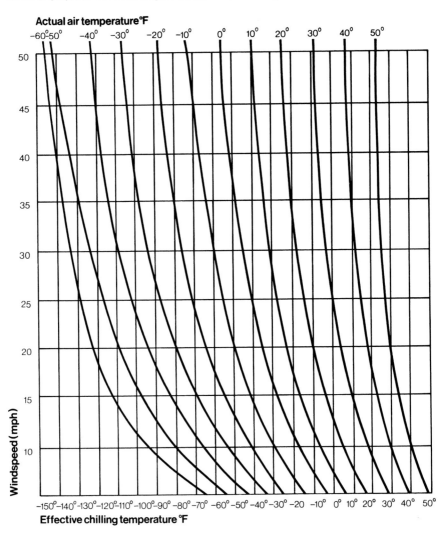

This illustration shows the effect of a wind, from the left of the drawing, on a party in line, following a compass bearing. Unless the rescue party can travel from one objective to another – e.g. a boulder at the limit of vision, etc., which is on the required bearing, the method of travel as shown on right should be adopted (R Turner)

This shows the leap-frog method of progression when there are high side winds. The man at the rear can shout (or have it relayed) to the man who has just moved up front, when he is in line, by a visual check along the line and also by use of the compass. If only one compass is available in the party this should always be kept to the rear of the line. In such conditions GPS is invaluable and is used by many rescue teams as well as SAR aircraft (R Turner)

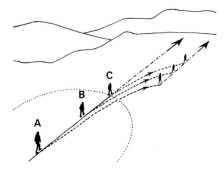
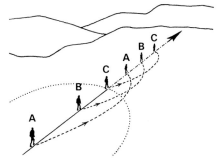

Table of wind force

This table is based on a position 10 m above flat ground

Beaufort number	Description of wind	Equivalent mean speed in knots	Limits of mean speed		
			Knots	Statute miles per hour	Metres per second
0	Calm	0	Less than 1	Less than 1	Less than 0·3
1	Light air	2	1–3	1–3	0·3–1·5
2	Light breeze	5	4–6	4–7	1·6–3·3
3	Gentle breeze	9	7–10	8–12	3·4–5·4
4	Moderate breeze	13	11–16	13–18	5·5–7·9
5	Fresh breeze	19	17–21	19–24	8·0–10·7
6	Strong breeze	24	22–27	25–31	10·8–13·8
7	Near gale‡	30	28–33	32–38	13·9–17·1
8	Gale	37	34–40	39–46	17·2–20·7
9	Strong gale	44	41–47	47–54	20·8–24·4
10	Storm	52	48–55	55–63	24·5–28·4
11	Violent storm	60	56–63	64–72	28·5–32·6
12	Hurricane	68	64	73	32·7

Lowering a casualty, in casualty bag, with the rescuer suspended from the same lowering cable and using a sit harness (L Gramminger)

Wire ropes

Norse links: These links can be purchased in stainless steel. They are used mainly for yachting purposes

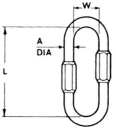

Wire ropes

Steel ropes are used widely throughout the world for rescue purposes. They have the advantage of combining great strength with small bulk and they are more resistant to abrasion than synthetic fibre ropes.

They have, however, certain handling disadvantages, as well as necessitating special clamps and attachments that cannot always be used on climbing ropes. Climbing ropes usually have to be taken on a rescue in any case.

If a rescue team in a given area has a great number of cliff evacuations, then wire rope equipment has points in its favour, but it is slowly being phased out. This is due mainly to handling problems and the lack of versatility compared with the new synthetic fibre ropes, which can be used more readily for rescue team access and special rigs. The wire has an advantage as it does not stretch so much as even the non-stretch synthetic fibre rope, obtainable for rescue work.

Size	A mm	L mm	W mm	Breaking Load kg	kN
5	4·7	62	15	1816	18
6	6·0	68	17	2724	27
8	8·0	83	24	4540	45
10	9·5	105	28	9080	89

Quick links. These links are excellent for use in rescue work due to their strength and locking nut. The 9 mm link has a breaking strain of over 50 kN (5000 kg) and is no heavier than a screwgate karabiner. They can be obtained in stainless steel and with large openings (Tirfor Ltd)

Sizes of wire rope

Wire rope is measured by diameter and the measurement should coincide with the diameter of the circle which encloses the strands of the rope. Anyhow, for rescue purposes only a few sizes are in fact used.

On the continent of Europe mainly 2·5–3 mm are used. 5 mm ropes are used for cableways whilst in other countries 6 mm diameter wire rope is used for cableways, of 6 × 19 (12/6/1) fibre core construction (i.e. the rope is made from six strands, each with 19 preformed wires).

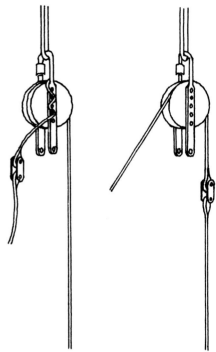

Above right: Joining two wire cables together using a coupling. Note that whilst the coupling operation is taking place the wire is locked on the pins of the brake block (left figure). A small coupling can be allowed to run round the brake block
(K Spence)

Opposite page: Changing ropes at a new belay position. The centre man is seen with a quick link at the end of the wire rope ready to attach this to the triangular quick link of the casualty bag suspension slings (see inset). The wire rope is already locked on the pins of the brake block. When the weight goes on the new rope, the top one is then uncoupled. The new section of lower continues with the minimum of delay. It can sometimes be difficult to get ledges on the correct descent line suitably located for this technique. Rescuers on these lower ledges must also beware of possible stonefalls (G Hunter)

Right: Norse terminal for wire cable joints. The two ends, when fitted together, are locked by a screw pin and this forms a very compact joint. Though they are simple to fit it is better to ask your wire rope supplier to fit these, or a similar terminal (G Hunter)

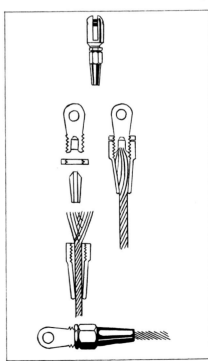

322

Below: A rescuer is lowered to casualty on ledge on wire rope and administers first aid (L Gramminger)

Below right: If the casualty is a 'walking' case, it is possible to winch both casualty and rescuer to top of cliff (L Gramminger)

Opposite page: A rescuer being lowered with casualty using a tragsitz (L Gramminger)

Opposite page, inset: Considerable strain is put on the rescuer using a tragsitz with patient. Feet must be placed apart and the legs kept as close to the right angles to the rock face as possible (L Gramminger)

Below: A ball bearing swivel as used for long lowers to prevent casualty from rotating when hanging free (H MacInnes)

Left: A horizontal lower using nylon rope. Patient is in a casualty bag suspended from slings (L Gramminger)

Below: Lowering a 'casualty' in a rope basket. Rope 1 goes to a separate figure of eight descender, but the belayer on the right is in control of both ropes (H MacInnes). Figure of eight descenders are not in common use for cliff lowers as often they don't provide sufficient friction for a controlled lower

A snow lower. Two wire ropes, from two separate brake drums, are being used. The 'barrow boy' is attached to the stretcher and lowering rope and he is using a harness (L Gramminger)

The lay of this rope is right hand ordinary lay and it should be galvanised or zinc plated. Stainless steel wire ropes are of course desirable, but are much more expensive.

Lengths of wire ropes

The length of the ropes required will be determined largely by the type of mountain country in which your rescue team is operating. It will obviously be easier to have reasonably long cable lengths when long lowers and cableways are being used, but the cable length must be considered with its weight in respect to portability. The lengths in common usage are as follows:

Steel wire cables in common use in rescue work

2 cables 100 m long and 1 cable 50 m long of 5 mm diameter 7/19 construction, galvanised aircraft cable min. breaking strength 18·67 kN (1800 kg), wt. = 9·5 kg per 100 m.
1 cable 250 m long of 3 mm diameter 7/19 construction galvanised aircraft cable wire min. breaking strength 8.896 kN (900 kg).

Joining wire rope

There are various methods of coupling wire ropes. The type of work to be done with the ropes will determine the best type of coupling for your particular purpose.

For example, if the wire cable is to be used mainly for a suspension wire for cableways, probably an eye splice at each end of the rope will offer the best compromise. This will enable it to be lashed easily to the belay at the static end of the rope, whilst at the other a lever winch can be used for tensioning.

Below: Cableway evacuation, using the suspension rope tensioned through a pulley using block and tackle. By altering the tension of the suspension rope the casualty can be placed with accuracy on a given ledge or on the ground, in line with the suspension rope. The dotted outlines of the stretcher indicate the positions of the stretcher during the lowering operation. Two jumar-type clamps are used for the lowering rope /stretcher attachment sling (or Prusik knots). Take great care that the suspension rope is not over-tensioned, and the block and tackle mustn't be used to tension then be tied off (E Grieve)

Right: Using a double pulley on a cableway suspension system. The single top rope is for pulling stretcher/casualty as well as acting as a safety rope. If enough rope is available always try to use double rope for cableway. To avoid suspension rope twisting under tension use wide, double-rope pulley. NB This pulley was designed for yachting purposes. Several yachting pulleys are suitable for MR work and can be modified so that they don't have to be threaded onto the rope. Carbon fibre pulleys are now available. (H MacInnes)

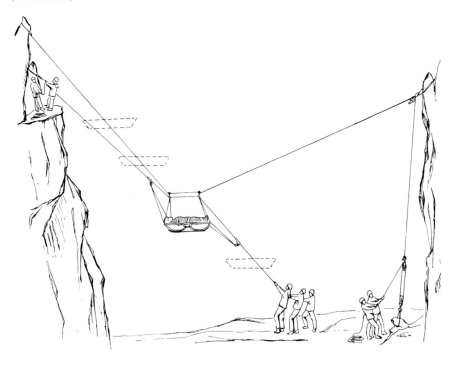

This illustrates another type of wire rope spool holder mounted on a pack frame. The operator of this feeds the wire rope out to the belayer at the brake block, allowing plenty of slack for more even running of rope round brake block. The belayer is wearing a harness and both men are belayed to the face. Note, both helmets and gloves should be worn on actual rescues and training exercises (L Gramminger)

Using a Simpul Sport winch for tensioning cableway. The two locking clamps can be seen in this photograph. The winch can be clipped onto the rope at any point (H MacInnes)

Below: Tensioning a cableway using a lightweight block and tackle. If a climbing rope is used for reefing the blocks this will also act as a shock absorber for the wire rope. Always use separate slings for attaching cableway ropes to belays (K Spence)

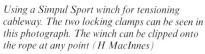

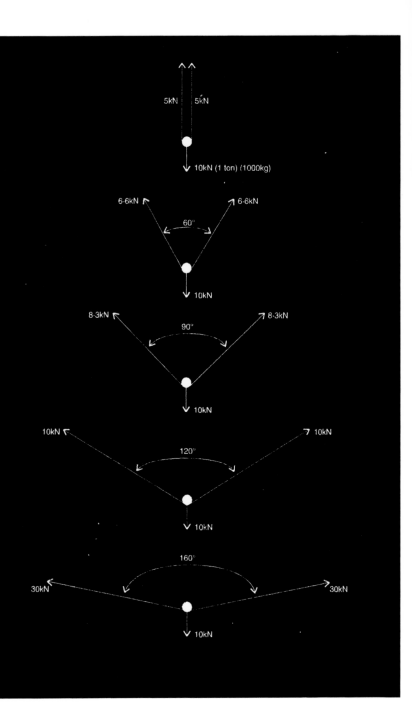

Opposite page: Suspension ropes for cableways. This series of illustrations shows the overloading which can occur on a rope due to the use of taut suspension wires. The table showing rope angle/rope tension at the bottom of this page should be studied before any cableways are rigged (G Hunter)

Right: A This illustration shows a two single block and tackle, and B a double and single block and tackle. Allowing 10 per cent per sheave for friction, the effort required to raise the weight on A would be 2·96 kN (300 kg). The loading on its belay B would be 5·94 kN (600 kg). The theoretical gain is 2 to 1. P = haulage rope.

The theoretical gain on B is 3 to 1. This means that the effort required to raise the weight, allowing 10 per cent per sheave for friction, would be 2·42 kN (240 kg) and the loading on the belay, 8·90 kN (850 kg). P = haulage rope (K Spence)

Below: The loading on a pulley and its belay, with the rope at various angles. The arrow indicates the haulage rope with a load of 5 kN/504 kg being exerted on it (K Spence)

0° = 10·0 kN (1000 kg)
30° = 9·5 kN (950 kg)
60° = 7·5 kN (750 kg)
90° = 7·0 kN (700 kg)
120° = 5·0 kN (500 kg)
150° = 2·5 kN (250 kg)

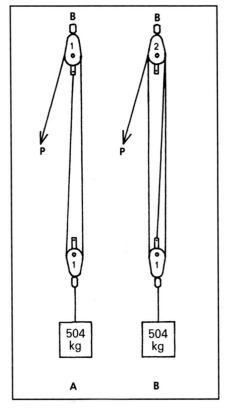

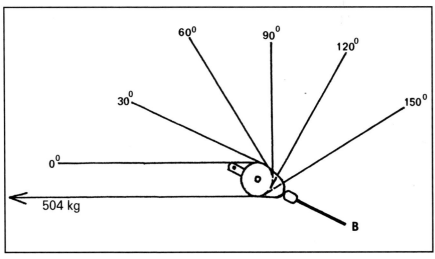

Rigging cableways

Great care must be exercised when evacuating a casualty on a cableway. It is very easy to over-tension cableway ropes. These must be suitable for the purpose, preferably the long, low extension ropes (in good condition) as described in this book. Ideally, two cableways suspension ropes should be used in conjunction with wide pulleys for the stretcher carriage. Tandem or double tandem Prusik's should be used instead of rope clamps on cableways with Load Releasing Hitches on anchors. If possible purchase a basic dynamometer for monitoring tension on the cableway ropes – see illustrations. Study the tables on pre-tensioning and always consult a team member with a knowledge of engineering/physics to mastermind the operation.

Stretcher lowering on 5 mm wire rope

Sample calculated based on 100 m of 5 mm diameter, 6 × 19 steel wire rope with fibre core (average breaking strength 1,610 kg/15·8 kN).

Rigged with an initial pre-tension not exceeding the values T_i as shown, the above rope will support a suspended safe load of 115 kg* any point along its length.

The suspended safe load of 115 kg creates in the rope, rigged as shown, a maximum tension of 268 kg/2·63 kN which gives a safety factor of 6.

*Safe Load = 115 kg in still air
      or = 114 kg in 72 kph crosswind
      or = 98 kg in 144 kph crosswind

Methods of checking pre-tension are shown on A

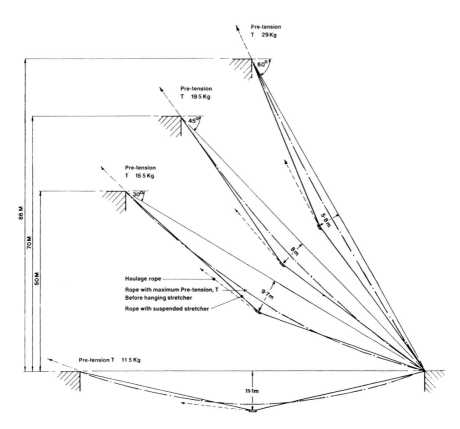

Checking pre-tension

It is important to avoid over-tensioning the wire rope span before suspending the stretcher.
A rigged wire rope may be checked for correct pre-tension by pulling at 'A' (5 m from the top end) or at B (10 m from the top end) with a force of anything between 0·5 to 1 kN (50 to 100 kg) and observing the deflection or play 'd' from the initial free hanging position. The deflection must be more than the figures shown in acompanying table

	Span Inclination			
	hori- zontal	30°	45°	60°
Minimum Deflection 'd' at A	3 m	3 m	2.5 m	2 m
Minimum Deflection 'd' at B	3 m	3 m	3 m	2·5 m
Pre-tension T does not exceed	11·5 kg 0·11 kN	13·5 kg 0·13 kN	18·5 kg 0·18 kN	14·0 kg 0·14 kN

Span declination	Max permitted pre-tension T	
Horizontal	·11 kN	(11·5 kg)
30°	·15 kN	(15·5 kg)
45°	·19 kN	(19·9 kg)
60°	·28 kN	(29·0 kg)

Position of haulage/lowering rope H

When the stretcher is near the top of the suspension wire, direct pull of the haulage rope adding to stretcher weight is avoided by arranging the haulage/lowering rope no further from the suspension rope than shown at H

333

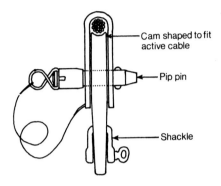

Cam shaped to fit active cable

Pip pin

Shackle

Left: The end elevation of the Russian wire grip. The main wire rope passes between the lever-cam and the U section of the grip (R Turner)

Below: Russian wire grip. This is a cam-lever wire locking clamp which has been developed in the USSR. The cam-lever 3 holds the main wire rope 6 when the anchoring wire 5 is under tension. The shackle 2 can be used in several positions on lever 3 for various tensions. 1 is a Pip-Pin, or some similar high tensile locking pin. 4 is the U shaped holder between the sides of which the cam-lever 3 operates and in which the main wire rope 6 passes. The anchoring wire 6 also passes between two faces of 4 and the Pip-Pin at this point acts as a pulley (R Turner)

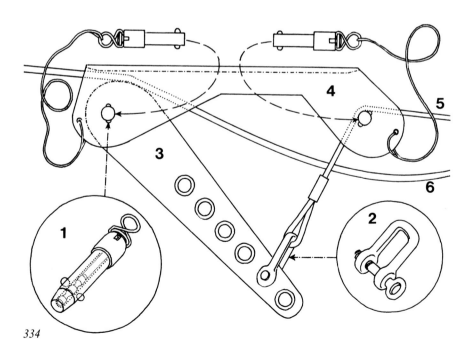

WARNING

Great care should be exercised in tensioning cableway ropes. As mentioned in the text, double suspension ropes should be used whenever possible. Cableway ropes should never be tensioned using vehicles.

When using **low stretch fibre ropes** the elongation of the rope/s should be taken into account. For example the 10 mm commonly used **Viking plaited polyester mountain rescue rope** has approximately a 2·5% elongation at 150 kg load. On the other hand, **Viking super speleo (kevlar core)** of 11 mm diameter has an elongation of about 1% at 150 kg load. The proposed European Standard (prEN 1891) allows a maximum elongation of 5% at 150 kg load.

For joining wire ropes with end splices, 'quick links' offer the best and safest method. These links are very strong and pulleys can be made which will allow the 'quick link' joint to run over the pulleys easily. A spanner should be carried for undoing 'quick links' or 'Norse links'.

There are various compact, smooth terminals available for joining wire rope which are quick to use but care should be exercised when used over pulleys or brake blocks. Despite this, splices, terminal fittings, or swageing should be done by qualified personnel and preferably by the suppliers of the wire rope. Ensure that all equipment comes up to national or international specification and that it is either stainless, zinc, or cadmium plated to suitable specifications. These terminals will run round wire rope brake drums as used for lowering. Ensure that galvanic action cannot occur at end terminals.

Attaching wire ropes to belays

The end of a wire rope should never be wrapped round a belay and separate belay slings should be used for this purpose, or wire slings with eye splices of various lengths are excellent. Such wire slings can be of plastic coated wire rope to avoid damage by abrasion on rough belay anchors and the eye ends can be spliced by the Talurit system (see below).

Talurit splicing

This splice requires very little rope. The end of the rope is threaded through a non-corrosive alloy ferrule of suitable size and then threaded back on itself through the ferrule to form a loop.

The ferrule is then put in a hydraulic press between two dies and pressure is applied. The pressure does not harm the rope, neither is the lay disturbed. Such splices are excellent for slings etc., but an eye splice is recommended for the main cable-ends, or for terminals. Copper ferrules are used for swageing stainless steel cable.

Care of wire rope

There are simple but important factors in respect of wire rope maintenance, which can materially extend the service life of a rope. Rope dressing can be obtained from the manufacturer and this should be applied at intervals. This coating should remain flexible and fully protective over the full range of temperatures likely to be encountered in service.

The wire rope inevitably becomes coated with foreign matter, which is often highly abrasive, and therefore the rope should be cleaned (two wire brushes intermeshed and attached to a board are suitable for this; the rope is pulled through between the brushes). Under corrosive condition, e.g. sea cliff rescue work, there is always the possibility of internal and external corrosion. Stainless steel wire should be used for sea cliff rescue work. It is not always easy to dry off a rope before applying rope dressing, and a dressing should be used which will displace moisture from internal and external surfaces.

Below: Wire rescue rope on spools. The holder frame is seen on the right and the brake drum in centre of picture (A Contamine)

Bottom picture: A spare wire rope spool made from two discs of aluminium alloy, mounted on a central spindle for carrying on a pack frame (H MacInnes)

Always consult the rope manufacturer regarding your personal problem as he will be only too happy to advise on the care and maintenance of your ropes.

Inspection of wire rope

The wire ropes should of course be dried after a rescue and inspected for damage. If more than three or four wires of a strand are damaged the rope should be renewed. Care should be taken in coiling the wire rope (see illustration), as kinks can damage a rope and can hinder the free movement of pulleys.

Minimum breaking load

This is the breaking load below which the rope will not fracture when tested to destruction in the prescribed manner. The value is calculated from the product of the square of the nominal diameter of a rope, the tensile grade of the wire and the coefficient appropriate to the construction of the rope.

Actual breaking load

The maximum load obtained in testing a sample of the wire rope to destruction in the prescribed manner.

Calculated aggregate breaking load

The value of force calculated from the product of the sum of the cross-sectional metallic area of the individual wires in the rope and the tensile grade of the wire. The metallic area can be associated directly with the square of the nominal diameter.

Factor of safety

This is the ratio between the minimum breaking load and the operating tensile load in the rope.

Spools for wire rope

These can be made up quite easily in the same fashion as those suggested for long synthetic fibre rescue ropes. However, it is

Below: The end pulleys of the edge roller are made with deep sides to allow bigger couplings to pass over. The centre part of each pulley tapers each side towards the central wire location groove. Normal lightweight rescue pulleys are not suited for wire rope. Special pulleys designed for the higher loading of the wire are available and some of these are now made from carbon fibre. Probably the best source of supply are yacht chandlers

Bottom diagram: The Glencoe edge roller: This is a simply made device for avoiding wear and friction of wire or nylon rope when it runs over an edge. The links between the rollers ensure that it conforms to the shape of the edge. The top and bottom rollers should have deeper cheeks to avoid the rope coming off

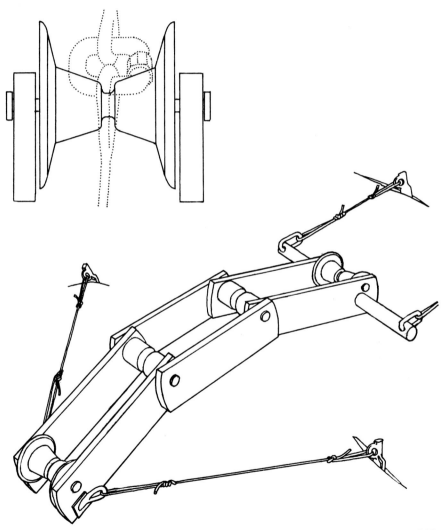

Below: Tensioning the bottom end of a long cableway using a Simpul Sport winch. This is a light-weight double acting lever winch, which can be used in any position. It operates two clamps, one in each direction of movement of the lever, and it can be used on either synthetic fibre rope or various sizes of wire rope. 1 indicates the winch lever and 2 shows a Norse link and sling keeping the cableway low at bottom end for ease of winching. The Simpul winch is slow operating for direct lifting – 1 m/min (H MacInnes)

Below: A brake block being used on a rescue on the east face of the Grepon, French Alps. Note that the brake block is bearing on the rock face, which prevents jerky lowering. With new brake drums, lowering can be often jerky; glacier cream on the block can sometimes help to lubricate it. The rescuer on the left is feeding the wire to the rescuer at the brake block. The rescuers should be wearing gloves for this operation. Should the brake block lowerer wish to halt the descent, or couple another length of rope, the wire can be taken out and in the pins on the top side of the brake block until this operation is completed. Couplings will pass round the brake block. Only a single turn round the brake drum is necessary if the casualty is light and the slope moderate. Two turns will be necessary on steep faces and with heavier casualties (A Contamine)

Opposite top: An injured climber being taken up the summit snow field of the Eiger North Wall on a tragsitz. A further rescuer is ahead on a separate rope and is in radio communication with the summit party (Alex, Grindelwald)

Opposite page, bottom left: Preparing for a large scale rescue operation on the summit of the Eiger, Switzerland (Alex, Grindelwald)

Opposite page, bottom right: Rescuer preparing to descend the Eiger North Wall. In the foreground an edge roller is seen (Alex, Grindelwald)

better if the spool has a removable spindle, which can be used in extra spools when required. Several of these are illustrated throughout the text. For transporting it is better to have the spool detachable from the winding bracket so that it lies flat on the carrying frame, fairly high with the centre of gravity close to the body.

Shock loading on wire rope

Considerable forces can be generated in a wire rope with shock loadings and these must be avoided. Care must be exercised, especially in a lower, where a terminal, or a quick link joint, may snag then suddenly free when jammed in a crack or fissure.

Clamps and attachments

There are several types of locking clamp available for holding wire rope at any given point. These are illustrated in the text. Probably the Russian clamp is the most useful and gives a very positive grip over a wide range of rope diameters.

The Simpul Sport is also very useful for locking and tensioning the rope (it uses a larger diameter wire rope and has to be connected to the active rope via a coupling/clamp), and for cableway work it is probably the easiest to operate as it both tensions and holds the rope at any given point from any angle of belay. However, the end of the active rope should be further secured round a brake drum etc. in case of rope 'creep'.

The simple 'U' wire rope grip should not be used on a rescue rope as this can damage it.

Blockstops

These are made by the Tirfor Company and though they are made for use with 8 mm wire rope they can be very useful for fixed rescue cableways. The end of the rope must be threaded through the Blockstop and therefore eye splices could not be used with Blockstops.

Wire rope swivels

These should be incorporated in the rig for stretcher-patient suspension lifts and lowers. They will prevent twisting action caused by the wire rope and be especially useful when free lowers and lifts are being done. The type incorporating a ball-thrust bearing is best.

Wire rope, pulleys

Excellent pulleys can be made for use with wire rope from single Tufnol pulley sheaves as used for yachting. These can be purchased in various diameters for different thicknesses of rope. Should quick links be used for couplings, then special wider pulleys with a locating centre groove must be used. See illustration (on page 93).

Tufnol pulleys are self-lubricating and if two sections of flat steel or alloy rectangular bar are used, each with three holes (one at each end and one in the middle), the centre hole will locate the pulley shaft and the other two can be used for karabiner attachments when required. As the two plates can move around the central shaft independently, quick attachment to the main steel cable can be made. The diagrams and photographs in this book should be studied for different forms of rigging with pulleys for stretchers etc.

The minimum recommended pulley diameter for 5 mm steel wire rope is approximately 85 mm.

APPENDIX 1

Rescuers' Rough Guide to S.I.Units

1.Introduction

The International System of Units (= Systeme Internationale = S.I.) defines and governs the application of all measurement units throughout the entire physical world. It came into being as a single worldwide system to replace the pounds-feet and several metric systems previously in use. The rate of adoption has been different from country to country but now, after many years it is the preferred and indeed, principal language for technical communication throughout most of the world.

There are exceptions such as aviation and marine operations bedded in the well established older units (particularly feet, miles, nautical miles and knots) and unlikely to change.

Whilst the design and performance of mountain rescue equipment is not affected by the changes to measurement units, such equipment is being increasingly specified, labelled and instructed in S.I. units. The most noticeable changes are to do with length and load. For length related measurements the metre and its multiples and sub divisions replace the foot based units to bring the imperial and USA systems into line with the S.I. (and existing metric) systems. These changes are well understood in the main and by now the more common units are in general use. Load, a term long used to embrace several meanings, particularly mass, weight and force all measured in the older systems by apparently the same unit (lb. or kg.), needs a closer look particularly when used in the sense of force for which a new unit, the newton (N) appears.

Considering that ropes, karabiners and all other load carrying equipment are now rated in newtons it is vital to be able to relate such ratings in N to the weights needing to be handled, usually expressed in kg or lb units.

(For example: are you sure it is safe to suspend 25cwt on a rope rated at 4kN? – or a 45gallon drum of water on the same rope?)

All forces in whatever direction whether pulling or pushing, upwards, downwards or sideways are best expressed in newtons and not in pounds or kilograms, though when it comes to the forces exerted by the human frame it is recognised that kilograms and pounds are likely to be the first to mind. Again, no problem so long as the conversions can be applied when needed.

A conversion between newtons and kilograms is given in section 2.

S.I. Units are described more completely in the chapter on Testing and Evaluation where conversion factors are given with exactitude appropriate to rigorous calculation.

On the following pages is a selectionof S.I. units and conversions from the imperial and previous metric systems units thought to be useful in the context of mountain rescue operations.

The constants, taken from standard reference works, are rounded for convenience and are thus rarely exact.

Along with some of these conversions are suggested a few close approximations (hence the term "Rough Guide") helpful to quick reckoning in converting from the less familiar to the more familiar units so that initially strange numbers can be accepted with some confidence. These are denoted {**rg:**..........}.

The selection of units includes: length and its derivatives (area, volume, speed and acceleration), mass, force and its derivatives (pressure, stress and torque/moments), temperature.

2.The Newton (N)

The newton is defined as the force that gives a mass of 1 kilogram an acceleration of 1 metre per second per second.

($1N = 1kg \times 1m/s^2 = 1kgm/s^2$).

Relating this to the Earth's gravitational acceleration taken, for the purposes of this guide, as a constant* $9.81m/s^2$, the gravitational force acting on a mass of 1kg is 9.81N which allows the statement that:

a force of 1 newton is equivalent to the weight of a mass of about 0.1kilogram.

For simplicity in the following lists, the conversion

$$1N = 0.102kg$$

is used.

[*near enough, the maximum deviation anywhere on the Earth is believed to be less than 0.5%]

3.Length and its derivatives
3.1.Units of Length

The S.I. unit of length is the metre (m). The preferred multiple is the kilometre (km) = 1000m.
The preferred subdivision is the millimetre (mm) = 1/1000m = .001m = 10^{-3}m.

[The centimetre (cm) and decimetre (dm), are not preferred units but, as will be seen as we go along, are used where convenient. This is particularly evident in the units for area and volume.
1cm = 1/100m = 0.01m = 10mm
1dm = 1/10m = 0.1m = 100mm].

These compare with:
the yard(yd) = 3feet(ft) = 36inches(in) and the mile, where 1mile = 1760yd.

Converting:
SI Unit to Imperial to SI Unit
1m   = 39.37in
        = 3.281ft
        = 1.094yd
1in   = 0.0254m = 25.4mm
1ft   = 0.3048m = 304.8mm
1yd   = 0.9144m
{rg: 1m=1.1yd=3 1/3ft=40in
3m=10ft; etc.}
– for distances:
1km   = 0.621mile
        1mile = 1.609km
              = 1609m
Also,
1UK nautical mile (nm) = 1.1515mile
                       = 1.8532km.

{rg:1km=5/8mile; 8km=5mile;
1600m=1mile; 800m=1/2mile;
400m=1/4mile; etc}

– for smaller measurements:
1mm = 0.0394in
    0.010in = 0.254mm
    0.001in = 0.0254mm
           = 25.4 micron
– and for fractional inch sizes:
0.3969mm = 1/64in (= 0.015625in)
                  (= 15.625thou)
0.7938mm = 1/32in (= 0.03125in)
                  (= 31.25thou)
1.5876mm = 1/16in (= 0.0625in)
                  (= 62.5thou)
3.175mm = 1/8in (= 0.125in)
                  (= 125thou)
                     etc.

{rg: 40thou = 1mm;
    20thou = 1/2mm;
    10thou = 1/4mm;
    1in = 25mm; 4in = 100mm;
    6in = 150mm; etc}

3.2.Units of Area
The unit of area is the square metre
(m^2 or sq m)
$1m^2$ = 1000000 mm^2(=10000cm^2)
$1km^2$ = 1000000 m^2

$1m^2$ = 1550.00in^2
     = 10. 76ft^2
     = 1.196yd^2
        1yd^2 = 0.8361m^2
        1ft^2 = 0. 0929m^{2}2
{rg: 1m^2 = 10ft^2; 10m^2 = 12yd^2;
1yd^2 = 5/6m^2; etc.}

– for larger areas:
100m^2 = 1are (a);
100a = 1hectare(ha) = 10000m^2
100ha = 1km^2
hence:

1ha = 11960yd^2 (= 2.471acres)
    1acre = 4047m^2(= 0.4047ha)
    1sq mile = 2.59km^2(= 259ha)
(ref: 1sq mile = 640acres;
    1acre = 4840yd^2)
{rg: 1ha = 2.5acres; 1km^2 = 250acres;
1sq mile = 2.5km^2; etc.}

– for smaller areas:
1mm^2 = 0.00155in^2
1in^2 = 645.2mm^2 = 6.452cm^2
{rg: a 1in dia circle= 0.8in^2
                    = 500mm^2;
a 1/4in dia circle   **= 1/20in^2**
                    = 32mm^2; etc.}

3.3.Units of Volume and Capacity
The unit of volume is the cubic metre
(m^3 or cu.m). For capacity, the litre (l)
is also used.
1cu.m = 1000 l
and 1l = 1000millilitres(ml)
= 1000cubic centimetres(cm^3,cc).
The cubic decimetre (dm^3) may also be
found, 1dm^3 = 1l).
1m^3 = 1.308yd^3
     = 35.31ft^3
1l = 61.02in^3
        1in^3 = 16.39cm^3
        1ft^3 = 28.32 l
        1yd^3 = 0.7645m^3
– for capacity:
[Note; gallons (gal), quarts (qt) and
pints (pt) need to be identified as UK
or US because of the size difference.
1UKgal/qt/pt = 1.201USgal/qt/pt.]

1m^3 = 220UKgal (= 264.2USgal)
1l = 0.22UKgal(= 0.2642USgal)
1l = 1.76UKpt (=1.057USqt)
1l = 35.2UKfl oz

```
1UKgal  = 1.546 l
1USgal  = 3.785 l
1UKfl oz = 28.41ml (cc)
(ref: 1UKpt  = 20UKfl oz)
1UKgill = 5UKfl oz)
{rg: 1UKgal = 41/2l;
 220UKgal = 1m³;
 1USgal = 5/6UKgal
       = 3.3/4l;
 1USqt  = 1l; etc.}
```

3.4.Other Length-Related Units

Linear velocity and acceleration and volume flowrate conversions follow logically from the above. However, because the time component of velocity and volume may be commonly expressed in seconds, minutes or hours there is a large number of possibly useful conversions to be considered. Thus the best rough guide here is to avoid too many conversions, concentrate on only the figures specific to the operation in hand and do not mix the measures for time [i.e. convert all velocities/flowrates to the same per sec or per min or per hour basis to make for simpler memorizing and comparison].

3.4.1.Linear Velocity (Speed)

The unit of velocity is the metre per second (m/s), thus the conversions to and from in/s, ft/s, yd/s and so on use the same factors as for the length conversions.
Also,
$1\text{m/s} = 3.28\text{ft/s}$
$= 196.9\text{ft/min}$
$= 2.237\text{mile/h}$
$1\text{km/h} = 0.6214\text{mile/h} = 0.2778\text{m/s}$

and $1\text{ mile/h} = 26.82\text{m/min}$
$= 0.447\text{m/s}$
[ref: 1mile/h = 88ft/min = 17.6in/s]
[and 1nm/h = 1knot(kt)].
{rg: decide what length and time units you want to work with and devise your own rough guide.}

3.4.2.Linear Acceleration

The unit of acceleration is the metre per second squared (m/s^2).
$1\text{m/s}^2 = 3.281\text{ft/s}^2$
$1\text{ft/s}^2 = 0.3048\text{m/s}^2$
Standard, or gravitational acceleration*, sometimes referred to as 'g'
$= 9.81\text{m/s}^2$
$= 32.2\text{ft/s}^2$
$= 386\text{in/s}^2$
[* see note in section 2].

3.4.3.Volume Flowrate

The unit of volume is the cubic metre per second (m^3/s or cu.m/s), thus the conversions to and from in^3/s, ft^3/s, yd^3/s and so on use the same factors as for the volume conversions.
Also,
$1\text{m}^3/\text{s} = 35.31\text{ft}^3/\text{s}$ $(= 2119\text{ft}^3/\text{min})$
$(= 127100 \text{ ft}^3/\text{h})$
$(= 13200\text{UKgal/min})$
$1 \text{ l/s} = 13.2\text{UKgal/min} = (791.9\text{UKgal/h})$
$1\text{UKgal/min} = 4.546 \text{ l/min}$
$= 75.76 \text{ cm}^3/\text{s}$

3.4.4.Mass Flowrate (of water)

Taking the density of freshwater to be 1kg per litre,* ($=1000\text{kg/m}^3$ or 1t/m^3).
hence,
$1\text{m}^3/\text{s} = 1\text{t/s} = 60\text{t/min} = 3600 \text{ t/h}$
{rg: as for Linear Velocity above.}
[*Also $=10\text{lb/UKgal} = 62.5\text{lb/ft}^3$]

4.Mass, Force and their derivatives
4.1.Units of Mass
The unit of mass is the kilogram (kg).
1000kg=1tonne(t);1kg=1000grams(g)

1kg	=	2.205lb
50kg	=	110.2lb
100kg	=	220.5lb
1t	=	2205lb
1t	=	0.9842ton*

1lb	=	0.4536 kg
1 stone(14 lb)	=	6.350kg
1 cwt (112 lb)	=	50.80kg
1 ton*	=	1016kg
1USton*	=	907kg

[Note;* the primary unit of mass in the USA has been the pound (lb) as in the UK but the multiples differ. The UK or Imperial ton (ton)=2240lb; the USA ton (USton)=2000lb; these are also known respectively as long and short tons].

{rg: to convert to kg from lb divide by 2 then subtract 10%.
to convert to lb from kg, multiply by 2 then add 10%.
50kg = 1cwt = 8stone;
100kg = 2cwt = 16stone, etc.
1tonne = 1ton = 1.1USton }

– for smaller measure:

100g	=	3.527oz
500g	=	1.102l lb

1 lb(16oz)	=	453.6g
1oz	=	28.34g
4oz	=	113.4g
8oz	=	226.8g

{rg: 100g = 3.5oz; 200g = 7oz; etc.}

4.2.Units of Force
The unit of force is the newton (N).
From Section 2, use the conversion
$$1N = 0.102kg$$

Hence,
1 decanewton(daN)[*1] = 10N = 1.02kg
1kilonewton(kN) = 1000N = 102kg
10 kN = 1020kg = 1.02t
1meganewton(MN) = 1000kN = 102t

[Note: kg and lb (together with oz, cwt, ton), when used in the sense of force, are often followed by 'f', (kgf, lbf). For simplicity this is generally not observed in this guide. Also, the term 'kp' (kilopond) is used instead of kgf in parts of Europe, where 1kp=1kgf.]

1N	=	0.2248 lb
1kN	=	224.8 lb
10kN	=	1.004 ton[*2]
1MN	=	100.4 ton

1 lb	=	4.448N
1cwt	=	498.2N
1ton	=	9964N
	=	9.964kN

[Note [*1]: Though non- preferred, the decanewton (daN) is to be found on some mountaineering equipment labels and may be useful and easier to memorize for being nearly 1kg.
Note [*2]: UKton = 2240 lb. See 4.1.]

{rg: 1. For converting between kg and N, round up the gravity constant to 10.
Hence, 1kg = 10N = 1daN;
100kg = 1kN; 1t = 10kN = 1000daN.
2. For converting between lb, cwt, ton, etc and N, either (a)convert into kg and proceed as 1 above, or (b)particularly for larger weights, convert directly using 1kN = 224lb = 2cwt = 16stone; 50daN = 112lb = 1cwt = 8stone 10kN = 1ton(2240lb)}.

4.3.Other Force-related Units

4.3.1.Pressure

The unit of pressure is the Pascal(Pa).

1Pa=1Newton per square metre

$1Pa = 1N/m^2$

[Note; this is a very small unit for normal usage and so is frequently used in kilo-(kPa) and mega-(Mpa) forms.]

1kPa = 1000Pa

1MPa = 1000kPa = 1000000Pa

Also used is the bar [increasingly common on hydraulic equipment].

1bar = 100kPa; 1MPa = 10bar

1Pa	=	$0.0209lb/ft^2$	
1kPa	=	$0.1450lb/in^2$ (psi)	
100kPa =	14.5psi	=	1bar
1MPa	= 145psi	=	10bar
10MPa	= 1450psi	=	100bar
			= 689.5kPa

{rg: 1psi = 7kPa;
1000 psi = 7MPa = 70 bar}

– for liquid columns:

1mm Hg(mercury) = 133.3Pa

1mm Hg = $13.60mmH_2O$ (water)*

$1mm H_2O^* = 9.81Pa$

1in Hg   = 3.386kPa

$1in H_2O$ =   249.1Pa

[* Taking water as 1kg per litre.]

-for atmosphere:

'standard atmosphere' (atm)

1atm = 760mm Hg = 101.325kPa

= 1.013bar = 14.69psi

'technical atmosphere' (continental Europe) (at)

1at = $1kg/cm^2$ = 98.10kPa

= 0.981bar = 14.5psi

{rg: 1atm = 1at = 1bar = $1kg/cm^2$
= 100kPa = 15psi}

– for underwater (freshwater) the pressure, additional to the prevailing atmospheric pressure,

at a depth of 1m = 9810Pa = 0.0981bar

at a depth of 10m = 98.1kPa = 0.981bar

{rg: for every 10m of depth the pressure rises by 1bar
(or 1 atmosphere)}

4.3.2.Stress (of materials)

The unit of stress is the pascal (Pa) as for pressure though magnitudes are frequently greater and the alternative form, newtons per square millimetre (N/mm^2) is often used.

$1N/mm^2 = 1MN/m^2 = 1MPa.$

Also: $1ton/in^2$ = 15.44MPa

4.3.3. Moment of Force, Torque

The unit of moment of force, or torque is the newton metre (Nm)*.

Supersedes 'pounds feet' (which may be found written as lb ft or lbf.ft) or 'kilogram metre'(written usually as kgf m* or kp m).

1Nm = 0.7376 lb ft)

1 lb ft = 1.356Nm

or, for the older metric system,

1Nm = 0.1020 kgfm(kilogram metre)*

1 kgf m = 9.81Nm

{rg: 1lbft = 4/3Nm; 1kgfm = 10Nm}

[*Note; The units of Nm and kgf m for torque are unfortunately written the same as for 'Energy' (see below) where the meaning is quite different. Beware! The pound foot system, if used correctly, differentiates by using 'lb ft' to denote torque but 'ft lb' to denote energy.]

4.3.4. Energy

The unit of energy is the joule (J).
Mechanical Energy = (force x distance)
1 J = 1Nm (newton metre)*
Electrical Energy = (power x time)
1 J = 1Ws (watt second)
Strain Energy = (pressure or stress
x volume)
1J = 1Pam³ (Pascal cubic metre)

– for the foot, pound conversion,
1J = 0.7376ft lb (foot pounds)
1ft lb = 1.356J
and for the older metric system
1J = 0.1020 kgf m
             (kilogram force metre)*
1 kgf m = 9.810J
(* see note in 4.3.3 above for
alternative uses of these terms).

5. Temperature

The unit of temperature interval is the
degree Celsius (°C).
For all practical purposes,
1°Celsius = 1°Centigrade = 1°C
1°C = 9/5°Fahrenheit(F).
5°C = 9°F
       1°F = 5/9°C
Both Celsius and Centigrade are in
use at the present time. Both are
written as °C.

To convert Fahrenheit to Celsius,
subtract 32°F then multiply by 5 and
divide by 9.
For example,
68°F = [(68 -32) x 5/9]°C
       = [36 x 5/9] = [180/9]
              = 20°C
{rg: subtract 32°F then divide
by 2 then add 10% of this.
For example,
68°F; stage 1, 68 - 32 = 36
       stage 2, 36 ÷ 2 = 18
       stage 3, 18+(10% of 18)
              = 18+1.8
       = 19.8°C
To convert Celsius to Fahrenheit,
multiply by 9 then divide by 5 and add
32.
For example
20°C = [(20 x 9/5) + 32]
       = [(180/5) + 32] = [36 + 32] = 68°F.
{rg: multiply °C by 2 then
subtract 10% then add 32.
For example,
20°C; stage 1, 20 x 2 =40
       stage 2, 40 - (10% of 40)
              = 40 - 4 = 36
       stage 3, 36+32 = 68°F
Alternatively, simply memorise a few of
the easy and most used conversions, for
example

°C	°F
100	212
36.9	98.4
28	82
16	61
10	50
0	32
-18	0
-40	-40

– then add or subtract to get to where
required using 5°C = 9°F.

APPENDIX 2

New Developments

1

2

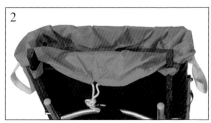

5

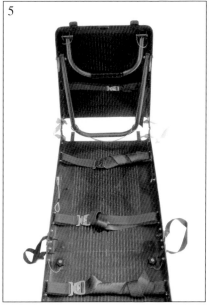

4

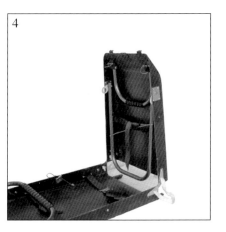

6

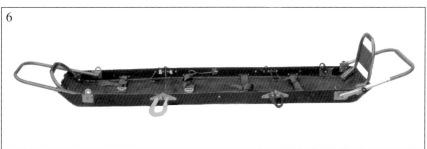

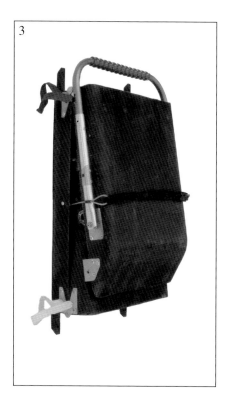

3

The MacInnes Mk 7 Stretcher

It is probable that all future mountain rescue stretchers will deploy space-age materials. The 11kg MacInnes Mk 7 stretcher is such and has taken several years to develop. It is constructed of a new very strong composite material through which, if necessary, the patient can be x-rayed. Titanium is used for shafts, etc. A six-point lifting harness for winching / lowering and a light-weight alloy wheel can be fitted in seconds.

At the rear, titanium clip-on extension shafts can be used, to which the pack frame can be attached for long evacuations. The illustrations show the sequence of unfolding the stretcher for use.

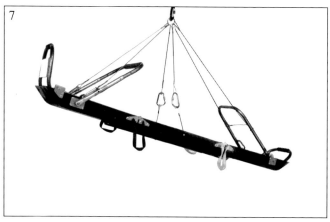

7

Addenda

Conversion formulae

To convert diameter into circumference × 3·14159

To convert circumference into diameter × 0·3183

Metric measures to imperial measures

Kg	to	Pounds	×	2·204724
Kg	to	Cwts	×	0·019685
Kg	to	Tons	×	0·000984
Millimetres	to	Inches	×	0·039370
Millimetres	to	Feet	×	0·003281
Millimetres	to	Yards	×	0·001094
Millimetres	to	Fathoms	×	0·000547
Metres	to	Inches	×	39·370113
Metres	to	Feet	×	3·280842
Metres	to	Yards	×	1·093614
Metres	to	Fathoms	×	0·546807
Kg per lineal metre	to	Pounds per foot	×	0·671999
Kg per lineal metre	to	Pounds per yard	×	2·015998
Kg per lineal metre	to	Pounds per fathom	×	4·031997
Kg per sq. mm	to	Tons per sq. inch	×	0·634997
Kg per sq. cm	to	Lbs per sq. inch	×	14·22
Grs per sq. cm	to	Ozs per sq. foot	×	32·771
Sq. mm	to	Sq. inch	×	0·001550

Imperial measures to metric measures

Pounds	to	Kg	×	0·45357
Hundredweights (cwts)	to	Kg	×	50·80
Tons	to	Kg	×	1016·00
Lineal inches	to	Millimetres	×	25·3999
Lineal feet	to	Millimetres	×	304·7997
Lineal yards	to	Millimetres	×	914·3992
Lineal fathoms	to	Millimetres	×	1828·7964
Lineal inches	to	Metres	×	0·0254
Lineal feet	to	Metres	×	0·3048
Lineal yards	to	Metres	×	0·9144
Lineal fathoms	to	Metres	×	1·8288
Pounds per lineal foot	to	Kg per metre	×	1·4881
Pounds per lineal yard	to	Kg per metre	×	0·4960
Pounds per lineal fathom	to	Kg per metre	×	0·2480
Ozs per sq. ft	to	Grs per sq. cm	×	0·0305
Lb per sq. inch	to	Kg per sq. cm	×	0·07
Tons per sq. inch	to	Kg per sq. mm	×	1·5748
Sq. inch	to	Sq. mm	×	645·1549

'24 Hour' clock system

0100 = 1 am
0200 = 2 am
0300 = 3 am
0400 = 4 am
0500 = 5 am
0600 = 6 am
0700 = 7 am
0800 = 8 am
0900 = 9 am
1000 = 10 am
1100 = 11 am
1200 = 12 noon
1300 = 1 pm
1400 = 2 pm
1500 = 3 pm
1600 = 4 pm
1700 = 5 pm
1800 = 6 pm
1900 = 7 pm
2000 = 8 pm
2100 = 9 pm
2200 = 10 pm
2300 = 11 pm
2400 = 12 midnight

Comparison in feet, inches, centimetres

feet	inches	centimetres
	1	2·54
		(cm's rounded below here)
	2	5
	3	8
	4	10
	5	13
½	6	15
	7	18
	8	20
	9	23
	10	25·40
1	12	30
	15	38
1½	18	46
	20	51
2	24	61
	25	64
2½	30	76
	35	89
3	36	91
	40	102
3½	42	107
	45	114
4	48	123
	50	127
4½	54	137
	55	140
5	60	153
	65	165
5½	66	170
	70	178
6	72	183
	75	191
6½	78	197
	80	203
7	84	214
	85	216
7½	90	229
	95	241
8	96	244
	100	254
8½	102	259
	105	267
9	108	274
	110	282
9½	114	289
	115	292
10	120	305

Comparative measurements

1 centimetre	=	·3937 inches
1 inch	=	2·54 cm
1 metre	=	39·37 inches
1 yard	=	·9144 metre
1 kilogramme	=	2·2046 lb
1 pound	=	·4536 kilo

Percentage equivalents of degree slope angles

degree	per cent	degree	per cent
1	1·74	31	60·09
2	3·49	32	62·49
3	5·24	33	64·94
4	6·99	34	67·45
5	8·75	35	70·02
6	10·51	36	72·65
7	12·28	37	75·35
8	14·05	38	78·13
9	15·84	39	80·98
10	17·63	40	83·91
11	19·44	41	86·93
12	21·26	42	90·04
13	23·09	43	93·25
14	24·93	44	96·57
15	26·80	45	100·00
16	28·67	46	103·55
17	30·57	47	107·24
18	32·49	48	111·06
19	34·43	49	115·04
20	36·40	50	119·18
21	38·39	51	123·49
22	40·40	52	127·99
23	42·45	53	132·70
24	44·52	54	137·64
25	46·63	55	142·81
26	48·77	56	148·26
27	50·95	57	153·99
28	53·17	58	160·03
29	55·43	59	166·43
30	57·73	60	173·20

Standards and Industry Ratings:

ASTM- Association of Standard Testing Methods is the largest standards setting organisation in the world and a not-for-profit corporation. They provide a forum for development of voluntary test methods. All actions are conducted through full consensus of the membership. The F-32 Committee is currently working on standards for search and rescue.

C.E.N.- European Community Law has dictated that climbing equipment be subject to uniform C.E.N. standards in order to be distributed in European Market Countries. C.E.N. has adopted common labeling, terminology, and strength ratings for all classes of products. Equipment is marked 'CE'.

D.I.N.- Deutsches Institut Fur Normung is the German institute that establishes safety standards for mountaineering equipment. Climbing equipment must meet D.I.N. Standard and marked as such to be sold in Germany.

ISO 9002- International Standards Organization Category 9002 (design and manufacture). To qualify, certain test methods, standard quality control procedures, and documentation must be met. Any product manufactured in an ISO 900 factory can be traced back to a specific product 'batch'.

NFPA- The National Fire Protection Association develops standards and operating guidelines for the fire service. *NFPA 1983 Standard On Fire Service Life Safety Rope, Harnesses, and Hardware*; covers high angle rescue equipment used on the fire ground.

U.I.A.A.- Union International D'Association D'Alpinisme. One of the original groups that established common test procedures and minimum standards for rope, helmets, harnesses, ice axes, and Karabiners. The UIAA serves merely in an advisory capacity.

3 Sigma- A rating system derived from established and accepted statistical principles and engineering practices in the USA. The average, or mean (breaking strength) is first calculated by a uniform test method along with the standard deviation. This deviation represents a variable range of breaking strengths within the group of products tested. If a manufacturer chooses to rate his products three deviations (3 sigma) less than the average breaking strength, statistics dictate that 99·87 per cent of all products will exceed this value. A three deviation rating standard has been proposed within ASTM.

Bibliography

Alta Avalanche Study Center,
Miscellaneous Report No. 13
Optimum Probing for Avalanche Victims
US Forest Service, Wasatch National
Forest, Salt Lake City, Utah, 1967

Alta Avalanche Study Center,
Translation No. 4
A Primer for the Avalanche Dog Leader
US Forest Service, Wasatch National
Forest, Salt Lake City, Utah, 1964
(first published as **Das ABC des
Lawinenhundeführers** by Osterreichischen
Bergrettungsdienstes, 1962)

American Alpine Club
**Accidents in North American
Mountaineering**
113 East 90th St, New York, NY, annual
reports

Barton, B & Wright, B
A Chance in a Million
Scottish Avalanches

Blackshaw, A
Mountaineering
Penguin Books Ltd, Bath Road,
Harmondsworth, Middlesex, 1966

Brey, C and Reed, L F
The Complete Bloodhound
Howell Book House Inc, 730 Fifth Ave,
New York, NY, 1960

Bridge, L D
Mountain Search and Rescue
Federated Mountain Clubs of New
Zealand, PO Box 1604, Wellington, 1961

Brower, D (editor)
Manual of Ski Mountaineering
Sierra Club, San Francisco, California,
1962

Daffern, A
Avalanche Safety for Skiers and Climbers
Rocky Mountain Books, Calgary, 1983

ESC Publications
Technical Rescue (Magazine)
Wheatsheaf House, 1a The Market Sq.,
South Petherton, Somerset TA13 5TB,
UK

Fraser, C
Avalanches and Snow Safety (originally
Avalanche Enigma)
John Murray Ltd, 50 Albemarle St,
London W1, 1978

Freudig, T & Martin A
Bergrettung
Lehrbuch der Bergwacht, Freudig/Martin
GBR, Rettenberger STR.27, 87509
Immenstadt i Allgau

Fyffe, A & Peter, I
The Handbook of Climbing
Pelham Books, 27 Wrights Lane, London
W8 5TZ

Gallas, F E
Land Search and Rescue
Federated Mountain Clubs of New
Zealand, PO Box 1604, Wellington, 1980

Kearney, J
Tracking
Pathway Press, 525 Jeffree St, El Cajon,
California, 1975

LaChapelle, E R
ABC of Avalanche Safety
The Mountaineers, Seattle, Washington,
1978

LaChapelle, E R
Field Guide to Snow Crystals
University of Washington Press,
Washington, 1969

Langmuir, E
Mountain Leadership
Scottish Sports Council, 1 St Coln St,
Edinburgh

Manning, H
Mountaineering, the Freedom of the Hills
The Mountaineers, Seattle, Washington,
1962

March, B
**Modern Rope Techniques in
Mountaineering**
Cicerone Press, Manchester, 1976

Mariner, W
Mountain Rescue Techniques
The Mountaineers, Seattle, Washington,
1963 (first published by the
Oesterreichischer Alpernverin, Innsbruck)

National Mountain Safety Council
Mountaincraft
NMSC, Wellington, New Zealand, 1971

Perla, R I and Marintelli, M Jr
Avalanche Handbook
Agriculture Handbook 489, US
Government Printing Office, Washington
DC, revised ed. 1978

Ravlat, C
Secours en Montagne
Didier-Richard, France

River Rescue
Appalachian Mountain Club Books

Seligman, G
Snow Structures and Ski Fields
International Glaciological Society,
Cambridge, England, 1980

Setnicka, T J
Wilderness Search and Rescue
Appalachian Mountain Club, Boston,
1980

Syrotuck, W G
**A Statistical Analysis of Lost Persons in
Wilderness Areas, No. 2**
Arner Publications, 8140 Coronado Lane,
Rome, NY, 1973

INDEX

NOTES